Assessing Writers

Carl Anderson

HEINEMANN
Portsmouth, NH

KH

Heinemann
A division of Reed Elsevier Inc.
361 Hanover Street
Portsmouth, NH 03801–3912
www.heinemann.com

Offices and agents throughout the world

The author and publisher wish to thank those who have generously given permission to reprint borrowed material: Figure 7.3 adapted from *How's It Going?* by Carl Anderson. Copyright © 2000 by Carl Anderson. Published by Heinemann, a division of Reed Elsevier, Inc. Portsmouth, NH. All rights reserved.

Library of Congress Cataloging-in-Publication Data
Anderson, Carl.
   Assessing writers / Carl Anderson.
     p. cm.
   Includes bibliographical references and index.
   ISBN 0-325-00581-8 (alk. paper)
    1. English language—Composition and exercises—Ability testing.
2. English language—Composition and exercises—Study and teaching (Elementary). 3. Lesson planning. I. Title.
LB1576.A61585 2005
372.62'3—dc22
                                            2005003037

Editor: Kate Montgomery
Production: Elizabeth Valway
Cover photography: Donnelly Marks
Cover design: Jenny Jensen Greenleaf
Composition: House of Equations, Inc.
Manufacturing: Louise Richardson

Printed in the United States of America on acid-free paper
09 08 07 06 05 RRD 1 2 3 4 5

1/24/06

For Anzia
who is becoming a lifelong writer
(and so much more)

your dad is very proud of you

Contents

Acknowledgments

I want to thank my mentor, Lucy Calkins. I appreciate the ongoing intellectual, professional, and personal support she has given me over the past decade. I am proud to say that this book stands on the shoulders of Lucy's work, as well as the work of the Teachers College Reading and Writing Project community that she leads. I hope this book honors the ongoing work of the project.

Several other colleagues at the project have made key contributions. I appreciate Laurie Pessah's steady faith in me—communicated in so many of her famous phone calls over the years—as well as her ability to make me laugh and not take things too seriously. Kathleen Tolan, an extraordinary teacher and staff developer I have admired for the past decade, epitomizes for me the kind of reflective practice that I describe in this book. Isoke Titilayo Nia's intellectual rigor has strengthened my own thinking, particularly in the areas of genre studies, curriculum, and independence in the writing workshop. And Janet Angelillo has been a thoughtful and respectful sounding board for my ideas about teaching writing, as well as the work we do in schools.

I am also grateful for the conversations I have shared with many other colleagues at the project, including Pam Allyn, Jane Bean-Folkes, Lydia Bellino, Jenny Bender, Linda Chen, Mary Chiarella, Grace Chough, Rory Freed Cohen, Mary Ann Colbert, Kathy Collins, Colleen Cruz, Kathy Doyle, Mary Ehrenworth, Ian Fleischer, Mark Hardy, Amanda Hartman, Lynn Holcomb, Ted Kesler, Holly Kim, Christine Lagatta, Gaby Layden, Paula Marron, Medea McEvoy, Leah Mermelstein, Annemarie Powers, Anna Reduce, Barbara Rosenblum, Hannah Schneewind, Emily Butler Smith, Ruth Swinney, Miriam Swirski, Kim Tarpinian, Cheryl Tyler, and Patty Vitale.

I appreciate the hard work done by the office staff at the project— Amber Boyd, Maurie Brooks, Denise Capasso, Karen Currie, Wairimu Kiambuthi, Tasha Kalista, Mary Ann Mustac, and (especially) Beth Neville—who again and again made my work at Teachers College and in the New York City schools go smoothly.

I also need to thank several colleagues who left the project before I started writing this book for the impact they had on my thinking about teaching writing while they were at the project. Thanks, then, to Randy and Katherine Bomer, Teresa Caccavale, Sharon Hill, Shirley McPhillips, Kate Montgomery, Katie Wood Ray, Donna Santmann, and Brenda Wallace.

During the 2000–2001 and 2001–2002 school years, I had the privilege of heading two project leadership groups focusing on writing assessment. Thanks to the teachers and staff developers in these groups: Jacqueline Allen-Joseph, Christina Bookout, Katie Brennan, Will Citrin, Susan Fox, Michele Helfman, Nina Ishmael, Grace Lee, Christy Malko, Maggie Moon, Cristina Narváez, John Otterstedt, Sarah Picard, Barbara Rossi, Jennifer Serravallo, Lis Cristina Shin, Rosie Silberman, Emily Butler Smith, Emily Steele Kirven, Patty Tabacchi, and Daira Tramontin. You'll see our conversations reflected on every page of this book.

Over the past few years, I have done my most satisfying work as a staff developer at P.S. 321, in Park Slope, Brooklyn. I'm grateful to the teachers there for being such good learning companions, as well as to the principal, Liz Phillips, and assistant principal, Beth Handman. And, as a parent in the P.S. 321 community, I am especially thankful for my daughter Anzia's remarkable teachers—Bill Fulbrecht, Andrea Rousso, Kelsey Goss, and Kristen Rost—who have made such a profound difference in her life.

During the past several years, I've crisscrossed the United States and Canada to work with teachers, literacy coaches, and principals in their schools and to speak about teaching writing in workshops. None of this work would have been possible without the hard work of Tracy Heine, at Heinemann Speakers, and Cherie Bartlett and Pat Goodman, at Heinemann Workshops.

I want to thank the educators with whom I've developed ongoing professional relationships. In the Boston Public Schools, Ann Deveney and Jane Skelton. In the Providence Public Schools, Barbara Halzel and Sandy Rainone. As part of my work with All Write!!!—a consortium of school corporations in northeastern Indiana that are implementing writing workshop with the generous support of the Dekko Foundation—Ruth Ayres, Kathy Douglas, Mary Helen Gensch, Karla Hayden, Mindy Hoffar, Jane Hormann, Valerie Hutton, Sandie Kern, Celena Larkey, Crystal Leu, Julia Nixon, Tammy Shultz, and

Tammy Taylor. In the Half Hollow Hills School District on Long Island, Sheldon Karnilow and Gloria Smith, as well as the principals, teachers, and students (some of whom appear in this book) with whom I've been privileged to work. And at the Lovett School in Atlanta, Mary Baldwin.

Several friends and colleagues volunteered to read first drafts of various chapters of the book. Thanks to Janet Angelillo, Robin Epstein, Barbara Halzel, Mindy Hoffar, Leah Mermelstein, Julia Nixon, Hannah Schneewind, and Artie Voigt.

And when I completed the manuscript, several friends and colleagues read it closely and gave me invaluable feedback. Thanks to Lucy Calkins, Robin Epstein, Mindy Hoffar, Cristina Narváez, Julia Nixon, and Brenda Wallace.

I appreciated every comment that my two Heinemann reviewers, Katherine Bomer and Sandra Wilde, made. This book is stronger because of their close reading and thoughtful insights.

I could fill up another book with praise for my editor at Heinemann, Kate Montgomery. Her unflagging enthusiasm for this project kept me going, especially when my energy for writing was low. Her gentle but firm nudges to keep to my writing schedule helped me finish on deadline. Her numerous suggestions about the manuscript made the book far, far better than it would have been without her input. (And when I decided to take a month off from writing to read George R. R. Martin's Song of Ice and Fire fantasy series, she understood, since she's a Martin fan, too!)

And I am grateful for Alan Huisman's thoughtful editing of the manuscript, as well as for the care Elizabeth Valway gave the book as it moved through each stage of production.

My final thanks are for each of the members of my family.

My son, Haskell, made his way into the world two months before I finished the manuscript. Amidst the pressures of getting revisions done, I was glad for the moments of joy that holding him and gazing at him gave me.

My daughter, Anzia, to whom this book is dedicated, was a constant source of laughter and love and wonderment throughout the years that I worked on the book.

My wife, Robin, has been at my side since the beginning of my teaching career. She has always seen more in me than I have seen myself and has helped me grow in ways that I couldn't have imagined nineteen years ago. For that and many other reasons, I love her passionately and deeply.

Introduction

Our research data show that entire years—or even school careers—can be wasted if we don't let our students teach us.
—DONALD GRAVES, A Fresh Look at Writing

For eleven years, my job has been to help teachers become excellent writing teachers. First as a staff developer for the Teachers College Reading and Writing Project at Columbia University, in New York City, and then as a consultant for urban, suburban, and rural school districts across the United States, I've spent thousands of hours with teachers who have created writing workshops in their classrooms. As part of this work, I've demonstrated teaching methods and coached teachers as they taught, and I've talked with teachers about the teaching of writing in study groups and presentations.

By *writing workshop,* I am referring to a daily block of time (usually forty-five minutes) devoted to teaching students to become skilled writers. Writing workshop usually begins with a *minilesson,* a ten-or-so-minute whole-class lesson in which the teacher teaches students something about writing—having a purpose, how to write strong leads, a revision strategy. The minilesson is usually part of a *unit of study,* a sequence of minilessons on one aspect of writing that lasts two to six weeks. A unit of study might delve into a particular genre, focus on using a writer's notebook as a tool for rehearsing writing, or zero in on punctuation.

After the minilesson, students work for half an hour on their writing. Depending on their grade level, students may work on a piece for a single writing workshop period (in kindergarten) or for several weeks (in upper-elementary and middle school grades). Children learn to take their piece through each stage of the writing process—rehearsal (or prewriting), drafting, revising, editing, and publishing. While students write, teachers move around the classroom conducting *writing conferences.* In these one-on-one conversations, teachers teach each student about an aspect of writing that meets that student's needs as a writer.

The writing workshop ends with a *share session*, which usually takes five minutes. In some share sessions, teachers highlight the work one or two students did in response to that day's minilesson. In others, students read their writing aloud to the class to get feedback from their classmates.

Teachers ask me lots of questions about every aspect of writing workshop. I'm especially glad when they ask, "What minilessons should I be teaching in my current unit of study?" and "What kinds of writing conferences should I be having with my students?" I like these questions because they open the door to a discussion of my favorite aspect of teaching writing—assessing student writers.

Assessment is the challenging intellectual work of getting to know students as writers and using what we learn about them to help us decide what they need us to teach them next. Assessing students well is essential if we're going to be excellent writing teachers. Linking what we learn from our assessments to our decisions about what to teach in minilessons and writing conferences is essential if we are going to be the kinds of teachers who are able to design whole-class and individual instruction tailored to students' needs.

The terms *assessment* and *high-stakes literacy tests* are often used interchangeably these days. While it's true that standardized tests can and do give us some information about our students as writers (particularly if we are involved in the scoring of the exams), this book is not about those tests. I believe that the day-to-day work of gathering information about our student writers is the most useful kind of assessment for making decisions about what to teach our students in writing conferences and units of study. And I believe that daily assessment has the most impact on students' growth as writers.

Educators in many different roles are hungry to learn more about writing assessment, and I've written this book with all of them in mind. For example, you may be an experienced writing workshop teacher who has numerous units of study in your curricular repertoire and who has been conferring with students about their writing for years. But you're still striving to improve yourself as a teacher of writing and thus would like to become more skilled at assessment. I've written this book for you.

Or perhaps you're a brand-new teacher, or a teacher in a preservice program. You've learned that getting to know your students as writers is key to becoming a good writing teacher. But you aren't sure what you should be looking for when you talk with students and read their writing, nor are you sure what to do with the information you gather. I've written this book for you.

Or maybe you're a literacy coach trying to help teachers improve their assessment of students as writers. But you aren't sure how to explain all the assessment you do intuitively with students in writing workshop so that teachers can benefit from your expertise. I've written this book for you.

Or possibly you're a principal. As the instructional leader of your school, you want to stress to your staff the importance of using what they learn from their assessment of student writers to inform what they do in writing workshop each day. But you need a clear image of the assessment work that should be a hallmark of day-to-day workshop teaching and of how excellent writing teachers connect their assessment to their teaching. I've written this book for you.

Exploring the topic of writing assessment in its entirety is way beyond the scope of this book. My goal is to help you, my imagined reader, learn about the kinds of information you should be gathering about students, where to find these kinds of information, and, ultimately, how to use that information to decide what to teach students in writing conferences and units of study. The teachers I've worked with who have honed their assessment abilities have some of the most successful writing workshops I've seen, and I hope this book helps you join their ranks.

The first two chapters of the book discuss central assessment concepts. In Chapter 1, I discuss how assessment is an everyday habit of mind for good writing teachers. Everyday assessment makes it possible for them to decide exactly what to teach in writing conferences and units of study. In Chapter 2, I talk about how assessment begins with developing a vision for who we want our students to become as writers and how that vision helps us decide what kinds of information we need to value when we assess students. I describe my own vision for the kind of writer that I hope students become, which I call the *lifelong writer*. I explain what kinds of information I gather about students to assess how they're becoming lifelong writers and to figure out what they still need to learn to achieve that goal.

The next three chapters discuss the three traits of the lifelong writer and how to assess students for these traits. Chapter 3 covers assessing students' initiative as writers (the reasons students write and the audiences for whom they write). Chapter 4 is a discussion of assessing how well students write. And Chapter 5 focuses on assessing the effectiveness of our students' writing processes.

The last three chapters discuss how to link assessment to our day-to-day teaching in writing workshop. In Chapter 6, I talk about how to use our assessments of students to design individual learning plans for them. These individual learning plans help us have effective writing conferences with students, which is the subject of Chapter 7. And these individual learning plans also help us design units of study for the whole class, which is the subject of Chapter 8.

There are several ways you might read this book. If your main purpose is to learn how to use assessment to tailor your writing conferences to students' individual needs as writers, I suggest you read Chapters 1, 2, 6, and 7. If your main purpose is to learn how to decide which minilessons to teach in the units of study that make up your whole-class writing curriculum and to make these units more responsive to your students' collective needs as writers, then I suggest you read Chapters 1, 2, 6, and 8.

Whatever your purpose for reading the book, by the time you reach the end of Chapter 2, you may realize that you also need to read Chapters 3, 4, and/or 5 before you proceed to Chapter 6. If, after reading the first two chapters, you want to deepen your ability to assess your students' initiative as writers, read Chapter 3. If you are especially interested in assessing how well your students write, read Chapter 4. If you want to focus on assessing the effectiveness of your students' writing processes, read Chapter 5.

As you read each chapter, you'll find that I've included many "actions" you can take in response to the material I've presented. I imagine that you might take these actions on your own or together with colleagues (in conversations about writing assessment in study groups or in grade-level or departmental meetings).

This book will not make assessment easy. After nineteen years of working with student writers, I still find assessment to be the most challenging intellectual work I do as a writing teacher. But this book will equip you to assess your students with more wisdom and confidence. And it will help you use what you glean about students to decide what to teach them. That's my goal—to help you make your assessment more effective, thereby helping you become an excellent writing teacher.

Reference

Graves, Donald. 1994. *A Fresh Look at Writing*. Portsmouth, NH: Heinemann.

Assessing Writers

Why Assess?

1

Since my daughter, Anzia, was born, I've kept a journal in which I've recorded things in her young life that I don't want to forget: milestones in her development (beginning to walk at fourteen months, her first sleepover at age five), favorite books (Rosemary Wells' Max books when she was two, Cynthia Rylant's Poppleton series when she was three), charming questions (*Did you pick me at the daughter store? Why doesn't the sky fall down?*).

A few months into her kindergarten year at P.S. 321, in Park Slope, Brooklyn, I began to notice Anzia doing all sorts of new things as a writer, and of course I wrote them down in my journal. That she was doing these new things didn't surprise me—Anzia's teachers, Bill Fulbrecht and Andrea Rousso, had a writing workshop in their classroom several days each week. So I wrote that on our walk home one afternoon, Anzia told me that writing workshop was her favorite part of school because she got to tell true stories about herself—like the ski lessons she took on Whiteface Mountain in Lake Placid over Christmas vacation and her exploits with her cousin Zivia Bea. I wrote about her letter to Santa Claus asking for a purple fairy doll and her note to her mom asking permission to watch a video (she didn't want to interrupt while her mother was working on the computer). I noted how Anzia worked hard to sound out the words she didn't know how to spell, instead of begging me to give her the spellings. And so forth.

As I wrote about Anzia in my journal that year, I was composing a mental image of the kind of writer she was becoming: one who found value in writing about her own experiences, one who understood the power of written words to move other people to do things for her, one who was developing a repertoire of strategies for composing drafts.

As Anzia continued to grow that year and in subsequent grades, I continued to record things I noticed about her as a writer—and to develop my image of the kind of writer she was.

In other words, I started assessing her as a writer. Before you jump to the conclusion that I'm one of those persons so obsessed by my work that I can't separate my professional life and family life, understand this about me that year: I wasn't aware at first that I was assessing Anzia. After spending nineteen years in writing workshops as a teacher and staff developer, whenever I'm around kids who are writing, I assess them. It's a habit of mind.

Taking an Assessment Stance

Good writing teachers assess student writers *every day*. One of the most important things, if not *the* most important thing, that defines good writing teachers is that they are constantly learning about their students as writers. For good writing teachers, writing assessment is a habit of mind.

Notice that I said that good writing teachers assess student *writers*. Writing assessment is often equated with reading through a set of finished pieces of writing, usually during a prep period or at home on the weekend, separate from the day-to-day activities of a writing workshop. I equate assessment with gathering information about students as writers. To gather this information, we must not only read student writing but also observe students at work and talk with them about their writing in conferences. And the only way for us to be able to gather information about students in all these ways is to assess them when they're in writing workshop.

To help me gather this information, I've developed what Peter Johnston (1997) describes as a "disposition" to see children as rich sources of information about themselves as writers. That is, I've become the kind of teacher who takes an assessment stance whenever I'm with student writers.

Reaping the Payoffs

There are three payoffs to taking an assessment stance in the writing workshop. First, assessment enables us to get to know students' strengths and needs as writers and thus to design individual learning plans for them. Second, assessment helps us tailor our teaching to students' individual needs in writing conferences. And, third, assessment helps us design units of study that focus on the collective needs of the children in our own classrooms.

Ultimately, assessment helps us figure out answers to what may be the most critical question we can ask ourselves: *What do I teach this child?* This question motivates us to construct a learning plan for every student. We need to answer this question in every writing conference we have with a young writer. And answering this question for all of our students helps us decide which minilessons we're going to teach in a particular unit of study. James and Kathleen Strickland (2000) write, "Assessment gets to the heart of teaching and lets us decide how and when to offer support to writers" (66).

Assessment Enables Us to Design Individual Learning Plans

It's common for teachers to refer to writing workshop as a child-centered approach to teaching writing. What does this mean? My answer is that good writing workshop teachers *get to know* their young writers. That is, over time, they construct multidimensional images in their mind of their students as writers. They learn about why their students write and for whom. They learn about what their children know about writing well. And they learn about their students' writing processes.

Good writing workshop teachers also imagine who they want their students to become as writers in a few months and by the end of the school year. These exemplary teachers have clearly defined goals in mind for students that they plan to work on with each of them in writing conferences and with the whole class in units of study. These teachers want to help students explore new purposes for writing and communicate with new audiences. They want students to deepen their knowledge of what it means to write well. And they want students to develop even more effective writing processes. Having goals in mind for students is essential to helping them grow in significant and appropriate ways during the school year.

In practice, creating individual learning plans for students is an extension of the work teachers are already doing in their writing workshops. Take the individual learning plan I designed for Syeda, a third grader, during visits to her classroom in the first few months of the school year (see Figure 1.1).

On the left side of this form, labeled *What am I learning about this student as a writer?* I recorded what I learned about Syeda in writing conferences, what I taught her in those conferences (the teaching points), and things I noticed as I observed her at work and read her writing. In other words, I constructed an image of the kind of writer Syeda was in the early part of third grade—one who saw writing as retelling every detail of an event, one who could sequence the events

Assessment Notes For _Syeda_   **Dates** _9/5 – 10/5_

What am I learning about this student as a writer?	What do I need to teach this student?
9/15 topic = "My vacation in D.C." - she's writing an "all about" entry in her writers notebook, events in time order - What's her point? She "likes to be with her cousin Amanda, who is like a sister." Ⓣ write entries about small important moments, not the whole topic 9/23 draft "Seeing Amanda in Washington D.C." - has written (mostly) about the parts of the trip connected to Amanda - is "adding detail" to her draft - wants to share her piece with "the class" Ⓣ writing can go beyond the class into the world (to Amanda!) 9/25 observe: peer conferring with Bonnie 10/5 topic = "Getting My Brother Into Trouble" - she says she wants her piece to be about "how much I love getting my brother in trouble" - wants to share her piece with other kids with siblings - eager to jump into her draft Ⓣ write a plan before drafting	Ⓖ write to get a point across about a topic Ⓖ write about the parts of an experience that help you get your point across Ⓖ write for audiences outside of "the class" Ⓖ strategies for planning a draft

Ⓣ is the symbol for teaching point.   Ⓖ is the symbol for instructional goal.

FIGURE 1.1   Assessment Notes for Syeda

she wrote about in the order they occurred, one who considered her class to be the audience for her writing.

In response to the information I was gathering, on the right side of the form, labeled *What do I need to teach this student?* I jotted down some goals for her—to learn that people write to communicate a meaning about their topic, to focus on the important parts of an event in a

TEACHER ACTION 1.1

Try out the thinking teachers do to construct individual learning plans for students.

- Think about one student in your class. Make a list of the things you know about this student as a writer. Read over the list when you finish; then make a new list of the goals you think you should set for this student.

- Read through your record-keeping forms. What kinds of things have you noted about your students as writers? Based on these notes, what do you think you should teach them?

piece (the parts that help a writer communicate meaning), to write for audiences beyond the classroom, and to make a plan for a piece of writing before drafting. Some of these goals had an immediate impact on my conferences, during which I looked for evidence that Syeda was trying to narrow her topics (she was) and considering audiences in addition to her entire class (with a little nudging, she came up with the idea of sharing her piece about her little brother with classmates who also had pesky younger siblings).

To become the kind of teacher who designs learning plans for individual students, as I did for Syeda, I first had to see the information I was recording not as an end in itself but as a means to setting some concrete goals. That is, I had to learn to take the time to make meaning out of all the information I had been collecting about children as writers since I launched my first writing workshop.

Assessment Helps Us Confer with Students Effectively

Ever since Donald Graves published the first major book on writing workshop in the elementary school, *Writing: Teachers and Children at Work* (1983), writing teachers across the United States have understood that the most important teaching opportunity they have is the conference. In a writing conference, the teacher meets with a student one-to-one to talk with him about his writing and to teach him something he needs to become a better writer. (In Australia, educators recognize the importance of the writing conference by referring to writing workshop as the "conference method" for teaching writing.)

The effectiveness of a writing conference depends on the teacher's ability to assess the writers in her class. With her individual learning plan for a child in mind—the result of her ongoing assessment of that child—a teacher knows beforehand several possible directions she may want to take. And once the conference has begun, her assessment skills are even more critical. In my own book on conferring, *How's It Going? A Practical Guide to Conferring with Student Writers* (2000), I talk about how in those first few minutes, the teacher's job is to discover what kind of writing work a child is doing—thinking about which audience with whom to share a piece, making a plan for the piece, developing a scene by adding precise detail—and assess what the child understands about doing that work. Lucy Calkins (1994) refers to this initial assessment as the "research" part of the conference.

What a teacher knows about a child before a conference and what she learns about him during the conference makes it possible for her to tailor her teaching to his particular needs as a writer. That is, in each writing conference, a teacher is able to differentiate her teaching in response to what she has learned about a student from her assessment. It's this opportunity to differentiate instruction that makes the writing conference such a powerful teaching method.

On an early October day, I visited Jeanne Maggiacomo's first-grade classroom at the Robert F. Kennedy Elementary School, in Providence, Rhode Island, and had a conference with Kayla. This was the first time I had worked with this particular student, but I had asked Jeanne beforehand to tell me about Kayla as a writer. She said that while Kayla drew very detailed pictures of her subjects before she wrote, she tended to write very short texts. One of Jeanne's goals was to nudge Kayla to write longer, more detailed texts.

Come sit next to me as I talk with Kayla, so you can see how assessment helps me decide what to teach her. As the conference unfolds, keep several questions in mind:

- What do I learn that confirms what I already know about Kayla?
- What do I learn that deepens my knowledge of her as a writer?
- How does what I decide to focus on connect to Jeanne's individual learning plan for Kayla?

I sit down next to Kayla after she and her classmates have been busy working on their pieces for fifteen minutes. Kayla is working intently on a drawing of herself playing with her Barbie dollhouse (see Figure 1.2).

ME: How's it going?
KAYLA: Good.
ME: Good? How about you talk about what you're doing?
KAYLA: I'm playing with my dollhouse.
ME: You're not really playing with your dollhouse right now! What are you working on?

Figure 1.2   Kayla's Drawing

KAYLA: I'm still working on [the sketch].

ME: Let me see if I understand this. What you're doing is sketching yourself playing with your dollhouse. [*Kayla nods.*] Have you done any writing yet?

KAYLA: [*Shakes her head*] I'm still working on [the sketch].

ME: OK. What I'm noticing about your sketch is that you have a lot of detail in your picture . . . there are so many things in that dollhouse. [*Kayla beams.*] The thing to remember is that the sketch is really just to get you to jump into your piece with lots of things to write about. So what do you want to write about playing with your dollhouse? [*Kayla thinks for a few moments.*] Look at the sketch while you're thinking.

KAYLA: I want to write . . . I like to play with my dollhouse.

ME: OK. And what are you going to say about that?

KAYLA: It's a lot of fun.

ME: It's a lot of fun. . . . [*Kayla nods.*] OK. But you know what? If you write, "I like to play with my dollhouse. It's a lot of fun," your words aren't going to tell me much about what it's like for you to play with your dollhouse. Here's where this sketch you're making can help you put details in your writing that would help me get a better picture in my mind. [*Kayla nods. I point to her sketch.*] Tell me about playing with your dollhouse.

KAYLA: This is a bed. . . . This is a jewelry box, but you can't really see it. . . . That's one of Barbie's jewelry boxes.

ME: Oh, this is a Barbie dollhouse? [*Kayla nods.*] So this is a picture of your Barbie dollhouse. It seems like there are a lot of things you can write about what you do with your Barbie.

KAYLA: [*Smiles*] I lay a Barbie in there [*She points to the bed.*] . . . and I put a Barbie in the chair. . . .

ME: Kayla, the detail you're giving now is just great. And if you write those kinds of details down, your words are going to help me know about how you play with your Barbie dollhouse. See how when you look closely at your sketch, you get a lot of ideas of things that can go in your piece? [*Kayla nods.*] I know you want to finish your sketch, but I do want you to do some writing now. You can go back to your sketch later on if you want. Go back and write and use your sketch to help you remember the things you just said. Are you ready to try this?

KAYLA: Yes.

ME: Good talking with you.

Conferring with Kayla, I learn so much about who she is as a writer at this moment. Some of this confirms what Jeanne has already told me. I see that Kayla's writing process consists of at least two steps. Like many first-grade writers early in the school year, Kayla draws her subject before she writes about it. Because she spends a lot of time working on her drawing (fifteen minutes today, and she still wants to keep at it) and because of the amount of detail she puts into it, I conclude that she values drawing as her primary way of communicating what she wants her say about her topic.

I also learn some things about Kayla that deepen what I know about her as a writer. When Kayla tells me that she plans to write, "I like to play with my dollhouse. It's a lot of fun," I realize that, for Kayla, the purpose of the writing she does after completing a drawing is to caption the drawing. Writing serves the drawing. This explains why the writing that Kayla is planning isn't going to contain much detail: in her mind, her drawing is the primary means for communicating meaning to readers.

This conference is congruent with the direction that Jeanne has already imagined taking Kayla in. Her individual learning plan for Kayla includes the goal that she learn to write longer texts. After gathering and synthesizing this information, I decide to teach Kayla to see the drawing she's done as a *rehearsal* for writing. That is, I want to help her begin to see this kind of drawing as a means to an end—writing a detailed piece—instead of an end in itself. With my support, Kayla is able to look at her sketch and get ideas for a longer, more detailed piece of writing (see Figure 1.3).

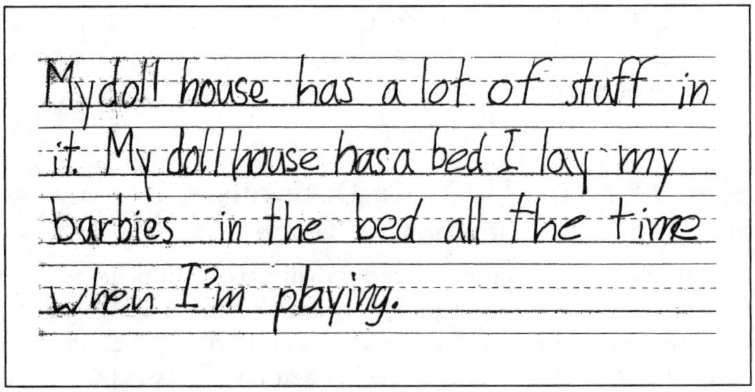

> My doll house has a lot of stuff in it. My doll house has a bed I lay my barbies in the bed all the time when I'm playing.

FIGURE 1.3   Kayla's Piece

Writing assessment—both the assessment Kayla's teacher had done prior to my conference and the assessment I did during the conference—helped me tailor my teaching to Kayla's needs as a writer.

This assessment paid off in future conferences with Kayla as well. In the weeks that followed, Jeanne brought what we had learned from my conference with Kayla into her own conversations with her. She began these conferences wondering whether Kayla was putting more value on her writing as a way of communicating meaning and whether she was using her drawings to help her get ideas for her writing.

In every conference, writing assessment—during the conference as well as during the days, weeks, and months before the conference—

TEACHER ACTION 1.2

Try out the thinking teachers do to connect their ongoing assessment to their writing conferences.

- Make a list of the things you know about one student in your class as a writer. Read over the list, and then make a list of some of the things you would like to teach him in future writing conferences.

- Have a writing conference with the student you wrote about. Afterward, reflect on the conference by asking yourself these questions: *What did I learn that confirmed what I knew about him as a writer? What new things did I learn about him? Was what I taught him one of the things I hoped to confer with him about?*

helps us tailor our teaching to fit the needs of each writer. In other words, writing assessment helps us answer the question: *What does* this *writer need me to teach her today?*

Assessment Helps Us Make Decisions About Which Minilessons to Teach

Taking an assessment stance in the writing workshop helps teachers decide what to teach their students in each of the units of study that make up the writing curriculum. As with conferring, the effectiveness of a unit of study depends on a teacher's ability to assess the needs of the individual writers in her class.

As a teacher assesses her students, she notices that many of her students have similar needs as writers. The goals she has set for one student in his individual learning plan is the same one she has set for another student, and another, and another. She's noticed, for example, that many of her students write bed-to-bed pieces—in which they include every detail they can think of about an event—and need to learn how to include only the details that help them get across a meaning about the event to readers. She's noticed that many of her students overuse dialogue and need to learn how to use this kind of detail effectively. She's noticed that many of her students put periods after a dependent clause (creating sentence fragments) and need to learn how to use a comma to connect dependent and independent clauses. And so on.

A teacher *could* address students' needs entirely in conferences. But why give the same lesson to twenty students in twenty conferences? It makes much more sense for a teacher to gather her students together and address shared needs in minilessons. Think of a minilesson, then, as a writing conference with the entire class. (Of course, there will be needs that only a few students in a class have in common or that only one student has; these needs are best addressed in conferences.)

Once again I'm going to invite you to sit next to me, this time as I review the assessments I've made of all the students in a class and use them to help me decide what to focus on in an upcoming unit of study. I've already read through each of my record-keeping forms on the students in the class and noted on a checklist which goals I've set for them. Now I'll look for patterns of needs throughout the class. These common needs will become the focus of the upcoming unit of study.

The checklist in Figure 1.4, which I filled out after the first month of school, enables me to see that I've checked off a number of similar goals for students: to learn to communicate meaning in their writing, to focus on the parts of the topic they're writing about that will enable

Assessing How Well Students Write

Trait	Goal	Jimmy	Allison	Jade	Michael	Jane	Jacob	Jack	Anna	Matt	Molly	Ruby	Robin	Terri	Harry	Isabel	Robert	Annabel	Sophia	Max	Alex
Meaning	The student communicates meaning in her writing.	+	+	+	+	+	⊕	⊕	+	⊕	⊕	+	+	⊕	+	⊕	+	+	+	+	+
	The student's meaning influences (or controls) other decisions she made in composing her pieces.	+	+	+	+	+	⊕	+	+	⊕	+	+	+	+	+	⊕	+	+	+	+	+
Genre	The student's writing has the typical features of the genres in which she writes.	+		+	+	+	⊕	⊕	+	⊕	+	+	+	⊕	+	⊕	+	+	+	+	
	The parts of the student's writing each help develop meaning.		+	+	+	+	⊕	+	+	⊕	+	+	+	+	+	⊕		⊕	⊕	+	+
	The student's pieces contain the kinds of parts specific to the genres in which she writes.	⊕	+				⊕	⊕								⊕					
Structure	The student orders her writing in genre-specific ways.		⊕		⊕			⊕				⊕	⊕			⊕		⊕	⊕		⊕
	The student writes leads and endings that guide readers toward meaning.	⊕	⊕				⊕					⊕							⊕		⊕
	The student uses transitions effectively.										⊕										
	The student weighs parts that are most important in developing her meaning.					+	+	+	+	+				+		⊕					
Detail	The student includes details in her piece that help develop meaning.	+	+	+	+	+	⊕	⊕	+	⊕	⊕	+	+	+	+	⊕	+	+	+	+	+
	The student writes with a range of genre-specific details.	+	+	+	⊕	+	⊕	+	+	+	⊕	+	+	+	+	⊕	+	+	+	+	+
	The student embeds and connects details in her sentences effectively.							⊕			⊕		⊕	⊕							
	The student uses specific words in her details.				⊕			⊕		+				⊕		+					+
Voice	The student uses a variety of sentence structures to give voice to her writing.	⊕	⊕	⊕	⊕	⊕	⊕	⊕								+					
	The student uses a variety of punctuation marks to give voice to her writing.						+														
	The student includes details that reveal who she is as an individual.	⊕					⊕	⊕													
	The student uses techniques to create intimacy between herself and readers.		⊕	⊕		⊕															
Conventions	The student uses punctuation marks correctly in the kinds of sentences that she is writing.	≠	≠	≠	≠	⊕	≠	⊕	≠	⊕	≠	≠	≠	≠	⊕	⊕	⊕	≠	⊕	≠	⊕
	The student uses grammatical conventions correctly in the kinds of sentences she's writing.				≠		≠					½				½	½	½	½	½	

+ Goal for student   ⊕ Goal achieved   1 's, " 's, etc. Convention student needs to work on   Ⓣ Goal achieved

FIGURE 1.4   Assessing How Well Students Write

Teacher Action 1.3

Try out the thinking that teachers do to connect their ongoing assessment to their units of study.

- Make a list of some of the needs you've noticed many students in your class share. Then make a list of some of the minilessons you could teach in your next unit of study that could address these needs.

- Read through your record-keeping forms. As you read, make a list of the needs that you notice many of your students have in common. Then list several minilessons you could teach in your next unit of study that would address these needs.

them to communicate their meaning, to develop a wider repertoire of details, and to paragraph their writing.

Realizing that I have the same goals in mind for many of the students in this class, I begin to think about which minilessons I want to teach in the next unit of study. I decide that I'll present some minilessons on how writers figure out what they want to say in a piece of writing and others on how writers get what they want to say across. Some of these minilessons will be about how writers focus on the aspects (or parts) of their topics that help them say what they want to say. Others will be about the kinds of details that writers use to achieve this focus. And at the end of the unit of study, when the students are editing their pieces, I'll give a few minilessons on paragraphing to help students learn how to use this convention in their writing.

During the school year, when teachers decide what to focus on in their units of study, they're most likely to make accurate decisions when they know a lot about the writers in their class and the needs that they have in common. And they're going to know about these shared needs only if they're the kind of teachers who've taken an assessment stance in their writing workshops.

References

Anderson, Carl. 2000. *How's It Going? A Practical Guide to Conferring with Student Writers.* Portsmouth, NH: Heinemann.

Calkins, Lucy. 1994. *The Art of Teaching Writing.* Portsmouth, NH: Heinemann.

————. 2003. *The Nuts and Bolts of Teaching Writing. Units of Study for Primary Writers: A Yearlong Curriculum*. Portsmouth, NH: *first*hand, Heinemann.

Graves, Donald H. 1983. *Writing: Teachers and Children at Work*. Portsmouth, NH: Heinemann.

Johnston, Peter H. 1997. *Knowing Literacy: Constructive Literacy Assessment*. Portland, ME: Stenhouse.

Strickland, Kathleen, and James Strickland. 2000. *Making Assessment Elementary*. Portsmouth, NH: Heinemann.

2

Getting Started
Developing an Assessment Lens

One starts with the end—the desired results.
—GRANT WIGGINS AND JAY McTIGHE,
Understanding by Design

I've lost count of the number of times people have asked me why my wife, Robin, and I named our daughter Anzia. Anzia is named after Anzia Yezierska, a Jewish writer who, during the 1920s, wrote about the experiences of Jewish immigrants to New York City's Lower East Side. In her novels—most notably *Hungry Hearts*—she portrays the lives of poor and striving factory workers with empathy and compassion.

Robin and I named our daughter after Anzia Yezierska because we hope when Anzia grows up and comes into her own as a Jewish woman, she will have compassion for people who are less fortunate than she is and be able to make a keen analysis of their situation. These qualities are an important part of our vision of the kind of person we hope Anzia will become.

Our vision for Anzia shapes how Robin and I parent her. Living in New York City, we encounter people on the margins of our society almost every day. Since she was three, Anzia has been curious about the men and women who stand on sidewalks in our Brooklyn neighborhood and ask for money from passersby. Although it's not a comfortable topic to discuss with a child, Robin and I have responded to Anzia's questions by helping her try to imagine the kinds of lives that people who ask for money might lead. And at her synagogue, Robin has encouraged Anzia to participate in the Jewish tradition of *tzedakah*—giving money that will be used to help poor people—as one way of teaching Anzia that she has a responsibility to try to make a difference in the lives of people who are less fortunate than she is.

In other words, because we have a vision of who Anzia will become, Robin and I pay special attention to any of Anzia's actions that connect in some way to that vision. We try to teach her to live in ways that are consistent with our hopes for her. Our vision for Anzia shapes how we see and respond to her.

Good writing teachers, like parents, have a vision of the kind of writers they hope their students will become someday—a vision that is essential to their ability to take an assessment stance in their writing workshops. In his book *Student-Centered Classroom Assessment* (1996), educator Richard Stiggins writes that high-quality assessment starts with a vision of success. That is, taking an assessment stance begins with thinking about who we hope a child will be *someday* before we start to think about who a child is *now*. To be able to assess—and use what we learn to design individual and whole-class instruction—we start by looking forward in time instead of at the here and now.

Our vision of who we want our students to become is a lens through which we can look at student writers. It helps us decide which information we should value when we observe students writing, when we talk with them in writing conferences, and when we read what they have written. We look for evidence that students are already exhibiting some or all of the characteristics of the kind of writers we hope they will become—in developmentally appropriate ways, of course—so that our teaching can help them strengthen those characteristics. And we also think about which characteristics they aren't yet exhibiting so that our teaching can help them begin to grow in these ways as writers.

Becoming good at assessing student writers, then, begins with each of us thinking hard about the kind of writers we want our students to become.

Becoming a Lifelong Writer

I use the term *lifelong writer* to describe the kind of writer I hope students will someday become. It's my vision for students that each will grow up to be the kind of person who uses writing across her or his entire adult life. Donald Graves has a similarly ambitious vision for students. In his book *A Fresh Look at Writing* (1994), Graves writes that he hopes each student in a writing workshop will become someone who uses writing as part of his or her everyday life to think, to learn, and to communicate—in other words, a lifelong writer.

My own way of describing a lifelong writer is someone who exhibits three characteristics:

- The lifelong writer initiates writing.
- The lifelong writer writes well.
- The lifelong writer has a writing process that works for him or her.

The Lifelong Writer Initiates Writing

To me, the most fundamental characteristic of a lifelong writer is that he initiates writing throughout his life. Donald Graves (1994) writes, "The most important [characteristic], the one that underlies all the others, is 'child initiates.' When the child initiates writing, she shows an understanding of what writing can do for her as author and for her audience" (155).

A writer who initiates writing is someone who understands that the written word has the power to *do* things in the world, that writing is a way to achieve many important purposes. He might write to make sense of life's experiences. She might write to teach others about one of her passions. He might write to try to correct an injustice.

A writer who initiates writing has a repertoire of genres she writes in to achieve her purposes. In order to share epiphanies about her life, she might write memoir or poetry. To communicate the results of research projects, he might write reports or publish an article in a professional journal. To urge her congressman to support legislation, she might write letters to that congressman or op-ed pieces for her local paper.

A writer who initiates writing understands that writing is an act of communication and thus writes for real audiences. He writes a eulogy for his father to help family and friends gathered at the funeral celebrate his father's life. He writes emails to members of his congregation to let them know about upcoming gatherings. She writes the president of the United States, urging him to reconsider his position on an issue.

Above all, a writer who initiates writing throughout his life is someone who finds writing meaningful. He may or may not love to write—I can't say that I *love* to write—but he finds satisfaction in discovering new meaning as he writes and in communicating his thoughts to others.

The Lifelong Writer Writes Well

By writing well, I don't mean a lifelong writer has to be good enough to win a Pulitzer prize. I am a lifelong skier, but I'll never win a gold medal at the Olympics. But I am able to ski well enough to achieve my two main purposes, which are to get down a mountain without breaking my neck and to have a good time while doing it.

A lifelong writer writes well when he is able to communicate with his audience effectively. But what exactly do writers *do* when they write well? Many educators have given answers to this question, usually in the form of lists of traits or qualities of good writing. (Several are discussed in Chapter 4.) These traits are descriptors of what writers do when they write well. Good writers *communicate meaning* when they write. Good writers *structure* their writing. Good writers *use the conventions* of standard written English. And so forth. In her book *Creating Writers Through 6-Trait Writing Assessment and Instruction* (2001), Vicki Spandel writes:

> [These qualities] are an inherent part of what makes writing work, and they have been around virtually as long as writing itself. We might think of them as distant planets—always there, awaiting discovery. What teachers and writers *have* invented is a language for *describing* the qualities, or traits, that most other teachers, writers, and readers think are important in good writing. (40)

It's helpful to be familiar with a number of these lists. They can give us the words we need to define what it means to write well. And many of the qualities or traits on these lists now show up on district or state writing rubrics. It's good to know that these lists originated in conversations that stretch back several decades.

Ultimately, in order to assess how well students are writing, each of us needs to think hard about what it means to write well. Some of us might use a list of traits that we learned about in a professional book or workshop or that our colleagues in our school or district use. And some of us might put our personal imprint on these lists. Over the course of the nineteen years that I've been a teacher of writing, I've created a version of the qualities of good writing that works for me when I assess how well students write (see Figure 2.1), a version that I discuss in detail in Chapter 4. While my list doesn't differ radically from the standard ones, it uses the language that makes the most sense to me when I consider what writers do when they write well.

A Lifelong Writer Writes Well When She:
- Communicates meaning
- Uses genre knowledge
- Structures her writing
- Writes with detail
- Gives her writing voice
- Uses conventions

FIGURE 2.1

The Lifelong Writer Has a Writing Process That Works for Him

A lifelong writer is someone who has developed, over time, a writing process that works for him. Those last two words—*for him*—are important. While writers generally go through the same series of steps in the process of making a piece of writing—rehearsal (or prewriting), drafting, revising, editing, and publishing—how one navigates these steps varies from person to person.

In his guidebook for student writers, *How Writers Work: Finding a Process That Works for You* (2000), Ralph Fletcher writes, "Certain people talk about the 'writing process' as if there is one, and only one, process for writing. . . . True, there are interesting similarities in how various writers work, but each writer uses a process slightly different from that of other writers . . . For every writer who works one way, you'll find a writer who works in another" (3–4). Some writers, for example, keep a writer's notebook in which they regularly write entries about topics that later become published pieces of writing. Other writers keep a running list of ideas to write about in a file on their computer. Some writers write about a topic extensively in their writer's notebook before they draft, using this writing to figure out what they want to say about the topic and to find their voice in talking about the topic. Other writers plunge right in, discovering what they want to say about the topic and finding their voice as they draft and revise. Some writers edit their pieces by reading them aloud over and over again. Other writers rely on editors to read their work—their spouses, friends, or colleagues.

If each writer's writing process is individual, how do we know whether or not the process *works*? If a writer consistently produces well-written pieces, then whatever process enables her to make those pieces is most likely an effective one. Conversely, if a writer more often than not writes pieces that aren't well written, then it may be that his writing process is an ineffective one.

Developing Your Own Vision

When I share my vision of the lifelong writer with teachers in workshops, they usually tell me that it makes sense. And they tell me that they're eager to try out my vision as an assessment lens when they return to their writing workshops.

In response, I tell them that I think it can be a valuable first step to use someone else's assessment lens for a while. Sometimes the lens someone else has already developed works perfectly well for us, too. But for others of us, trying out someone else's lens is a means to

Develop (or further develop) your vision of who you want your students to become as writers.

- *Think about yourself as a writer.* Jot down on a piece of paper some words that describe you as a writer. In which ways would you like your students to be like you (or different from you)? Which words do you use to describe yourself as a writer that you might want to use to compose your vision of a good writer?

- *Talk to—or read about—other writers.* Think about the ways in which you would like your students to be like them. Which words describing these writers might you want to include in your vision of a good writer? One starting place for reading about a writer is her or his website. You can also read books, such as *Author Talk* (Marcus 2000) or *Speaking of Poets 2* (Copeland and Copeland 1994), that recount numerous details about the writing lives of many writers.

- *Read other educators' visions.*[1] Which aspects of their vision for student writers are congruent with your vision? Which aspects of their vision differ from yours and could lead you to rethink aspects of your own? Are you comfortable with the words they've chosen to describe their vision? Do you want to use some of these same words in yours?

- *Read your district and state standards.* The educators who have penned writing standards over the past decade have done so in order to provide a local or statewide vision of who students should become as writers. An important reason to become familiar with the standards in your district or state is to be aware of the words that other teachers will be using in conversations about student writers and what those words mean. While you may decide to use synonyms for these words in your mind or in your teaching, you'll need to know them in order to have conversations with your colleagues.

---

1. See, for example, Don Graves' vision, in *A Fresh Look at Writing* (1994), pages 154–56, and Katie Wood Ray's, in *Wondrous Words* (1999), pages 212–14.

developing our own individual assessment lens. Notice that I used the word *individual*, not *unique*. In my conversations with writing teachers around the country, I've noticed that most have similar hopes for the student writers they teach. However, some teachers put more—or less—emphasis on one or another of the characteristics. Or they use different words to describe them.

Gathering Information About How Our Students Are Growing into Lifelong Writers

Teachers who take an assessment stance are constantly gathering information about their student writers, or, as Don Graves (1994) says, constantly letting the students in their writing workshops teach them what these students know about writing. They see what's going on in their writing workshop in the way that Dorothy saw Oz when she first walked out of the door of her family's house after the twister deposited it there: a place full of interesting things to notice, to be intrigued by, to marvel at, and to be moved by.

Of course, there's so much going on in a writing workshop that it would be easy to become overwhelmed by too much information. Anayra is chewing on her pencil eraser. Tory and Jeff are huddled together, talking about how Karen Hess has crafted one of her picture books. Danya begins her draft with the words, "Ding, dong, the doorbell rang." Is all of this useful information? Is any of it?

Having an assessment lens helps us decide what information we should pay attention to and what information we can disregard. When I'm working with students in a writing workshop, I gather information about the ways that they are beginning to resemble lifelong writers. How are they initiating their writing? What do they do to write well? What writing processes are they using? I tap three sources.

Source Number 1: What Students Are Doing

The first source is what students *do* when they write, information we can gather by using our eyes to observe what students are doing while they are writing and our ears to listen to what students are saying about their writing—what Yetta Goodman (1985) describes as "kidwatching." James and Kathleen Strickland (2000) write, "Teachers who believe in supporting learners use assessment by observation on a daily basis; they are continuously searching for patterns, supporting students as they take risks and move forward, and watching in order to better facilitate further learning" (21).

Kind of Information We Want to Gather	Examples of What We Might Notice or Hear
Information about students' initiative as writers	• A student gets right to work after the minilesson (or doesn't). • A student stays focused on his writing for most of writing workshop (or doesn't). • A student seeks out peers for response to a work in process.
Information about what students know about writing well	• Two students talk in a peer conference about what they're doing to try to make their pieces good writing.
Information about students' writing process	• The writing strategies students use as they write (rereading a draft, talking with classmates about one's writing, reading a draft aloud to listen for errors in spelling and punctuation). • The kinds of writing tools students use to help them navigate the writing process (a writer's notebook, a touchstone text, sticky notes added to a draft, revision and editing checklists).

FIGURE 2.2

Observation takes two general forms. Sometimes we decide to watch a child (or several children in a peer conference or response group) for several minutes as he works on his writing. And sometimes we happen to notice something intriguing about a child while we're in the midst of doing something else, like walking around the classroom in between our writing conferences. By using just our eyes and ears, it's possible to gather information about how students are approximating all three characteristics of the lifelong writer (see Figure 2.2).

For example, we'll notice that some students get right to work and stay focused on their writing for most of the workshop. From this we can infer that these students are probably initiators of writing and find writing meaningful. We'll notice that some students stop writing occasionally and reread what they've written so far. This tells us something about these students' writing processes. From the talk we overhear in a peer conference, we'll learn something about what students think it means to write.

Source Number 2: What Students Are Thinking

The second source is what students are thinking—about what they're doing when they write and about their writing as they write. The best way to discover what students are thinking is to listen to them talk about their writing in conferences. Peter Johnston (1997) writes that "the ability to listen is a teacher's most important assessment skill. Actively listening to what a child has to say about her own . . . writing enables us to understand the logic of her literate behavior" (9).

Writing conferences, then, are windows into a young writer's mind. When we sit down and ask a student, "How's it going?" we might learn why he's writing the piece he's working on and with whom he intends to share it. We might learn where he is in the process of writing the piece and the tools and strategies he's using to navigate that particular step. And we might find out what he's trying to do to write well. This information contributes to our understanding of how he is becoming a lifelong writer.

Let's look at the transcript of the first part of a conference I had with Eric—the "research" part of the conference, as Lucy Calkins (1994) describes it. As you read the transcript, think about the kinds of information that can be gleaned from what Eric is sharing.

ME: What are you doing as a writer, Eric?

ERIC: I just started doing a better draft of my piece called "When We Went to the Beach."

ME: That sounds like a lot of fun.

ERIC: Yeah.

ME: You said you're working on a better draft? What do you mean by that?

ERIC: Well, I've looked over it more, and I think I'll add some more details, like Cynthia Rylant does in *The Relatives Came*.

ME: Details?

ERIC: Well, one thing I thought I could do is talk about how I played my Gameboy in the car. Oh, and about how my sister threw up, too. She got carsick.

ME: [*Skimming Eric's piece*] Why do you think writers add details to a part of a story, Eric?

ERIC: [*Thinks for a moment*] Because it would paint a picture in a reader's mind?

ME: So you add more details because you want to paint a picture in our minds. [*Eric nods.*] I'm curious, Eric. What do you think are the really important parts of your piece?

ERIC: Where we were on the beach . . . right here [*points*] . . . where we went in the water. That was fun.

ME: I had a feeling you were going to say that part is an important one.

As Eric and I sit together and talk about his writing, he teaches me a lot about himself as a writer. For example, I learn something about Eric's writing process. His concept of what you do with a draft when you finish it is to "look it over more" and write a "better draft." He also thinks about the writing of another writer, Cynthia Rylant, when he's trying to decide what changes he needs to make. I also learn a little about what Eric thinks is necessary to write well. His desire "to add some more details" tells me he knows about the importance of detail in telling about an event in his life.

Not all students are able to talk about their writing in the ways that Eric did in this conference. It's important to note that their inability (or in some cases, unwillingness) to talk is not necessarily evidence that they don't know very much about writing. Instead, their silence when we ask, "How's it going?" may simply mean they need our help in learning about the ways writers think and talk about what they do.

Conferring with students is an indispensable source of information about them as writers—information that's available to us if we listen hard to what students are saying about their writing as we talk with them.

Source Number 3: What Students Are Writing

The third source is student writing, by which I mean much more than finished pieces. We can gather information not only from finished pieces but also from the writing that students do in the process of making their finished pieces—their writer's notebooks and their rough drafts, with revisions and edits visible. In fact, in the day-to-day life of the writing workshop, it's this kind of writing that teachers see most often. And we can also gather information from the writing that students do *about* their writing—the table of contents in their writing folder, their written reflections about individual pieces and their portfolio.

Each of these kinds of student writing can give us certain kinds of information (see Figure 2.3). When we look at students' finished drafts, for example, we get a picture of what a student does when he tries to write well. Writer's notebooks let us see what students do in the process of rehearsing a piece of writing and how their knowledge of writing well shapes their rehearsal process. The changes that students make to a piece of writing—rewriting a lead, reorganizing a piece,

Type of Student Writing	Kind of Information We Can Learn
Final, or published, pieces	• What students do when they try to write well • With some genres (such as letters to the editor), who the intended audience is
Writer's notebooks	• What students do in the rehearsal process (find topics, gather information about a topic)
Revised and edited drafts	• What students do in the process of revising and editing drafts • What students do to write well • Students' knowledge of the language system—grammar, mechanics, spelling
The table of contents in student's writing folders	• Which audiences students share their writing with during the year • The range of genres that students write in during the year
Students' written reflections about their writing (individual pieces and their writing portfolios) and about their writing histories	• Why students have written pieces, and for whom • What students think it means to write well • The process students went through to write their pieces • Students' assessments of their writing and of themselves as writers

FIGURE 2.3

adding information to a section—tell us what they think they need to do in order to write well. And students' written reflections about their writing can give us information about all aspects of them as writers. We might find out why a student wrote a piece or what a student thinks a collection of his pieces says about his strengths as a writer.

TEACHER ACTION 2.2

Ask yourself about the sources of information you rely on to assess students.

- What kinds of things do you tend to notice about your students as you observe them at work in your writing workshop? What else could you focus on? How does what you observe affect what you teach in writing conferences? How does this information help you in your whole-class teaching?

- What kinds of things do you learn about students when you confer with them? What other things could you learn? How does what you learn help you teach students in conferences? How does what you learn help you in your whole-class teaching?

- Which kinds of student writing do you read to assess students (final drafts, writer's notebooks, drafts with revisions and edits, writing students do about their writing)? What other kinds of student writing could you read? What kinds of things do you learn about students when you read their writing? How does this information help you confer with them? How does it help you in your whole-class teaching?

- Is there one source of information that you rely on most to gather information about your student writers? Why? Is there a source you tend to overlook?

- How do you record information you learn about students? How do you use what you record in your day-to-day teaching? How else could you use this information?

In this book, when I talk about reading student writing, I mean primarily the writing that students do in the process of composing a piece as well as their finished drafts—the two types of student writing teachers read most often.

I also think it's useful to have students write about their writing— beginning-of-year surveys, midyear and end-of-year reflections on themselves as writers, reflections on individual pieces, and reflections on the writing they decide to include in their writing portfolios. There are good books in the professional literature on this.[2]

---

2. See, for example, *Portfolio Portraits*, edited by Donald Graves and Bonnie Sunstein (1992), *The Portfolio Standard*, edited by Bonnie Sunstein and Jonathan Lovell (2000), and *Making Assessment Elementary*, by Kathleen and James Strickland (2000).

References

Calkins, Lucy. 1994. *The Art of Teaching Writing.* New ed. Portsmouth, NH: Heinemann.

Copeland, Jeffrey S., and Vicky L. Copeland. 1994. *Speaking of Poets 2: More Interviews with Poets Who Wrote for Children and Young Adults.* Urbana, IL: NCTE.

Fletcher, Ralph. 2000. *How Writers Work: Finding a Process That Works for You.* New York: HarperCollins.

Goodman, Yetta. 1985. "Kidwatching: Observing Children in the Classroom." In *Observing the Language Learner*, edited by Angela Jaguar and M. Trinka Smith-Burke. Newark, DE: International Reading Association.

Graves, Donald. 1994. *A Fresh Look at Writing.* Portsmouth, NH: Heinemann.

Graves, Donald, and Bonnie Sunstein, eds. 1992. *Portfolio Portraits.* Portsmouth, NH: Heinemann.

Johnston, Peter H. 1997. *Knowing Literacy: Constructive Literacy Assessment.* Portland, ME: Stenhouse.

Marcus, L. S., ed. 2000. *Author Talk.* New York: Simon and Schuster.

Ray, Katie Wood. 1999. *Wondrous Words: Writers and Writing in the Elementary Classroom.* Urbana, IL: NCTE.

Spandel, Vicki. 2001. *Creating Writers Through 6-Trait Writing Assessment and Instruction.* 3d ed. New York: Addison Wesley Longman.

Stiggins, Richard. 1996. *Student-Centered Classroom Assessment.* 2d ed. Columbus, OH: Merrill Education/Prentice-Hall.

Strickland, Kathleen, and James Strickland. 2000. *Making Assessment Elementary.* Portsmouth, NH: Heinemann.

Sunstein, Bonnie, and Jonathan Lovell. 2000. *The Portfolio Standard: How Students Can Show Us What They Know and Are Able to Do.* Portsmouth, NH: Heinemann.

Wiggins, Grant, and Jay McTighe. 2000. *Understanding by Design.* New York: Prentice Hall.

Assessing Students as Initiators of Writing

3

> *Children want to write.*
> —DONALD GRAVES, Writing: Teachers and Children at Work

> *Learning to use literacy to obtain or accomplish something*
> *is a cultural norm and a political predisposition,*
> *one that adults must pass on to children.*
> —RANDY AND KATHERINE BOMER, For a Better World

On the Fourth of July, Americans hang flags in their front yards, decorate their houses with red, white, and blue bunting, gather family and friends for backyard barbecues, and, in the evening, watch fireworks explode in the sky. We do all this to celebrate the declaration made by our founding fathers on July 4, 1776, that the thirteen colonies would be from that date on independent of England.

It pleases me that we have a national holiday to celebrate a piece of writing, the Declaration of Independence. The authors of the declaration knew that the written word has power and knew that they could use writing as a tool to achieve purposes that mattered to them. Therefore, we are celebrating people who were *initiators* of writing in their lives.

With increasing numbers of teachers conducting writing workshops in their classrooms, more and more American children have excellent writing instruction as part of every school day and thus have the opportunity to become initiators of writing, just as our founders were. That students can and do become initiators of writing has been well documented in numerous professional books and articles over the past two decades—see, for example, Nancie Atwell's *In the Middle* (1998), Lucy Calkins' *The Art of Teaching Writing* (1994), Judy Davis and Sharon Hill's *The No-Nonsense Guide to Teaching Writing* (2003), or Colleen Cruz's *Independent Writing* (2004).

Children who are initiators of writing in their lives *learn* to be this kind of writer. While, like Donald Graves (1983), I have observed—both as a staff developer in numerous primary classrooms and as a parent—that most children start school wanting to write, this desire doesn't mean that children intuitively know what writing can *do* for them. It's in the literate communities of which they are a part, in school, at home, and in the larger world, that they learn the range of purposes that writing can help them realize, the genres they can write in to help them achieve those purposes, and the kinds of audiences that their writing can affect.

Ultimately, our success as writing teachers can truly be measured only by how students use writing *after* being in our writing workshops. Nothing we teach about writing matters, nothing students accomplish while in our writing workshops matters, if they never do it again later in their lives. Judy Davis and Sharon Hill (2003) write, "The true test of whether Writing Workshop has made a difference is not whether all of our students become professional writers . . . but whether writing becomes a tool they use for responding to the world—to comfort, to convince, to pay tribute, to commemorate, to celebrate, and to speak out" (205).

If we're going to be able to help children learn to become initiators of writing—or writers who initiate writing for new reasons—we need to start by assessing students as initiators of writing. We need to figure out who students are *right now* as initiators of writing so that we can begin to imagine what we need to teach them *next* to help them grow as initiators of writing.

What Does It Mean to Be an Initiator of Writing?

A writer who initiates writing in his life finds the act of writing to be, first and foremost, a meaningful one—meaningful because writing can help him achieve purposes and communicate with audiences that are important to him. Someone who finds writing meaningful doesn't have to be a professional writer who writes books or who wins major literary prizes. All sorts of people who never write a book or an article or an essay find writing a meaningful thing to do—principals write memos to their staff, parents leave love notes in their children's lunch boxes, friends write toasts to give at their friends' weddings, citizens write letters to newspapers complaining about government policies they don't like.

Someone who finds writing meaningful may—or may not—love to write. Don Graves (1993) tells about beginning a speech to a student assembly by declaring, "I hate to write." When the students' applause died down (apparently many of them felt the same way!), he followed up with, "But I love *having written*," a line Don says he stole from writer Dorothy Parker. Don's message was that while he finds writing a "sweaty business," in the end he finds it worthwhile, because writing helps him realize purposes that are important to him. Don may hate to write, but he still initiates writing in his life.

What are the characteristics of someone who initiates writing? As I see it, an initiator of writing

- writes for various purposes
- has a repertoire of genres
- writes for real audiences

Writing for Varied Purposes

People write because they know—and believe—that writing can help them achieve something important, in their personal lives or in the world beyond. According to Katie Wood Ray (1999), "It is the good reason to write that will propel the experienced writer forward through all the processes necessary to move an idea to publication" (95). The "good reason to write" inspires people to initiate writing, even when it's hard work, even when they hate to write.

People write for many, many good reasons. One reason I have written this book is because I wanted to learn more about writing assessment, and I know that writing a book about something is one of the best ways to justify taking the time to really learn about that subject. Another is because I enjoy teaching, and writing a book is one way I can be a teacher. Still another is to argue that the foundation of good writing instruction is knowing students well as writers.

Reading what other writers have written about their writing lives has taught me many other good reasons that writers write. In his book *Crafting a Life in Essay, Story, Poem* (1996), Pulitzer prize–winning author Don Murray details twelve reasons he writes. One of them is "to say I am." Don explains, "When we write, we become visible, we are players in the game of life" (2). Another is "to testify." Don writes, "I also bear witness to the horrors of war, to the shame of describing a child who learns differently from others as 'stupid,' to the wonder of my unexpected life" (7). Yet another is "to celebrate". Don says, "Writing makes me aware of the extraordinary in the ordinary" (8).

I've detailed some reasons to write in Figure 3.1. It's instructive to compare them with the reasons many of us tell students that writers write: to tell a story, to inform, to persuade, and to respond to reading. These generic ways of talking about writers' purposes (which often are the words used in state standards) aren't specific enough to help students understand the varied reasons experienced writers write and thus to help them imagine all of the varied reasons they themselves can write.

Using a Repertoire of Genres

Initiators of writing have a repertoire of genres and a sense of what different genres can *do* for them. Genres, after all, are types of writing that members of a culture create as tools to help them achieve certain purposes (see Figure 3.2).

Some Purposes for Writing
- To celebrate an important person or event in your life
- To persuade someone to think like you do on an issue
- To bear witness
- To show how fascinating a subject is
- To let someone know how to do something
- To help create a better society
- To disagree with a position taken by others
- To make someone laugh
- To learn something about yourself or a subject
- To be understood by others for who you are
- To get someone to vote for you
- To teach a moral or lesson
- To complain about something
- To recommend an action
- To tell what happened
- To share a passion with others
- To explore an idea
- To imagine how your life could be different
- To make plans
- To imagine what it would like to be someone else
- To share how you feel about someone
- To make money
- To remember
- To heal
- To leave something behind of you for others

FIGURE 3.1

For example, people write personal ads to help them find a soul mate. People compose arguments to persuade others to think as they do about an issue that matters to them. People write book reviews to share their response to a book and to help others decide whether or not they should read the book. Charles Cooper (1999) says, "Genres develop in recurring, concrete social situations where people must communicate with one another in writing . . . in family and community life, school or college, the professions, government, leisure, religion, politics—all of the countless occasions for interaction and communication, for conflict and cooperation" (25).

In our culture, there are some purposes for writing that most initiators of writing have in common. Because most of us like to ex-

Genre	Some Purposes for Writing in the Genre
Memoir	• To reveal something important about yourself and your life • To leave something behind of you for others • To bear witness • To learn something about yourself • To celebrate an important person or event in your life
Feature article	• To share a passion with others • To show how fascinating a subject is
Short story	• To explore a theme • To teach a moral or lesson • To imagine how your life could be different
Op-ed piece	• To persuade someone to think like you do on an issue • To critique society • To disagree with a position taken by others • To help create a better world

FIGURE 3.2

press gratitude for gifts we receive or for interviews that we've been granted, most of us know how to write thank-you notes. And because most of us need to exchange information with others quickly, we've learned how to compose emails.

There are some purposes for writing, however, that are specific to who people are as individuals. Hence, some initiators of writing have genres in their writing repertoires that others don't. Teachers write lesson plans; doctors write prescriptions; members of the clergy write sermons; political activists write campaign literature; and so forth.

In the schools that many of us attended as children, we learned that genres were ways of classifying texts. In today's genre studies in writing workshops, children are not only learning about the features of certain genres, such as memoir or short story, but also learning through experience what purposes these genres can fulfill in their lives. In addition to developing their repertoire of genres, they're learning about the connection between purpose and genre, a connection that initiators of writing will make again and again.

Writing for Real Audiences

People initiate writing for real audiences. Without readers, a text is nothing more than a series of symbols. For a text to fulfill the purposes intended by its author—for it to *do* something in the world—it must be read by others.

Writers write for different types of audiences. For example, sometimes a writer writes a text with a specific person in mind. I've written letters to several of our presidents to let them know how I felt about their policies. And I have written emails to my daughter's teachers to give them information my wife and I thought they needed to know. Sometimes a writer is writing for himself. A person who keeps a journal usually doesn't intend anyone else to be privy to what he records in its pages. He might write in his journal as a way to help him reflect on ideas or remember events he doesn't want to forget.

Sometimes a writer writes a text with a specific subgroup of society in mind. For example, I have written this book for teachers who teach writing and for the administrators and literacy coaches who support them. Teachers write letters to the parents of the children in their classes. Sports columnists write for their fellow sports fans. People write petitions to be considered by their local school board or zoning commission.

And sometimes writers write with a general audience in mind. People write poems or short stories that can be read by anyone who reads the particular magazine or literary journal they appear in. Journalists write news articles that may be read by anyone who happens to pick up a newspaper on a given day or feature articles that may be read by anyone who picks up a magazine in a doctor's office or on an airplane.

Teachers who conduct writing workshops in their classroom expect that that their students will be writing for real audiences—a family member, a group of their friends who share a common interest, the readers of a magazine such as *Merlyn's Pen*. In contrast to many of our early experiences with writing in school, children today are learning through experience that writing is an act of communication with others.

Assessing Students as Initiators of Writing

Until teachers started launching writing workshops in their classrooms in the late 1970s, it didn't make much sense to assess students as initiators of writing, since most of the writing students did was in response to prompts designed by their teachers. The primary purpose students had for writing was to complete an assignment. "Writing to an assigned topic, no matter how 'good' the teacher thinks the assignment, is, from the writer's perspective, largely if not entirely an act of compliance rather than a linguistic *doing* meant to affect the world" (Bomer and Bomer 2001, 3).

The audience for this kind of traditional writing assignment was usually only the teacher, whose role was to evaluate whether or not students had gotten the assignment "right." In contrast, real audiences don't respond to a piece of writing by giving it a grade—they laugh or cry, change their mind about an issue, or express a sense of wonder at learning something they didn't know before.

Today, now that more and more students in the United States participate in a writing workshop each school day, they have the opportunity to learn to become initiators of writing. In part, that's because teachers who set up writing workshops no longer give students writing prompts. By giving students the opportunity to choose which topic to write about—and, often, which genre to write in—teachers are inviting students to have purposes for writing other than satisfying the requirements of a teacher-designed assignment. Teachers are also helping students find real audiences for their writing—other students in the classroom, people in the world outside the classroom. Phyllis Ryder, Elizabeth Vander Lei, and Duane Roen (1999) observe that the role of the teacher in a writing workshop has shifted from "judge" to "coach." They write, "Instead of responding to a text by saying, 'This is how it's done; these are the rules,' we can say, 'Your writing will probably affect your reader in X way,' and explain how the author might better reach that audience" (54).

Of course, participating in a writing workshop does not magically transform students into initiators of writing. Some students will have had little previous experience with writing and will therefore know little about what writing can do for them. It's imperative that we identify these students early in the school year so that we can help them find answers to the question: Why should I write?

Other students will have had writing experiences that have taught them about *some* of the purposes that writing can fulfill for them, *some* of the genres in which they can choose to write, and *some* of the kinds of audiences they can affect with their writing. It's important that we learn why these students write, which genres they usually write in, and who they expect will read their writing, so that over the course of the school year, we can help them explore other purposes, try unfamiliar genres, and reach new kinds of audiences.

How can we assess whether or not a student initiates writing in his life? How do we determine what writing purposes students already have, what genres are in their repertoire, and the kinds of audiences for which they have learned to write?

What Actions Indicate Students Are Initiators of Writing?

Initiators of writing act in certain observable ways. Most obviously, they *write*. They usually write because they want to, not because they are told to. Moreover, they usually have certain writing habits that help them get their writing done and that help them write well. People who initiate writing also share their writing with others.

Take me. If you had spied on me during the time I wrote this book, you would have noticed that I wrote several times during a typical week, whenever and wherever I could. I wrote in coffee shops on weekend mornings, on the train or plane as I traveled to work in various schools across the country, and in the morning at the dining room table while my wife and daughter were asleep. In fact, I looked at my calendar at the beginning of each week and figured out which days would be writing days. When the times I had scheduled for writing arrived, I usually got right to work and used the time I had as well as I could.

You would also have noticed that even when I wasn't writing, I was still doing things to help move this project along. I thought about what I was writing and frequently jotted these thoughts down in my writer's notebook while I was riding the subway, eating a slice of pizza, or reading the newspaper. I read professional books to help me deepen my knowledge of assessment. When I finished a draft of a chapter, I gave a copy to my wife, Robin; my editor at Heinemann, Kate Montgomery; and several other friends and colleagues, and waited eagerly for their responses. Then I revised what I had written so that what I was trying to say would be even clearer.

In short, I acted in many of the typical ways that people who initiate writing act; you could easily have observed my behavior and, in response, surmised that I was working on a project that was important to me.

Many children who have learned that writing can fulfill purposes important to them will act in similar ways when they are in (and outside) writing workshop. Observing this behavior, we can infer that these students may be initiators of writing. I use the word *may* because teacher pleasers act in similar ways even if they have no other motivation than to meet the requirement that they write in writing workshop. To be able to conclude more definitively that students have reasons of their own for writing, we need to consider some additional indicators.

How Students Use Their Time in Writing Workshop

One of the easiest things to observe is how well students use the time we give them to write. When I'm in a classroom, I watch how students get to work after that day's minilesson. Which students dig right in? Which ones are still having trouble getting started five or even ten minutes later?

I also look for how well students are able to sustain their writing. Which students stay focused, stopping for reasons connected to their writing, such as getting materials or having a peer conference? Which ones seem easily distracted and are constantly at the pencil sharpener or disappearing to the bathroom?

Whether Students Make Plans for Their Writing

It's important to notice which students think ahead and imagine when and how they're going to get their writing project done. A student who writes for important reasons of his own is more likely to figure out how to get a piece done so that he can get it out into the world to do what he wants it to do. Conversely, it's important to learn which students are passive with regard to time and don't seem to care when and how their writing will get done.

One way to find out whether students are the kind of writers who think ahead is to check whether they have written down their plans. In some classrooms, students fill out planning sheets to help them think out what they need to do to compose a piece of writing (see Figure 3.3). In Colleen Cruz's fourth-grade classroom, which she describes in her book *Independent Writing* (2004), her students used calendars to give themselves deadlines for projects; they imagined where they would be in the writing process on each date leading up to those deadlines.

To find out whether or not primary students are beginning to make plans for their writing, we can watch how they use their writing folders when it's time to wrap up their writing at the end of writing workshop. A student who is planning to work more on a piece will put her draft in the *not finished* side of her folder while a student who wants to write a new piece the next day will put that day's writing in the *finished* side.

Whether Students Have Good Writing Habits

People who initiate writing have certain writing habits that help them write well enough to communicate effectively with their readers. When they get to the end of a draft, they revise and edit it. They share their work in progress with others to get feedback. They look at the work

Planning Sheet

Name _____

Date _____

1. A brief description of my writing project:

2. What work am I planning to do in my writer's notebook to get ready
    to draft?

3. Which model texts do I plan to use to help me write my draft?

4. I expect to be done by this date: _____ .

FIGURE 3.3

of other authors for ideas on how they can craft their own writing. They genuinely want their writing to affect others, so they do things to ensure that their writing is as good as they can make it—things we can observe as students are busy writing.

We need to pay attention to which students have some or all of these writing habits—which revise, edit, have peer conferences, or look at model texts *on their own*. Some students, of course, do none of these independently. They write a draft, write "The End" on the bottom of the page in big letters, and announce, "I'm done." Many students write like this because they have no reason to write except to get it done as quickly as possible. Other students write like this because they haven't yet been taught to revise and edit, to collaborate with other students, or to use other authors as mentors.

Which Audiences Students Seek Out for Their Writing

We need to pay attention to whether students share their writing with others. Which students ask if they can read their finished pieces to a classmate in the corner of the classroom? Which students beg to read their writing to the class in share sessions? Which students have their writing finished on time for a whole-class writing celebration? Which students ask if they can take a piece home to share with a family member? Which students send their writing to the local newspaper or to a children's magazine?

Whether Students Make Time for Writing Outside Writing Workshop

Students who discover in writing workshop that writing can help them do things in their lives often continue to work on their writing during other parts of the day. For example, fourth-grade teacher Lindsay Caplin noted that soon after she introduced her writing workshop, some of her students begged her to allow them to work some more on their pieces during free time or over the weekend.

Which of our students are like Lindsay's? Which students ask for more time or continue to write even after we have announced that it's time to share? Which students put their writer's notebook in their backpack and jot down new ideas for writing when they're at home? Which students are visibly or vocally relieved that writing time is over?

While it's not possible for us to be with students after school, we can still see evidence that some of them write when they're at home. In Colleen Cruz's fourth-grade classroom, she helped her students envision that they could each become the kind of writer who writes pieces not just at school but also at home. During the year, her students wrote comic books, recipe books, short novels, fantasy stories, plays, songs, profiles, picture books, poetry collections, and many other genres in addition to the pieces they wrote as part of the units of study in Colleen's

TEACHER ACTION 3.1

Observe your students to find out information about them as initiators of writing. (You may want to use the checklist "Assessing Students' Initiative as Writers" in Appendix 1 to help you record your observations.)

- Periodically throughout the year, spend a writing workshop period observing your students at work. Which students get to work right away? Which take a while to get started? Which students stay focused on their work? Which are easily distracted? By what? Which students are revising or editing drafts on their own? Which students seek out peer conferences? Which students refer to texts written by other authors?

- In a whole-class meeting or in conferences, ask students whether they write outside school. Do they write in their writer's notebooks? Do they continue working on the drafts they're working on in school? Do they write additional pieces at home? Ask students to show you writing that they've done at home.

curriculum. Colleen invited her students to put these "independent projects" in a special box for her to read. A box for independent projects filling up with pieces—from two students one day, three the next, one the day after—is something that we can see and value as evidence that students are making writing part of their whole lives.

What Does Students' Writing Reveal About Them as Initiators of Writing?

By reading student writing—and the writing they do about their writing—we can gather information about the purposes for which students seem to be writing in their lives. Sometimes, too, we can learn about the audiences they seem to be trying to affect with their writing.

Reading to Learn About Students' Purposes

When I read a piece of student writing to learn about that student as an initiator of writing, I start by asking, "What is the genre?" Genres are tools that writers use to help them realize certain purposes. The genre a student chooses gives us information about her purpose for writing. For example, the piece in Figure 3.4, written by Xiomara, a fifth grader in Christy Bookout's class, is an op-ed, a genre that people often use to persuade readers to believe as they do. Because she wrote

---

Multicultural Teachers

Are you one of those kids that walks into a school and the only teachers you see are from one kind of race? Do you wish that your teachers could speak your language and be a part of your culture? I think there should be more multicultural teachers in New York City public schools. If teachers spoke two different languages it would improve the education of children that do not speak the English language. For example, if children could only speak Spanish they would not be able to learn all the other subjects we are taught. When they grow up they won't know that much. They will need to know the skills of reading, writing and math.

Also if we had more teachers that were multicultural our states would get stronger. How? All of the different racial teachers would have different ideas about how to teach children in classes and different systems could get built in order to teach children better. I think if we had multicultural teachers our world would be more peaceful and probably people will notice that all children are important in the world. It would also help the teachers. They would be able to learn better in a peaceful, multicultural environment.

In my class we have a lot of children that are from many different races. I think it's good that my classmates are from different countries because all of our cultures can unite and defeat anyone that is jealous of us and wants to make us segregate. Our class [would be] like one whole world making a difference.

FIGURE 3.4   Xiomara's Piece

an op-ed, we can say it seems that Xiomara intends to use her writing to persuade.

Notice that I have qualified my observation about her purpose for writing with the word *seems*. I've conferred with many children who were writing beautifully in clearly recognizable genres, which led me to think they had a purpose in mind that writers in that genre typically have. Yet when I asked them why they wrote the piece, they replied, "Because my teacher told me to," or "To meet the narrative standard."

Most often, I get this response when students have written a piece as part of a genre study. In a genre study, students are expected to write in that genre. Now, it's a good thing that students are expected to try the genre they are studying—if they don't, they won't learn what it can do for them. However, it's important not only to study the characteristics of a genre and the techniques writers in that genre routinely use but also to explore the reasons writers write in the genre, in order to help students envision what this kind of writing can do for them in the world.

To get the clearest picture of which purposes for writing truly seem to matter to a child, it makes sense to pay particular attention to the genres that students use *when they can choose any purpose for writing*. Take a look at the table of contents in Randy's folder of finished pieces (see Figure 3.5). The pieces Randy wrote that weren't part of a genre study— stories about his exploits as an athlete, a feature article on Yu-Gi-Oh! cards, an op-ed that his school's playground should be improved, and a short story called "The Champ"—are indicated in bold type. From these choices, we can infer that at the beginning of the school year, Randy probably already knew something about what writing stories and feature articles could do for him. We can also infer that the genre studies of op-eds (in January) and short stories (in March and April) got him excited about these kinds of writing, because he chose to write in these genres again in February and in May and June.

Table of Contents

Date	Title	Genre	Who Did I Share This With
9/26	**My First Home Run**	**Story**	**The class**
10/17	When My Team Won the League Championship	Story	The class
11/7	**All You Need to Know About Yu-Gi-Oh! Cards**	**Feature Article**	**The class** **Jake and Steve**
12/19	What Makes a Good Hitter?	Feature Article	The class My dad
1/30	Why We Should Have Less Homework	Op-ed	The class Ms. Foote [his teacher]
2/13	**The Playground Stinks!**	**Op-ed**	**Mr. Young** [the principal]
3/12	**When I Lost My Ski!**	**Story**	**The class** **My mom and dad**
4/9	The Big Bully	Fiction	The class
5/14	My Poetry Anthology	Poems	The class
6/18	**The Champ**	**Fiction**	**The class**

FIGURE 3.5

In some genres, writers explicitly announce their purpose for writing. When we read an op-ed, for example, we expect the author to tell us his opinion on an issue, and we can look for where in the text he lets us know it. In Xiomara's op-ed, she tells us her purpose in her third sentence: "I think there should be more multicultural teachers in New York City Public Schools."

As we read students' writing to learn their purposes, it's helpful to keep in mind all we know about each student as a person and how what she's writing connects with who she is. Knowing something about who and what is important to a child—family members and friends, hobbies and interests, places in the neighborhood and in the world, opinions about the world—can give us the context we need to understand why a child has chosen to write a particular piece.

Read the piece my daughter, Anzia, a first grader, wrote with the guidance of her teacher, Kelsey Goss (see Figure 3.6). Even if I didn't

Schools Need More Money
by Anzia Anderson

It will be a great day when schools get all the money they need and the air force doesn't have enough money to buy a bomb. It will be a very, very happy day. Almost everyone will be happy, but the air force won't be happy. We hope there will not be any more bombs dropping. If the schools get more money, they could clean the bathrooms more often. And they could have more blocks and more Legos and more K'nex and more fun!!

FIGURE 3.6   Anzia's Piece

know anything about Anzia, I could reasonably infer that because she wrote an op-ed, she knows that she can write to persuade others to believe what she believes—in this case, that we should choose to spend money on our schools instead of on our military. And indeed, since I know Anzia extremely well and know what's important to her, I'm confident that she did, in fact, genuinely write this piece because she wanted to express an opinion that mattered to her.

For example, when Anzia was five, she decided to become a vegetarian; she stopped eating meat because "it hurts animals." In early 2003, in the weeks before the start of the war in Iraq, Anzia overheard my wife and me talking about a peace march that was going to take place in Manhattan. Anzia asked if she could go, so one cold February Saturday, I took her to the demonstration. Afterward she asked us, "Did the march win?" Sadly, we had to tell her no.

You might be thinking that you aren't privy to the kinds of information that parents know about their children. To learn more about your students and their lives, I suggest that you read Don Graves' book *A Fresh Look at Writing* (1993), in which he discusses some strategies for getting to know our students so that we can appreciate how their writing is—or is not—growing out of their lives.[3]

Teachers who teach their students to keep a writer's notebook can learn a great deal about their students' lives when they read these notebooks. For example, Camilla, an eighth-grade student of mine when I taught in Bardstown, Kentucky, wrote in her writer's notebook many, many times about the pressures she felt as a teen. For example, she wrote about the pressure she felt from the media to look a certain way:

> I'd like to comment on teenagers in movies and T.V. shows. Why are they so damned *perfect*? Like for instance I remember one time there was this episode of, like, *The Wonder Years*, where Kevin gets one lousy pimple and is upset about one stinking zit. You know, I would be happy to have only one zit at a time (so would a lot of people). But no, when I break out, I BREAK OUT.

Because I read Camilla's notebook periodically during the school year and knew what was important to her, I wasn't surprised when the chose to write an op-ed piece titled "Under Pressure" (see Figure 3.7). I knew Camilla wrote this piece because she wanted to express an opinion that mattered to her.

Reading to Learn About Students' Audiences

Students tell me time after time that they are writing for "the class." While the class is a perfectly good audience, I want children to learn

---

3. See, for example, Chapter 2, "Learn from the Children."

Under Pressure

Is it just me, or does every teenager feel like they're being pushed into a corner? Like they don't have enough say in the way they lead their lives? Let's face it, as teenagers today, we're constantly being pressured to do things with our lives that we may or may not necessarily want to do. Sometimes it's kind of difficult to tell what's right and what's wrong.

There are lots of different kinds of pressure. Think about it. There's peer pressure, pressure from the media, pressure from our parents and teachers, etc., etc.

We're pressured to do almost everything, in one way or another. We're pressured to pass tests (usually we're bribed to do this), win that student council election, go to the moon . . . well, okay, maybe I'm exaggerating a little, but don't you agree that we get pushed around an awful lot?

Take our parents (please!). We know they love us, and want the best for us, but do you feel pressured by them? "Let's try to get at least an A on this History test." "Let's get into Harvard!" Of course, not all parents are like this, but you get the point. Why do parents expect so much from us?

Take, for instance, my father. He likes to wake me up bright and early every Sunday morning and drag my tired little old butt to Mass. I am not a religious person and he knows it, but he still makes me go to Mass. I guess he thinks that maybe a miracle will happen and I will suddenly decide to become a nun. (Right.)

What does this have to do with "parent pressure?" It's just an example of the many pressures that parents put on their teenage children.

Peer pressure is probably the type of pressure that you notice the most. How many times have you done, said, or worn something just because everyone else was? Probably a lot more than you realize.

We are also constantly being pressured by the media. Do we really need *these* shoes or *those* jeans? (Well, okay, so we do, or we think we do, at least.) Commercials really do influence what we decide to wear, eat, drink, and do. Come on, do people really think that Revlon products will make them look like Cindy Crawford? Well, yeah, probably some people do, but they're wrong. (They're also idiots.) So it's best to just ignore commercials and make your own decisions. (Does it seem like I'm trying to pressure you not to pay attention to commercials?)

So, class, what have we learned from this? All about pressure and about how much pressure can suck. It's everywhere, and you either have to learn to live with it, or just ignore it. That's really up to you, but take my advice if you want and ignore it. Be the best you can possibly be. That sounds like an Army commercial, but I really mean it. And please, please don't ignore positive pressure, like pressure NOT to use drugs, or NOT to do this or whatever, because if you did, you might get into big trouble for it, and I would feel guilty for persuading you to ignore pressure in the first place.

FIGURE 3.7 Camilla's Piece

that they can write pieces for specific individuals in the class (friends or classmates with similar interests) or outside the class (relatives or community leaders) and also for a more general audience (readers of the school or local newspaper). When a child is writing a story about a special trip she took with her family to Cape Cod, does she share it with her class *and* her family? When a child writes an argument that the school playground is in disrepair, does he share it with the class *and* the principal?

A simple way to discover the range of audiences with whom students share their writing is to have them record who these people are on the table of contents of their folder of finished pieces. Take another look at the one that Randy filled out (Figure 3.5). Glancing at the *Who Did I Share This With?* column, we see that Randy shared his writing with individual classmates, his whole class, his teacher, his parents, and the principal of the school—an admirable range of audiences.

Sometimes we can learn about students' intended audiences by reading their finished pieces. Some genres include "naming moves" that signal who the intended audience is and the writer's relation to that audience (Ryder, Vander Lei, and Roen 1999). The simplest naming move we make is beginning a letter or email with "Dear So and So." In other genres, writers use pronouns such as *you* and *your* or *we* and *our* to indicate their audience and their stance toward their audience. In this book, I frequently use the pronoun *we* to indicate that we share many things in common as writers and as educators. Writers also indicate which group (or groups) they're writing for, as I have done in this book when I wrote sentences like this from the book's introduction: "For example, you may be an experienced writing workshop teacher who has numerous units of study in your curricular repertoire and who has been conferring with students about their writing for years."

Take another look at Xiomara's op-ed (Figure 3.4), and notice the naming moves she makes throughout the text. In the lead of the piece, she writes:

> Are you one of those kids that walks into a school and the only teachers you see are from one kind of race? Do you wish that your teachers could speak your language and be a part of your culture?

In these first few sentences, readers learn that Xiomara's audience is other kids—and not any other kids, but those kids who wish their teachers were part of their own culture. And after she names her audience, she speaks directly to the members of that audience using the pronoun *we*: "Also, if we had more teachers that were multicultural, our states would get stronger."

TEACHER ACTION 3.2

Read students' writing to assess them as initiators of writing. (You may want to use the checklist "Assessing Students' Initiative as Writers" in Appendix 1 to help you record your observations.)

- Read some of your students' pieces. What genres are they? What do these genres tell you about the purposes the students probably had for writing these pieces?

- As you read student writing, see if you can find places in the text where students explicitly tell you their purpose for writing.

- Read through students' finished folders or portfolios. Notice the genres students use when they're not studying a particular genre. Assess the range of purposes students write for when it's up to them to have a purpose for writing. Students' decisions to write in a genre that they've studied earlier is evidence that they've learned about new purposes for writing.

- Read through a student's pieces. What do you know about this child that would help you understand why this child might have written each piece? Is what the child has written congruent with what you know about her?

- Look at the table of contents in your students' folders of finished work. Which audiences do they typically write for? Which audiences could you help them imagine writing for in the future?

- Read through student pieces. Which students include naming moves in their texts? What audiences are they writing for?

In genres in which people often write with a general audience in mind—story or poetry, for example—writers may not include these kinds of naming moves. When students are writing in these genres, we will have to get information about the audiences they're writing for from other sources.

What Does Students' Talk Reveal About Them as Initiators of Writing?

We can also ask students directly about their purposes for writing, the genres in which they're writing, and who they imagine sharing their writing with once they're finished. Writing conferences are the best times to ask these questions.

When I confer with students, I often ask early on why they're writing the piece they're working on:

- Why are you writing this piece?
- Why are you writing about this topic?
- What do you hope your writing will do to readers?
- How do you want people to react when they read your piece?

I also ask students to talk to me about the genres they're writing in (or the genres they think they might write in if they're in the very early stages of a writing project):

- What genre do you think you will choose to write in about this topic? Why?
- What genre are you writing in? Why did you choose to write in this genre?

Likewise, I ask students questions about the audience(s) for whom they're writing:

- Who are you writing this piece for?
- Can you tell me which people you hope will read this? Friends? Family? Other people?
- Who are you imagining your readers to be?

Asking these kinds of questions helped me learn about Montana, a fourth grader in Lindsay Caplin's class. When I sat down to confer with her, Montana was working on a story about the birth of her sister, Paige (see Figure 3.8).

Me: How's it going, Montana?

Montana: I'm revising my story.

Me: [*Skimming the first page of her story*] So this is a story about how you felt after your sister was born? [*Montana nods.*] I'm wondering about why you decided to write this.

Montana: I want kids to know that if they're getting a brother or sister, they should know that it's not so bad.

Me: So you're writing this story as a way of letting them know about what can happen. It's like you're going to teach them something?

Montana: Yeah, it's not bad, but it's not good.

Me: It's one of those good-and-bad kind of things, huh? So your story's got a moral to it, it's got a message for kids?

Montana: Yeah.

Me: Who do you want to read this when it's done?

Montana: [*Thinks for a moment*] My mom.

Me: Because she's your mom, and because she's the one who had your sister? You want her to know about how it felt for you?

Montana: Yeah! And any person who is going to have a new sibling.

My Sister Paige

One time, late at night, May 2nd, 1999, my little sister Paige was born. I was so excited and happy to have a new baby sister. Well, actually, just at first. Then, after Paige was about 6 days old, I started to get sick of her.

I got very jealous because my mom was spending all her time with Paige. At this time I was four and a half. My mom used to always be on time to drive me to school, but now, since she had to take care of that sister of mine, I was late. Then, oh my gosh! She was going to the refrigerator to get Paige food when my mom is supposed to be doing that for me! My mom was also giving Paige a nap and changing her diaper at the same time when we were supposed to cuddle on the couch and watch television together! Now I was filled with anger. I felt like I was going to go ballistic! My face was sizzling, boiling, hot, red.

I ran to my room as fast as I could and slammed the door shut super hard. I jumped on my bed, put my face in the pillows and cried. I ALWAYS liked to be the center of attention, but now it's like Paige was a huge block blocking me. I was furious. I stayed in my room for a half hour. Then my dad came in my room and spoke to me. He said, "Don't feel bad because other girls and boys have to deal with little brothers and sisters too." I said to myself, Oh yeah! I sat in my bed, and finally I understood what my dad said. Then I went to the kitchen where my mom was feeding Paige. I apologized to her and Paige. I think Paige said, "Yvlarmaylzmkjo," which probably meant she forgave me. We all laughed. Eventually, it turned out to be pretty cool. I got used to having Paige in the house. I think it's good now to have a sibling because if you're lonely, you will always have someone to play with.

FIGURE 3.8   Montana's Piece

ME: That makes sense. I wonder if there are any kids in your class who are about to have a new sister or brother who you could show this to . . . or if you know any other kids like that. [*Montana nods.*] Anyway . . . so you're revising this story.

MONTANA: Yeah, I think it needs more detail.

ME: More detail . . . let's talk about that.

Ideally, all children would have the sense of purpose and audience that Montana had with this story! With children like Montana, as I talk about why they're writing a piece, I usually restate their purpose: "It's like you're going to teach [kids] something?" and "So your story's got a moral to it, it's got a message for kids?" Sometimes I find it necessary to help children like Montana imagine a more specific audience. After Montana told me she wanted "any person who is going to have a new sibling" to read her piece, I nudged her to think about whether any kids in or outside her class fit into that category. And with children like Montana, once I finish talking about their reasons for writing—talk that usually takes no more than a minute or so—I focus the rest of the conference on teaching them about an aspect of writing well or about developing a more effective writing process. In the remainder of my conference with Montana, I taught her something about adding detail to her story.

Of course, not all children have learned to articulate their purpose for writing and intended audience the way Montana did. When I ask students why or for whom they're writing their pieces, often they don't respond or they shrug. While it would be easy to conclude from these responses that these children don't have purposes or audiences in mind—and sometimes this is the case—it's also possible that these children haven't yet learned how to talk about purpose and audience. In a conference like this, before teaching the child a writing strategy, craft technique, or language convention, I often take a minute to help her learn how to talk about why she's writing her piece. I might say, "I see you're writing a feature article about what it's like to be an only child. I guess that means you're writing this to teach people about what this is like." Then I might help her imagine whom she might share the piece with when she's done: "I know that there are a lot of people who will find this piece very interesting to read. Are there any kids in this class you hope will read it? Family members? People in the school? The community?"

TEACHER ACTION 3.3

Ask students to talk about themselves as initiators of writing. (You may want to use the checklist "Assessing Students' Initiative as Writers" in Appendix 1 to help you record your observations.)

- Interview students in your classroom about their reasons for writing, the genres in which they choose to write, and the audiences they hope to reach with their writing. Ask: *Why are you writing this piece? Why did you choose to write in this genre? Who do you want to read this piece?*
- Do the same at the beginning of your writing conferences.

In these conferences, it often helps to draw on all that I know about the child as a person. If I know he's an avid collector of Pokemon cards, and he's writing a feature article on these kinds of cards, I might say, "It seems you want to share all those amazing things you've learned from being a Pokemon card collector!" Or if I know that several of his classmates also collect the cards, I might say, "I bet you'll want to have Ricky and Desmond read this book when you're finished!"

When children seem as if they really don't have any purpose in mind except to complete an assignment—especially when they say they're writing because their teacher told them to do it or have little enthusiasm for what they're writing about—I usually devote the rest of the conference to helping them imagine good reasons for composing the piece they're working on and people with whom they can share it or to helping them find something else to write about. To me, not having good reasons for writing in a writing workshop is an emergency, and it's worth taking precious moments of a conference to address it.

Figure 3.9 lists several common issues that students wrestle with in relation to initiating writing and several lessons we can teach to help them become initiators of writing.

Do We Pay Sufficient Attention to Students as Initiators of Writing?

I've never met a writing teacher who doesn't consider teaching students to be initiators of writing an important goal. However, it's a challenge for many of us to give the same kind of attention to initiating writing as we do to how well they write and the effectiveness of their writing processes. Here's why.

Our Writing Histories

Many of us wrote in school in response to the prompts that our teachers gave us, and the main reason we completed these assignments was because we had to. For some of us, it's hard to imagine that children can and do write for a wide range of purposes and audiences and that they can develop—and draw purposefully from—a repertoire of genres. Because of our writing histories, it simply doesn't cross our minds to ask children about why they're writing, the genre in which they're writing, and for whom they're writing.

Even today, some of us don't see ourselves as initiators of writing in our lives. We write when we're required to—a paper in a graduate course, the expected letter home during the first week of school to introduce ourselves to parents, our lesson plans—but we rarely write without there being some authority telling us to do so.

Teaching Students to Become Initiators of Writing

If I see this . . .	I might . . .
A student is going through the motions with the piece of writing he's working on.	Help the student find topics to write about that give him genuine reasons for writing beyond meeting the requirement that he write.
Students write for the same reason again and again.	Talk with students about other reasons that writers write, and nudge them to try writing for one of them.
A student isn't sure about what genre in which she should write.	Ask the student why she's writing the piece she's writing and then suggest genres that writers typically choose to write in to fulfill that purpose.
Students write in the same genre again and again.	Discuss other genres with students and the reasons writers write in them and then suggest that they try out one or more of these genres.
A student isn't able to name an audience for his writing.	Brainstorm a list of people with whom the student can share his writing or places he could publish his piece.
Students usually name as their audience only the ones that we provide as part of our writing workshops (for example, the class for a writing celebration).	Discuss audiences outside of writing workshop with whom students can share their writing.

FIGURE 3.9

There has been much written during the past twenty years about how important it is for teachers of writing to *write*—at summer institutes, as part of an adult writing group, alongside our students. One reason these writing experiences are important is that through them we get a sense of what writing can do for us—and, by extension, what it can do for the children we teach. Teachers who see themselves as initiators of writing are much more likely to pay attention to the ways their students are initiators of writing and to find ways to help them grow as initiators of writing.

Standardized Tests

Another reason we sometimes don't pay as much attention to students as initiators of writing as we should is the pressure we feel from standardized tests. When evaluators score these tests, they usually look only at how well students write—how well a student organizes a piece, how much of a student's voice comes through, how well a student uses conventions, and so forth. Evaluators of these tests don't score students for their initiative as writers because they *can't*; students usually write in response to a prompt on these tests, for no reason other than they have to, in a genre defined by the test question, for an undefined or imaginary audience.

One of the unfortunate effects of these tests and the pressures they put on teachers and schools is that many of us focus our assessment primarily on how well students are writing. Since all that counts on the state test is how well students write, we quite understandably pay attention only to that aspect of our students as writers. Nevertheless, paying attention to students as initiators of writing will have beneficial short-term and long-term effects.

In the short term, if we can help students learn to write for reasons and audiences that matter to them, they'll be more receptive to the lessons we teach about how to write well—lessons they'll need to help them write in ways that will help their pieces do what they want them to in the world. And it's precisely these lessons that will help them perform better on a high-stakes test.

In the long term, if we can help students learn to write for reasons and audiences that matter to them, they'll be more likely to be initiators of writing in their adult lives. It's imperative that we keep in mind that *this* is our primary goal. If our students receive proficient scores on their standardized tests but end their school careers without a sense of what writing can do for them, we've failed them as writing teachers.

Too Many Genre Studies

Many times teachers' writing curricula include genre study after genre study. Sometimes their school district, in response to state standards that expect that students will become proficient at writing in various genres, mandates a year of genre studies. Other times teachers themselves feel most comfortable when students are all doing the same kind of writing and therefore find genre studies easier to teach.

If our writing curricula are stuffed with genre studies, it often seems beside the point to assess students as initiators of writing. If we ask, "Why are you writing in this genre?" we know that many of our students will answer, "Because you're telling us we have to."

While I believe that genre studies are a critical component of a rich writing curriculum in every grade, I also believe that it's important that there be several times during the year when students can choose for themselves the genres in which they write. It's then that students truly have the opportunity to initiate writing. And it's then that

Unit of Study	Dates	What Will Students Be Writing?
1. Launching the Writing Workshop	September 8–26	Genres of their choice
2. Personal Narrative	September 29–October 17	Personal narratives
3. Short Story (Fictional)	October 20–November 26	Short stories
4. Learning from Authors	December 1–23	Genres of their choice
5. A Study of Punctuation	January 5–16	Genres of their choice
6. Op-Ed Pieces	January 20–February 13	Op-ed pieces
7. Feature Articles	February 23–March 19	Feature articles
8. Improving Our Peer Conferences	March 22–April 2	Genres of their choice
9. Poetry	April 14–May 14	Poetry
10. Open Genre Investigation	May 17–June 23	Genres of their choice

FIGURE 3.10 Sample Curriculum Calendar

we can best assess the ways that students are initiators of writing and coach them to become even more purposeful about initiating writing.

There will still be a curricular focus during these times when students can choose genres—we can study craft, or conventions, or revision. (For a sample curriculum calendar that balances genre studies with times in which students can choose their own genres, see Figure 3.10.) Or, as Heather Lattimer (2003) and Judy Davis and Sharon Hill (2003) suggest, a series of genre studies can be followed at the end of the school year with time for students to revisit genres they have already studied or to explore those they haven't (see Figure 3.11).

If you work in a district that mandates a year of genre studies, remember how important it is to discuss in your minilessons the reasons writers write in the genres you study and help students write for one (or more) of these reasons. By writing in the genres they study and learning what these genres can do for them, students will have experiences that will inspire them to write in these genres (or in other genres for similar purposes) outside school or later in their lives.

Confusing Creating the Conditions for Initiative with Initiative Itself

Almost every writing workshop teacher with whom I work creates the conditions in his or her classroom for students to learn to become ini-

Writing Cycle	Length of Cycle	What Students Are Writing?
1. Setting Up the Writing Workshop	4–5 weeks	Personal narratives, poems, letters
2. Lifting the Quality of the Writer's Notebook	4–5 weeks	Personal narratives, poems, letters
3. Using Authors as Mentors	4–5 weeks	Personal narratives, poems, letters
4. Poetry	5 weeks	Poetry
5. Feature Articles	5 weeks	Feature articles
6. Picture Books	5 weeks	Picture books
7. Open-Choice Investigation	5–6 weeks	Magazine articles, advice columns, informational texts, poems, personal essays, letters to persuade, and more

FIGURE 3.11   Sample Curriculum Plan from Judy Davis and Sharon Hill's *The No-Nonsense Guide to Teaching Writing* (2003)

tiators of writing. These teachers give their students the opportunity to choose what topics to write about. And they provide opportunities for students to publish their writing, usually in whole-class writing celebrations in which students share their writing with one another. Because some teachers assume that with these conditions in place, their students will find purposes and audiences for their writing, they don't feel the need to ask students why they're writing their pieces or for whom they're writing.

However, simply creating these conditions in the classroom doesn't guarantee that all students will become people who write for reasons and audiences that matter to them. It's true that there are some students who already understand what writing can do for them, and they tend to thrive in a writing workshop from the beginning to the end of the school year. But it's equally true that we teach some students who write because they're in school and they feel compelled to do so, even though they can choose the topic to write about and even though they can share their writing with others. And it's also true that we teach students who see little or no reason to write and thus write little at all. It's often these students who ask again and again, "What do I write about?" I've come to believe they're asking for help not so much in finding a topic but in figuring out why they should write in the first place.

While it's essential to create the conditions in which students *can be* initiators of writing, we must also teach many of them to *become* this kind of writer. As the school year unfolds, we need to discuss, in minilessons, the reasons writers write and, in conferences, the reasons each student is—or could be—writing. We need to provide explicit instruction in genre, especially by including several genre studies in our yearlong curricula. And we need to discuss with students, both as a class and individually, the audiences with whom they can share their writing.

References

Atwell, Nancie. 1998. *In the Middle: New Understandings About Writing, Reading, and Learning*. Portsmouth, NH: Heinemann.

Bomer, Randy, and Katherine Bomer. 2001. *For a Better World: Reading and Writing for Social Action*. Portsmouth, NH: Heinemann.

Calkins, Lucy. 1994. *The Art of Teaching Writing*. Portsmouth, NH: Heinemann.

Cooper, Charles R. 1999. "What We Know About Genres, and How It Can Help Us Assign and Evaluate Writing." In *Evaluating Writing: The Role of Teachers' Knowledge About Text, Learning, and Culture*, edited by Charles R. Cooper and Lee Odell, 23–52. Urbana, IL: NCTE.

Cruz, M. Colleen. 2004. *Independent Writing: One Teacher—Thirty-Two Needs, Topics, and Plans*. Portsmouth, NH: Heinemann.

Davis, Judy, and Sharon Hill. 2003. *The No-Nonsense Guide to Teaching Writing: Strategies, Structures, and Solutions*. Portsmouth, NH: Heinemann.

Graves, Donald. 1983. *Writing: Teachers and Children at Work*. Portsmouth, NH: Heinemann.

———. 1993. *A Fresh Look at Writing*. Portsmouth, NH: Heinemann.

Lattimer, Heather. 2003. *Thinking Through Genre: Units of Study in Reading and Writing Workshops 4–12*. Portland, ME: Stenhouse.

Murray, Donald M. 1996. *Crafting a Life in Essay, Story, Poem*. Portsmouth, NH: Heinemann.

Ray, Katie Wood. 1999. *Wondrous Words: Writers and Writing in the Elementary Classroom*. Urbana, IL: NCTE.

Ryder, Phyllis Mentzell, Elizabeth Vander Lei, and Duane H. Roen. 1999. "Audience Considerations for Evaluating Writing." In *Evaluating Writing: The Role of Teachers' Knowledge About Text, Learning, and Culture*, edited by Charles R. Cooper and Lee Odell, 53–71. Urbana, IL: NCTE.

Assessing How Well Students Write

4

It's not what a piece of writing is about,
but how it's written, that makes good writing good.
—KATIE WOOD RAY, Wondrous Words

I became a struggling reader a few weeks into tenth grade, in my AP English class. Yes, I know—a struggling reader in an AP English class? Students in AP courses are supposed to be excellent readers.

Here's what happened. My teacher, Mr. Barra, assigned the first few chapters of Charles Dickens' *Tale of Two Cities*. I dutifully read the chapters and came to class prepared to talk about what had happened so far in the story. Mr. Barra, however, didn't want to talk about that. Instead, he asked who had noticed all the symbols that Dickens had embedded in the chapters. I had no idea what he meant. And, neither, apparently, did my classmates. For several long moments, no one raised a hand.

Finally, Melissa, the smartest student in the class, spoke up. "I think that the image of the wine spilling from the cart in Chapter 5 is a symbol of the blood that was spilled during the French Revolution," she asserted. "And the scene in which Madame Defarge is knitting is also deeply symbolic—of all the complicated schemes that the people involved in the revolution were weaving at the time." I stared at Melissa, amazed at her response and curious about how she was able to see things in a text that the rest of us couldn't.

This scene repeated itself many times that year. Sometimes Mr. Barra asked us to find symbols in the novel we were reading. On other days, he would ask us what themes the author was exploring in the text or how the setting enhanced the plot. Most often, his questions were greeted by silence, until Melissa would speak up and rescue us once again.

As the year went on, I felt a growing sense of inadequacy as a reader. Mr. Barra challenged us to think and talk about texts in ways in which I had little or no experience. I managed to muddle through the course, mainly because I had a private tutor—my mom, who taught high school English in my school district. However, even today, I still feel that I'm not a good reader. I still struggle when it comes to thinking and talking about books in the ways that Mr. Barra expected twenty-five years ago.

When I give workshops on how to assess how well students write, I often start with my story of being a struggling reader. I've worked with so many teachers who feel they struggle when they read their students' texts to assess how well they write; my story makes them laugh and puts them more at ease. Just as I had trouble analyzing aspects of the texts I had to read in high school, many teachers have trouble analyzing aspects of the texts that their students write.

The Traits (or Qualities) of Good Writing

Over the past three decades, it's become common practice for teachers of writing to zero in on certain *traits*, or qualities, of good writing when they assess how well students write. Just as a basketball coach assesses her players by focusing on how well each of them dribbles a basketball, plays defense, or shoots free throws, writing teachers get a picture of how well their students write by analyzing how well each of them organizes his writing, writes with detail, or uses punctuation.

One of the first educators to list the qualities of good writing was Paul Diederich (1974); in the early 1970s, he described them as *ideas, mechanics, organization and analysis, wording and phrasing,* and *flavor.* Eight years later, Donald Murray (1982) came up with his own list: *meaning, authority, voice, development, design,* and *clarity.* Shortly thereafter, a group of teachers in Oregon met in a study group and, with the assistance of their writing consultant, Vicki Spandel, devised a list of traits (see Figure 4.1) that has become highly influential in the United States. Known as 6 (sometimes 6 + 1) Trait Writing Assessment, it now shapes standardized writing assessments in more than forty states

---

The 6 Traits
Ideas
Organization
Voice
Word choice
Sentence fluency
Conventions and layout

(In 6 + 1 trait assessment, the seventh trait is *presentation.*)

FIGURE 4.1

and informs writing assessment in numerous school districts all over
the country (Spandel 2001; Culham 2003).

57

*Assessing How
Well Students
Write*

and informs writing assessment in numerous school districts all over
the country (Spandel 2001; Culham 2003).

More recently, educators at the National Center on Education
and the Economy and the University of Pittsburgh (1997) composed
a list of *writing performance descriptions* (see Figure 4.2) that have

---

The New Standards—Writing Performance Descriptions

Standard E2 Writing

E2a The student produces a report[4] that:

- engages the reader by establishing a context, creating a persona, and otherwise developing reader interest;
- develops a controlling idea that conveys a perspective on the subject;
- creates an oganizing structure appropriate to a specific purpose, audience, and context;
- includes appropriate facts and details;
- excludes extraneous and inappropriate information;
- uses a range of appropriate strategies, such as providing facts and details, describing or analyzing the subject, and narrating a relevant anecdote;
- provides a sense of closure to the writing.

Standard E4 Conventions, Grammar, and Usage of the English Language

E4a The student demonstrates a basic understanding of the rules of the English language in written and oral work, and selects the structures and features of language appropriate to the purpose, audience, and context of the work. The student demonstrates control of:

- grammar;
- paragraph structure;
- punctuation;
- sentence construction;
- spelling;
- usage.

---

4. These standards include writing traits that are genre specific; that is, they describe what it means to write well in certain genres. In the elementary performance standards, these genres include *report, response to literature, narrative account,* and *narrative procedure.* The middle school standards also include *persuasive essay,* as do the high school standards, which also include *reflective essay.*

FIGURE 4.2

informed conversations about what it means to write well in many school districts around the United States. And JoAnn Portalupi and Ralph Fletcher share their own list of traits in *Teaching the Qualities of Writing* (2004).

During the nineteen years that I've been a teacher of writing, I, too, have defined for myself what I think it means for someone to write well. Here's my list of the qualities of good writing:

Lifelong writers write well when they
- communicate *meaning*
- use *genre* knowledge
- *structure* their writing
- write with *detail*
- give their writing *voice*
- use *conventions*

As I composed my list, I chose what I consider to be the most precise words to describe what I think it means to write well. Some of these words are the same as those used in similar lists. And the rest aren't radically different—most are synonyms for the words that appear on other lists.

Meaning: The Most Important Trait

The reason a writer composes a text is to communicate *meaning* to his intended audience. For this reason, meaning isn't just one of the many qualities of good writing we consider when we assess whether or not a text is well written; meaning is the most important of the traits.

There are several terms that we use to refer to meaning. In general, we read a text expecting that the author has *something to say* or *a point to make* about his topic. Or when we read in certain genres, we expect to construct certain kinds of meaning. For example, when we read an op-ed piece by Maureen Dowd in the *New York Times,* we know that we will find out her opinion on an important national issue. When we read a column written by Dear Abby, we expect that we'll find out her advice about how to handle tricky life situations. Or when we read an article in *Language Arts,* we anticipate that the author will tell us the results of his research into teaching literacy. When a text is well written, the author satisfies our expectation that the text will communicate meaning.

Read the memoir "Why the Parents Say, 'Money Doesn't Grow on Trees'" written by Rusty, an eighth grader (see Figure 4.3). In this text, Rusty tells us the story of a time he helped his grandpa cut and load tobacco. As we read, expecting that Rusty will have something to say about this experience, we learn that the experience taught him the value of a dollar. *That's* the meaning Rusty communicates.

Why the Parents Say, "Money Doesn't Grow on Trees"

Money doesn't grow on trees? Well that's what the parents say.

"Mom, I can't go to the movies unless you give me some money," I'd ask.

"Money doesn't grow on trees, Rusty," she would reply.

I used to get this all of the time. I'd ask for money and I'd get the same answer over and over. I still ask for money, just not all of the time. Do you want to know why? Let me tell you.

It was late July or early August. I can't remember the date. I can tell you that it was a week when I was grounded. Anyway I was at a family reunion just goofing around. I heard my grandfather, alias Paw-Paw, talking about his tobacco.

"Paw-Paw," I asked, "Are you ready to cut and load your tobacco?"

"Yes I am," he replied with that rough voice of his.

I responded to his answer, "Can I go home with you and work?"

"I guess so," Paw-Paw said.

This excited me. I've only done little jobs up to then, but I felt that this year would be different. The long hours, great pay, and talking with the guys is what makes the job fun. So I went home with Maw-Maw and Paw-Paw. I only had a few clues of what lay ahead.

"Rusty," I heard Paw-Paw mutter, "Time to get up."

I wallowed around on the couch not wanting to get up. How early is it I thought to myself. Finally after about ten minutes the smell of bacon and eggs dragged me out of my bed.

"Finally up?" asked Maw-Maw as I walked into the kitchen.

I replied, "Guess so."

I was in the zombie zone as I ate my breakfast. I guess it was pretty good.

Paw-Paw hollered from outside, "Let's go!"

We were the first ones out there and had to wait for the other workers to come. It was about 8:30 a.m. when we were all there. It took another ½ hour to get to work.

I'm going to tell you the pay before the story. You get paid $7.00 an hour. That's 8½ min. of work for every dollar. You're probably thinking that's a lot for a little. You just wait and see.

Lifting the heavy tobacco over your head and onto a moving wagon isn't really fun. Especially when there are a trillion bugs crawling over the tobacco. They'll bite the heck out of you.

Lunch time came. It was 3 hours and $21.00 into the day. The temperature was steadily rising. Everybody was dog tired. We sat around for an hour eating and resting.

"Back to work!" hollered Paw-Paw.

Up we went. None of us wanted to go, but we had to. Though I wish we hadn't. It was about 100 degrees for the rest of the day.

It was about 7:00 p.m. when we quit. Everybody went home to rest up. I had $63.00 in my pocket.

The next morning went the same as the one before it. I was tired, but went anyway.

Hard work came early. They, the workers that is, were tired like me. It was to be scorching hot like the day before.

FIGURE 4.3 Rusty's Memoir

Pain mounted as well as heat and the money. Those five words my mom has been telling me were playing over and over in my mind.

The day was done at about 7:00 again. I was tired like the day before. Only new thing was I was finished.

"Come up for your money," hollered Paw-Paw. He's real abrupt.

I was next in line behind Stevie, my cousin. He made $100.00. I thought he had more than I did. I was wrong. I came out with $126.00 of sweat and pain. The trouble was worth it.

From that experience I've learned the value of a dollar. I know what my mom means about money doesn't grow on trees.

I've come out for the better. My new found knowledge will serve me for years to come. Hopefully I will use it wisely.

FIGURE 4.3 *Continued*

Figure 4.4 is a feature article by Helaina, a sixth grader. It doesn't take Helaina long to satisfy our expectation that she will have something to say about her topic. In her lead and again later on, in the ending, Helaina makes the point that grass has many essential uses.

Not all writers communicate meaning explicitly like this. In some genres, writers communicate meaning implicitly. In her story "The Pool" (see Figure 4.5), first grader Alexandra writes about having to swim across the pool during a swimming lesson. Early in the story, Alexandra tells us that she "clutched the wall with an enormous amount of fear." Then she vividly describes a short detour to the bottom of the pool before successfully getting all the way across. Details like these, followed by her final line ("I was so proud of myself"), help us understand that Alexandra overcame a difficult and frightening challenge.

The meaning that a writer wants to communicate influences almost every composing decision. Ralph Fletcher (1993) writes, "Every part, every *word*, depends upon its relationship to the whole" (4). For example, meaning helps a writer decide on which aspects of a topic to focus. Because Helaina wants readers to know about the essential uses of grass, she includes sections on some of those uses—how animals eat grass for food, how insects depend on grass for shelter, and so on. Helaina doesn't include a section on photosynthesis because that wouldn't have helped her explain what she was trying to say about grass.

Meaning also influences which details a writer includes in a text. Consider how Rusty chose to tell us about the bugs that were crawling on the tobacco as he was cutting it and loading it, the rising temperature, and how many minutes it took to earn each dollar. Ultimately, we understand what Rusty has to say about his experience, not just because he tells us that working for his grandfather taught him the value

What's Up in the Field of Grass?

When you think of grass, what comes to mind?

When asked, some people said they never even thought about it. "Green and onion, because of onion grass," said Carrie Bennet. "I also associate it with the outdoors and nature."

Nobody said anything about how important grass is, though. It's one of those things you take for granted in life. You don't really stop to think about or look at grass. Grass is used in so many ways, here are a few.

• Many animals, such as cows, eat grass and so do humans. Cows have little bugs in their stomachs to help them digest grass.

During the summer, cows chow on the green grass outside. In the colder seasons, farmers have to bring their cows hay, another type of grass.

Did you know that rice is grass? Yep, and sugar is made from a type of grass called sugarcane.

• Lots of little bugs depend upon grass as shelter. Spiders, beetles, crickets, grasshoppers and lots of other insects live among the thin, green blades. They use grass as a means of protection.

• Grass adds beauty to the world. Without grass, the world would be a desert of dark, brown dirt.

• Grass also helps prevent erosion. It keeps soil and sand tied to the ground. If we didn't have grass then when a wind picked up, woosh, there would go your front yard.

Grass is essential in more ways than one. I don't know where the world would be without it. Next time you pass a patch of grass, you should stop to think about how important it is, and be grateful that it's there.

FIGURE 4.4 Helaina's Feature Article

of a dollar but because, detail by detail, he shows us how he came to this understanding.

Meaning even influences how writers use punctuation. Take a close look at pages 9 and 10 of "The Pool," the turning point in Alexandra's story. Page 9 includes this sentence: "But then . . . I jumped . . . so I could get out of the bottom of the pool in the deep water." By using ellipses, Alexandra slows down the story at this critical point. Two sentences later, she uses an exclamation point to end the sentence: "I got out of that horrible dungeon!" The exclamation point signals us to give this important sentence—the moment where Alexandra turns what might have been a disastrous outing in the pool into a moment of triumph—added emphasis when we read it. The punctuation marks that Alexandra uses in "The Pool" help us construct meaning, even though Alexandra didn't tell us directly what the point of her story was.

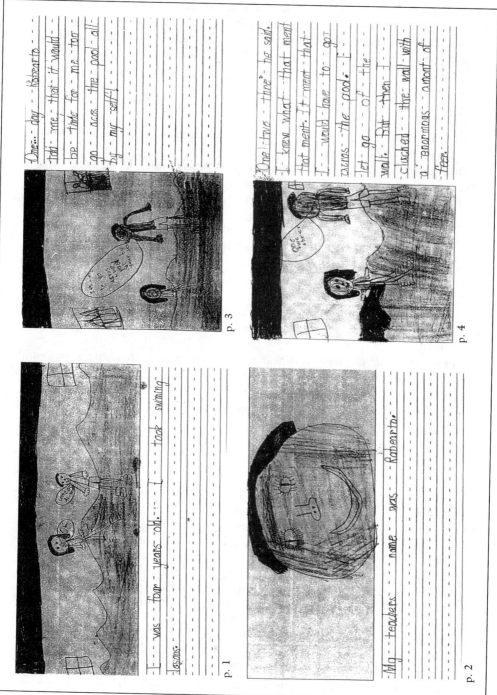

FIGURE 4.5 Alexandra's Story

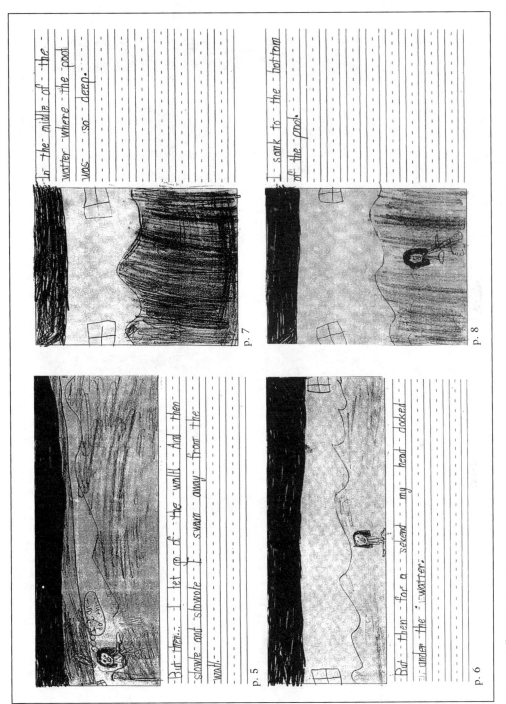

In the middle of the watter where the pool was so deep.

p. 7

I sank to the bottom of the pool.

p. 8

But then... I let go of the wall. And then slowle and slowote I swam away from the wall.

p. 5

But then for a sekent my head docked under the watter.

p. 6

FIGURE 4.5   *Continued*

63

I felt as though I was a tiny little fish that had just got eaten by a shark. But then... I jumped... so I could get out of the bottom of the pool in the deep watter.

p. 9

I did I got out of that horble dungah. I swam back with out going under watter.

p. 10

My swiming teacher said in astonishmint great: I was so proud of my self.

p. 11

FIGURE 4.5 *Continued*

> **My Aunt's Wedding**
>
> I went to Vermont for my aunt's Wedding. I was her jr. brides made with my cousin Amanda. The first day we went to a bridge waterfall the waterfall was beautiful. We went into the waterfall hole. We went tubing. The secound day we had the weding. I wore a green butterfly dress with a matching hat. And the third day we went horseback rideing. My hourse was named Chester. He was a brown and black horse. The next time I went there I had the same horse.

FIGURE 4.6   Katie's Piece

Not all children understand that writing is an act of communicating meaning. Instead of trying to make sense of an event or a subject for their readers, some children see writing as retelling everything they can think of about an event or every fact they've learned about the subject. (These are often referred to as *bed-to-bed* or *all-about* pieces.) Katie Wood Ray (1999) writes that for these students, the "act of writing, then, is simply one of faithfully recording these events in the order in which they happened," instead of "find[ing] what is important to say" (92).

For example, read "My Aunt's Wedding" (Figure 4.6), written by Katie, a fourth grader. In the piece, Katie tells us about many of the things she did during the weekend her aunt got married. She doesn't, however, seem to have something to say about the weekend. Was the weekend the best time of her life? Was she really nervous to be a junior bridesmaid? Was she excited that she got to spend so much time with relatives? It's difficult to glean a meaning from the piece because Katie needs to learn how to figure out what she wants to say about an experience or learn how to write a story in a way that communicates meaning or learn how to do both of these things. (The only way to know for sure whether or not Katie had a meaning she wanted to share with readers would have been to ask her, "What are you trying to say about your aunt's wedding?" in a writing conference.)

What I have said about communicating meaning in writing is specific to written English in the United States, where writers tend to communicate meaning very directly. This is important to remember when we work with ESL students from cultures in which indirectness is characteristic of written discourse (Indonesia or China, for example). When we assess the writing of students from these cultures, we have to know something about the rhetorical norms of these cultures. (Guanjun Cai's 1999 article on the writing of Chinese students is an excellent starting place.) Then, in order to teach these children to write

Teaching Students to Communicate Meaning in Their Writing

If I see this . . .	I might . . .
Students are writing bed-to-bed stories or all-about nonfiction pieces.	Discuss with the children what they want to say about their topic and then show them how to write a plan for their piece in which each part will help them say what they want to say.
The child's meaning is unclear or confusing (this applies to genres in which the writer typically makes her point explicit, such as memoir or feature articles).	Suggest that the child respond to the question: *What am I trying to say in my piece?* in her writer's notebook and then use this thinking to help her rewrite the part of her piece in which she is trying to make her point (usually in the lead or the ending).
The student knows what he wants to say about his topic, but he hasn't communicated his point anywhere in his draft (this applies to genres in which the writer typically makes his point explicit, such as memoir or feature articles).	Point out in a model text where the writer made his point (usually in the lead or the ending) and suggest that the student communicate his meaning in the same way.

FIGURE 4.7

well in English, we need to stress the ways writers *in this culture* communicate meaning in writing.

Figure 4.7 lists several common problems students have with communicating meaning in their writing along with lessons we can teach to help them overcome these problems.

Genre: The Vehicle for Conveying Meaning

Genres are created by the people in a culture to help them communicate certain kinds of meaning. When a writer in that culture chooses to write in a genre, then, he hopes to communicate a particular kind of meaning. When we read an editorial in a newspaper, whether it's the *New York Times* or the *Greensboro Record*, we understand we are going to read the opinion of the newpaper's editorial board on important issues of the day. When we read a recipe for Chicken Kiev in *The Joy of Cooking*, we know we're going to learn how to prepare the

Assess your students' writing for meaning. Gather several of your students' pieces. As you read them, ask yourself the following questions. (You may want to use the checklist "Assessing How Well Students Write" in Appendix 2 to help you record your observations.)

- What meaning is this child trying to convey about his topic? Are there places in the text where the child lets me know what he's trying to say? Or can I infer the child's meaning?

- Am I having trouble constructing meaning from this piece? Does the piece reveal that this child sees writing as retelling an event or listing everything she knows about a topic, instead of communicating meaning about the topic?

dish. When we read a piece of literature distributed by a political campaign, we understand we're going to learn why a political candidate and her party believe she should be elected to the office she is seeking.

Genres are easily recognized. Charles Cooper (1999) observes that "a genre cannot be reduced to a reproducible formula, yet its main features can be described" (26). Because genres have these predictable features, readers are able to comprehend a writer's meaning. We are able to understand what a memoirist has to say about his life because he includes stories that show us how he came to his epiphanies. We get the point a writer makes in a book review because the writer refers to passages in the text that support his interpretation. We comprehend the message in the president's annual State of the Union address because he includes facts and statistics about the lives of Americans, along with a few of their individual stories, to explain his position about how the nation is faring.

In a well-written text, the writer uses his knowledge of the genre he has chosen to write in to help him convey meaning to his audience effectively. Randy Bomer (1995) writes, "A sense of genre is one of the most important mental frames we use in our writing" (117).

In *What a Writer Needs* (1993), Ralph Fletcher writes about how important it is for a writer both to establish conflict (or tension) and to bring that conflict to some kind of resolution in a well-written story. When she wrote "The Pool" (Figure 4.5), Alexandra uses this genre knowledge to help her convey meaning. The conflict between Alexandra and the pool, and its eventual resolution, is the device that

Dear Mom,
I hate chicken soup. Please do not make chicken soup so much.
Here are my reasons.

1) You make it too much. Last month you made it 5 times.
   I don't like it that much.
2) You put too many vegetables. Last time you put
   tomatoes and cauliflower and I don't like them.
3) I do not like the skin of the chicken because it is all
   slimy. When I see the slimy chicken skin, I want to
   throw up. The worst thing I hate is the bones from
   the chicken because I feel like I am going to choke.
   Next time please do not make chicken soup again.

Love,
Valerie

FIGURE 4.8   Valerie's Letter

she uses to let us know that she overcame a difficult challenge. Or consider the persuasive letter that Valerie, a third grader, wrote to her mom (see Figure 4.8). To convince her mom to stop making chicken soup, Valerie includes several reasons, something we expect from someone who is writing to persuade.

When children write, they are approximating the genres they have read up to that point in their lives. As children become more and more proficient in writing in a particular genre—a proficiency gained by writing in the genre numerous times—they learn to incorporate more and more of the features of the genre. Thus, when I assess a student's piece for genre knowledge, I begin by asking, "What does this child already know about writing in this genre?" Then I ask, "What else does she need to learn about this genre to write well in it?"

For example, Katie brings some knowledge of personal narrative into "My Aunt's Wedding" (Figure 4.6). Just as we expect a writer of a story to do, she includes a series of scenes ordered in time. However, to be able to write a story that successfully communicates meaning, Katie still needs to learn to focus on an event that contains conflict or tension.

Now look at "The First Day of 4th Grade Seeing Ms. Levinson" (Figure 4.9). Clearly, Sean, a fourth grader, knows a lot about writing a story. Just as we expect, Sean focuses on a tension-filled event—the moment when she sees her third-grade teacher after a summer away from school and wonders whether Ms. Levinson will remember her. By setting up and resolving this tension, Sean communicates that this teacher is special to her. However, even though most fourth-grade

The First Day of 4th Grade Seeing Ms. Levinson

"Where is she?!" I asked Lisa.

"I don't know," Lisa says.

I am waiting in line, at my new 4th grade class, for my old 3rd grade teacher, Ms. Levinson. I thought, would she look different? Was her hair going to be blue? Was she going to have red little streaks? I wonder, I wonder.

I also wished I could have 4 eyes. One would look North, one West, one South, and one would look East so I could find her.

Then I saw her. I saw her smile. I thought, was she looking at me. She waved. I waved back. Now I knew she was looking at me.

I started to walk, then my walk, it got faster and faster, and then I started to run to her. While I was running I felt the old summer air blowing on my face. I closed my eyes, then I opened them. I saw a picture of me and Ms. Levinson giving each other big squeezy hugs. I knew that was going to happen in about 25 seconds.

I ran up the stairs and into the cafeteria. The white tables surrounded me. I was almost there. I looked both ways. I ran the way she was.

I shouted, "Ms Levinson." She turned her head.

I ran up to her and gave her a big squeezy hug. She gave me one too.

I said to her, "I missed you so much." I thought for a moment, did she miss me also?

She said, "I missed you too." Then I knew she missed me.

I asked her, "Can we have lunch today?"

She thought for a moment. "Sure," she said.

I said, "Great." I had to go because I had to get back in line. I also had to meet my new teacher. I started to run back to line.

I was really excited for lunch with Ms. Levinson. But I thought, was it just the two of us, or a lot of other kids?

FIGURE 4.9   Sean's Story

teachers would be overjoyed if all their students wrote like Sean, there are still places to take her. For example, had Sean been able to characterize Ms. Levinson more fully, perhaps by including some telling physical details about her (for example, her warm smile) or by flashing back briefly to an important moment in Ms. Levinson's third-grade class, she might have helped readers understand even more why she was so excited to see her teacher again.

TEACHER ACTION 4.2

Assess your students' writing for genre knowledge. Gather some of your students' writing. Try to select several genres. As you read each piece, ask yourself these questions. (You may want to use the checklist "Assessing How Well Students Write" in Appendix 2 to help you record your observations.)

- What genre is this piece?

- What does this piece reveal about what this child knows about writing in this genre? (Which genre features can I identify in the piece?)

- What does this child still need to learn about writing in this genre?

To assess a child's knowledge of genres, we must be familiar with those genres ourselves. Our own writing experiences, of course, give us one important source of information about genres. And over the past two decades, many educators have written extensively about the genres in which children write (or in which we want them to write). Figure 4.10 includes basic descriptions of several of the more common genres students explore in writing workshops. Figure 4.11 discusses some genre issues students encounter and some lessons that we can teach them to develop their genre knowledge.

Structure: The Parts That Make Up the Whole

When we read a text, we expect that it will go a certain way—that the writer will have structured her text in a way that will help us understand what she's trying to say. By *structure,* I mean the parts or sections of a text and their roles and interrelationships within the text.

In school, conversations about the ways children structure their texts are often oversimplified. Does a student's writing have a beginning, a middle, and an end? Is it sequenced? To assess what children know about structuring writing, however, we need to deepen our knowledge of structure.

Deciding Which Parts to Include

One of the most important structural decisions a writer has to make in composing a piece is which aspects of his topic he should include (or focus on) and which he will exclude. For example, of all the things that happened during the afternoon I spent with my family on the

Characteristics of Some Common Genres

Personal Narrative
- Tells a story about an event in the author's life.
- Establishes tension or conflict early in the story, which is resolved by the end.
- Focuses on one or more scenes, which are ordered in time.
- Develops characters and shows how main character (usually the author) changes during the event.
- Develops the setting.
- Implies or states the importance of the story.

Short Fictional Story
- Tells a story about an event in the main character's life.
- Establishes tension or conflict early in the story, which is resolved by the end.
- Focuses on one or more scenes, which are ordered in time.
- Establishes characters and shows how the main character changes during the story.
- Develops the setting.
- Implies or states the importance of the story.

Feature Article
- Focuses on an aspect of the topic the author is writing about.
- Gives information about the topic in a series of sections that are organized in a logical way.
- Includes facts, statistics, examples, anecdotes, and/or quotes from experts on the topic.

Opinion
- Clearly states the author's opinion.
- Gives reasons to explain her opinion.
- Develops her reasons with facts, anecdotes from her experience and/or that of others, statistics, and quotes from experts on the subject.
- Organizes the sections logically.
- May take into account opposing perspectives.

Literary Essay
- Advances an idea about a text (or texts) the author has read.
- May include a short retelling of the text(s).
- Organizes the sections of the essay in a logical, point-by-point way.
- The author develops his points by referring to parts of the text(s).

Figure 4.10

Teaching Students to Write Well in a Genre	
If I see this . . .	**I might . . .**
Students' writing contains some features of the genres in which they're writing but not others.	Show students examples of the genres, point out features that they need to learn to incorporate into their writing, and then nudge them to do so.
A student knows to incorporate a feature of the genre she's writing in into her writing but has more to learn about that feature.	Show the student an example of the genre she's writing in and discuss other aspects of the genre feature that she could include in her writing.

FIGURE 4.11

beach in Cape Cod, which parts of the experience should I put in my story and which parts should I leave out?

A good writer decides which parts of an experience or which aspects of a topic to focus on based on the meaning she's trying to get across. The role of each part of a text is to develop the writer's meaning. To help us understand how he learned the value of a dollar, Rusty tells us how hard it was for him to get up early in the morning and about the work he did cutting and loading tobacco on the two days he worked for his grandfather (see Figure 4.3). He doesn't tell us about the television shows he watched in the evening, because that won't help us understand what he has to say about his work experience.

Inexperienced writers sometimes include parts in their writing that don't seem to develop their meaning. They make surprising detours and go off on unexpected tangents. In other words, they lose control of their piece. For example, look at the story Quincy, a fifth grader, wrote about his family's Christmas (Figure 4.12). When I first read the lead, I thought his story would be about the anticipation he felt about his Christmas gifts and what he ultimately got. While most of the sections Quincy includes in the piece develop this meaning (getting money from his father, opening presents at his grandmother's house and at his home) he includes some things (his argument with his cousins and aunt over the toys he had brought to his grandmother's house on Christmas Eve) that seem tangential. Quincy needs to learn to read over a draft and ask himself whether or not each part of the piece helps him say what he wants to say about his topic.

Again, I use the word *seem*: it's possible that in a young writer's mind, these parts help him say what he's trying to say, but he doesn't yet possess the skill to write them in a way that advances his meaning.

Christmas Vacation

On Friday when I came home from school I bugged and bugged my mom to tell me what I got for christmas. She said "Quincy I don't know what you got, only Santa claus knows that." Mom I know there is no such thing as Santa claus so come on tell me, *please*. Quincy its supposed to be a surprise, my mom replied. So you do know what I got? Yes but I'm not telling you, now come on don't ruin it for your brother and sister. Aimee is still at that age where she's thinking about it. And Jack is on 3 he has a long way to go before he stops believing in Santa Claus. Alright, alright I'll stop asking you Mom, I say.

On Saturday my poppy sent me, my sister, and Jack 250 big ones. I got 1 hundred, Aimee got 1 hundred and Jack got 50 because he has a different father. With my 1 hundred I wanted to go see "Dude Where's My Car"? My sister didn't really want to go see it but she went anyway. I payed for me and my mom, my sister payed for herself and my brother was free. That movie was the stupidest movie I've ever seen! My mom agreed. For 20 dollars I could of played games at mutant mania, bought pokemon cards, and a toy wrestler. But, I'm glad I saw it, it was stupid but it was really funny.

On Sunday I went out to grandmothers for christmas eve. Me and my sister bugged and bugged my grandmother to open the presents under the tree. But, she didn't let us. I brought a 20 dollar army men toy to keep me and my cousins busy. When I got it out at my grandmothers house I went to the bathroom and my cousins opened it and left all the pieces all over the floor and I got blamed for the mess. My aunt told me to pick up all the pieces now! I said no! I didn't make the mess sam did. No he didn't, you brought it, you clean it up! So I with my bad tempure stormed out of there and headed for McKinley park. My mom chased me, and urged me to stop. But, I didn't want to hear anything. She told me she yelled at aunt joney and Grandma did to. She left with sam and antoine. So I went back with my mom and enjoyed the rest of the night. On christmas eve I got 2 N64 tapes, a remote controlled car, a basketball game, a gameboy pack, shampoo, conditioner and cologne and a loop earring from my mom. I really had fun that night.

On christmas day I woke up at 4:20 in the morning and screamed it's Christmas! I ran out to the living room and looked at everything I got. Six N64 tapes Supersmash brothers, donkey Kong 64, No Mercy, Hey you pikachu, war zone, and Batman Beyond. I also got Playstation 2 with Smackdown 2, and a simpsons trivia game. This christmas I really got a lot of stuff, this was a great christmas.

FIGURE 4.12 Quincy's Story

When I'm puzzled by why a student included a part in a text, I ask, in a conference, "Why did you include this section?" The response helps me decide whether I should teach how writers sometimes delete part of their drafts or teach how to write the part in a way that contributes to the meaning.

Ordering the Parts

Another important structural decision a writer has to make is how to order the parts of the text. (We also use the words *organization* and *sequencing* to describe this decision.) To decide on an order, a writer draws on his knowledge of the genre in which he is writing—that is, the order is genre specific. In general, in narrative genres (personal narrative, short story) the parts of the text are ordered in time. Each scene usually takes place after the one it follows. (Occasionally, a writer will flash back or forward from a point in a story, but those shifts are still made in relation to time.) In the first part of her story (Figure 4.5), Alexandra is perched on the edge of a swimming pool, scared to swim across when her instructor nudges her to do so. The next part focuses on the next few minutes, while she struggles to swim to the other side. The third and final part focuses on her subsequent moment of triumph, when she and her instructor react with joy at her accomplishment. The parts are ordered by the linear flow of time.

The parts of nonnarrative genres (feature article, op-ed pieces, literary essays, etc.) are ordered by logic. A writer in one of these genres usually communicates his meaning at the beginning of the text, and the parts that follow develop that meaning in a logical manner. At the beginning of her feature article (Figure 4.4), Helaina asserts that grass has many uses. One after another, she then presents parts that develop this assertion. Logic binds the parts of the piece together.

Many inexperienced writers have trouble ordering their texts. Their narratives may shift back and forth in time, seemingly without reason. In nonnarrative texts, the order in which they make their points may seem illogical. These writers need to be taught to order their texts in the genre-specific ways that help readers understand what they're trying to say.

Deciding What Kinds of Parts to Include

A good writer also has to decide what *kinds* of parts to include in his piece. For example, if I'm writing an op-ed's piece in which I argue in favor of the smoking ban in New York City's restaurants, I might mention the time a smoker sitting at the next table ruined my or a friend's meal. I might also include a section on the results of some research on secondhand smoke.

Again, a writer's knowledge of the genre he's writing in helps him envision the kinds of parts he can include. A writer who knows a genre inside and out and knows all the different kinds of parts he can include has a more extensive repertoire of ways to communicate meaning than a writer who is inexperienced in writing in the genre.

When I assess student writing for what it reveals about the writer's structural knowledge, I look for the kinds of parts she has included in her texts. Alexandra's pool story (Figure 4.5) starts with a part in which she introduces the main characters—herself and her swimming instructor. The rest of the story is a series of dramatic scenes—Alexandra clutching the edge of the pool, Alexandra swimming across the pool, Alexandra at the other side of the pool with her instructor.

Rusty's piece (Figure 4.3) shows he is aware that a memoir includes both reflection and narrative. In his lead and ending, he reflects on what he learned from the experience of working for his grandfather. In between the lead and ending, he includes scenes of what the work was like.

When I'm assessing a student's piece (or pieces—it's often more effective to look at several samples in the same genre), I also think about the kinds of parts that the child isn't yet including, parts I can later teach him so he'll be able to communicate meaning more effectively. Both Alexandra and Rusty, for example, could learn to include descriptions of the settings in which their stories take place.

Several structural parts that help guide the reader along the path toward meaning have special names: the *lead,* or *introduction;* the *ending,* or *conclusion;* and *transitions.*

LEADS   We often oversimplify the importance of leads by saying that they catch the reader's attention. While this is certainly what writers try to do in many genres, the role of the lead is actually much grander: it starts the reader on a journey toward meaning. Sometimes a writer's lead communicates meaning explicitly: see Helaina's feature article (Figure 4.4) or Valerie's letter to her mother (Figure 4.8). Other times the lead sets the reader on a journey toward constructing meaning that will take the entire piece to complete. Alexandra (Figure 4.5) establishes the conflict of her story—Alexandra versus the swimming pool—early on when she writes, "One day, Roberto told me that it would be time for me to go across the pool all by myself!" We aren't able to comprehend fully what the story is about, however, until Alexandra resolves the conflict at the end.

ENDINGS   When I was in junior high school, one of my English teachers told my class that the best way to end a piece is to rewrite the introduction. I did this dutifully, but I didn't understand the point of doing so. While I now understand she wanted us to learn that the ending is the last chance for a writer to get her meaning across, I can also see that like many of the writing lessons I received as a child, this one was an oversimplification. True, in many texts the writer explicitly states what he has to say about his topic in his lead and tells us once again in his ending. This is how Helaina begins and ends her feature article. But some writers don't explicitly tell us their meaning in their lead; they wait until their ending to make their point. And some writers don't ever explicitly tell us their meaning, either in their lead *or* in their ending, letting us take the final few steps toward meaning ourselves. In the ending of Alexandra's story—as in the ending of many stories—she resolves the conflict that she established in her lead. Through reading that she successfully made it across the swimming pool, we infer that Alexandra overcame a difficult challenge.

When I assess what children know about how to end pieces of writing, I don't look for whether or not a child rewrote his beginning but whether he wrote the ending in a way that helps readers glean meaning from the text.

TRANSITIONS   There are usually several parts to a text's structure between the lead and the ending. One of a writer's many jobs is to help readers navigate the shift from one part to the next without disorientation or confusion. A well-written text includes transitions to help readers make these shifts.

In narratives, most of the parts are *scenes.* A new scene begins when the story shifts forward or backward in time, to a different character's point of view, or to a different setting. Experienced writers have a repertoire of transitions. For example, they'll begin a scene with the words, "That afternoon" or "I walked outside," or they'll skip a space in the text in between scenes. However, many children's repertoire of narrative transitions is limited to "And then . . ." Marion Crowhurst (1987) found that 61 percent of the "temporal conjuctions" in the writing of sixth graders in the United States consisted of the word *then*!

In nonnarrative genres, one way experienced writers signal a shift from one section to the next is to write a topic sentence at the beginning of a section. They might also use headings (as I have done for each section and subsection in this chapter) or bullets. Helaina, for example (see Figure 4.4), signals shifts from section to section by using bullets and by writing topic sentences that let us know what each section is about.

When I assess what students know about shifting from one part of their text to the next, I am curious about their repertoire of transitions. I'm also interested in how effectively they use these transitions to help readers navigate from one part to another.

Weighting Some Parts More Heavily

Experienced writers develop some parts of their text more fully than others. They weight more heavily those parts that are more crucial to communicating meaning. For example, in an op-ed piece, a writer may think that one of the reasons he feels the way he does is more persuasive than the others and write more about that reason. Barry Lane (1994) explains that writers of narrative genres "explode moments." That is, when they write about the significant moments of a story—the ones that are most important in developing the meaning—they include more detail.

Inexperienced writers often give equal weight to every part of a piece of writing, or give more weight to sections that aren't as important. Consider Katie's piece about her aunt's wedding (Figure 4.6). Since the title is "My Aunt's Wedding," we expect that Katie will develop the part about the wedding more than other parts. However, she writes more sentences about going to the waterfall and going horseback riding than she does about the wedding! It's common for younger children to write only one sentence for each part. Teachers often refer to these pieces as "laundry lists."

Even writers who have learned to develop their sections with details sometimes need to learn to weight some sections over others. Did you notice that Rusty (Figure 4.3) develops the part of the story in which he woke up early at his grandparents house more fully than some of the parts later on in the piece in which he writes about cutting and loading tobacco? As a former middle school teacher, I appreciate how hard it is for some teenagers to get out of bed early in the morning. Still, as a reader, I expect someone who is writing about the

TEACHER ACTION 4.3

Assess how your students structure their texts. Gather some of your students' writing. Try to select several genres. As you read each piece, ask yourself these questions. (You may want to use the checklist "Assessing How Well Students Write" in Appendix 2 to help you record your observations.)

- Does each part of the piece help develop the student's meaning?
- Has the student ordered the sections in a way that makes sense?
- What kinds of parts has the student included in the piece? Which kinds of parts does this student need to learn to include when he writes in this genre?
- What does the piece reveal about what this student knows about the function of leads, endings, and transitions in a text?
- Does it seem as if the student has given sufficient weight to each part of the text?

challenges of getting tobacco ready for market to give more weight to the sections in which he discusses doing the work.

In conferences, I often ask children, "Which parts are most important?" or "How are you letting readers know which parts are important?" Their answers teach me what they understand about some parts of a text doing more work than others in developing meaning.

Figure 4.13 identifies some common structural issues students encounter in their writing and suggests ways to respond in minilessons and writing conferences.

Teaching Students About Structuring Their Writing

If I see this . . .	I might . . .
A student includes parts in his piece that seem to have little to do with what he's trying to say about his topic.	Discuss with the child how writers delete the parts of a piece that don't help them communicate what they're trying to say.
The way that students have chosen to order the parts of their pieces makes them confusing to read.	Look at examples of the genre and discuss how writers order the sections in this genre.
A student includes some of the kinds of sections that the genre typically includes but not others.	Look at examples of the genre and point out some other kinds of sections he can try in his piece.
Students' leads don't let readers know where they're going in their piece or launch readers on a journey toward meaning.	Analyze the leads of model texts to show students how to write their leads.
A student relies too much on the transition *then* in her narrative writing.	Teach the student other kinds of time transitions.
Students' nonnarrative writing shifts abruptly from one point to another.	Show students how to write subheadings, topic sentences, and/or bullets to help readers transition from one point to the next.
Each section of a student's piece gets the same weight as the others.	Ask the student what the most important parts of his piece are and then discuss how writers usually develop the most important parts of a piece more than others.

FIGURE 4.13

Details: The Particulars of a Text

How many times have you exhorted students to add details to their writing? Teachers know that for students to write well, they need to include the specifics of an experience or a subject. Don Murray (1985) says, "Effective writing is produced from an abundance of specific information" (10).

Learning to write well, however, involves doing much more with details than including a lot of them. When I am assessing how well a student uses detail, I think about whether the details she includes help develop her meaning. I think about the range (or kinds of) details a writer uses when he writes in a particular genre. I think about the student's ability to write complex sentences that allow her to signal the relationships between details. And I think about whether or not a student has learned to write precise, concrete details.

Including Details That Develop Meaning

In a well-written text, every detail counts. Each one plays a role in helping a writer develop what she's trying to say.

In Alexandra's story about swimming across the pool (Figure 4.5), we learn that she "clutched the wall with an enormous amount of fear," that she "sank to the bottom of the pool," and that she "was so proud of [herself]" once she made it safely to the other side. All these details help us understand that Alexandra overcame a difficult challenge.

Or consider the details Helaina included in her feature article about grass (Figure 4.4). We learn that many animals, including cows, eat grass. We learn that spiders, crickets, and grasshoppers "depend upon grass as shelter." And we learn that grass "keeps soil and sand tied to the ground." All these details help us understand Helaina's point that grass has many uses.

Many young writers need to learn about the role details play in developing meaning. Look at the first draft of a story written by fifth grader Megan about her uncle (Figure 4.14). I'm pleased with her lead: "My Uncle Brian can be very crazy sometimes." She has something to say about her uncle, and she knows she can use her lead to tell her readers this. I expect the rest of Megan's story will include details that will help me understand Megan's point about her uncle. However, while she certainly includes a lot of details—where the story took place (her grandma's house), what the weather was like (very hot), who was part of the story (Megan's brother, cousins, and uncle), what she and the other kids did (put seaweed on Uncle Brian's head, called him a seaweed monster)—they don't help me understand why Megan thinks her uncle can act crazy. In fact, they lead me to think that Megan, her

---

Seaweed

My Uncle Brian can be very crazy sometimes. My grandma lives upstate and half of her backyard is a lake, a very big lake.

Once when I was at my grandma's house for Easter all my family came. The weekend was very hot. So we went swimming with my cousins and my uncle. We were having a seaweed fight when my youngest cousin put seaweed on my uncle's head. Then me, my brother, and my other cousin joined in. Then we started calling him seaweed monster and kept jumping on him. We thought it was funny. Then my aunt got her camera and took a picture of all five of us when my uncle was wearing the seaweed. I think you can tell sometimes my Uncle Brian can be crazy.

FIGURE 4.14   Megan's First Draft

brothers, and her cousins are the ones who act crazy! After talking with me in a writing conference about the role that detail plays in helping a reader understand a writer's point about her topic, Megan revised her draft (see Figure 4.15), adding details (in bold) that successfully characterize her uncle.

Using a Range of Details to Develop Meaning

To write well in a particular genre, a writer needs to know about—and use—the kinds of details that are typically found in that genre. Barry Lane (1994) has defined the types of detail that writers use when they write in narrative genres: dialogue, characters' thoughts (which Lane refers to as *thoughtshots*), and descriptions of characters and their movements and of the setting (all of which Lane refers to as *snapshots*). Nonnarrative writers, too, include certain kinds of details. Writers of feature articles include facts, statistics, quotations from experts on the topic, sometimes even asides that reveal the author's reaction to a particular fact.

When I'm assessing how well a student writes with detail, I look for the range of details she typically includes in the texts she writes. When I read Sean's piece, "The First Day of 4th Grade Seeing Ms. Levinson" (Figure 4.9), I learned that when she composes a narrative, she includes many kinds of detail. She writes dialogue ("'Where is she?!' I asked Lisa"), her thoughts ("I thought, would she look different?"), her actions ("I started to walk, then my walk, it got faster and faster, and then I started to run to her") as well as Ms. Levinson's ("She turned her head"), and setting details ("The white tables surrounded me").

Seaweed

My Uncle Brian can be very crazy sometimes. My grandma lives upstate and half of her backyard is a lake. My family likes to go swimming in it.

Once, when I was at my grandma's house for Easter all my family came. The weekend was very hot, so me, my brother, my cousins, and my uncle went swimming in the lake. We were having a seaweed fight when my youngest cousin put seaweed on my uncle's head. Then my other cousin and I joined in. We started calling him seaweed monster, and kept jumping on him. **My uncle started to growl, and he laughed, and then we laughed, then he growled again, and we laughed even harder. Then he acted like a real monster.** My cousins, my mother and I ran away from him and screamed! **My uncle took off some of his seaweed and threw it at us.** The seaweed was very gross and slimy. We thought it was funny and so did my uncle. **My uncle ran away from us because he thought we would throw it back at him. He was kind of chicken.** Then my aunt got her camera and took a picture of all five of us when my uncle was wearing the seaweed.

I think you can tell my Uncle Brian can be very crazy sometimes, and a lot of fun!

FIGURE 4.15   Megan's Second Draft

Many children need to learn to add certain kinds of detail to their writing repertoires. In a memoir about her communion (Figure 4.16), Anya includes setting details ("It was terribly hot on Sunday morning"), descriptions of characters ("my sister and I were dressed in beautiful white dresses"), character actions ("My father also took a picture of Father Ray, my brother, my sister, and me"), and her thoughts ("I wondered if my sister would feel nervous too"). However, she doesn't include any dialogue, even though the memoir is about her sister's support being crucial to her getting through the service. Surely Anya and her sister said some things to each other during the morning! Learning how to write dialogue would give Anya another tool to help her develop meaning in her narratives.

Embedding and Connecting Details

Good writers can convey a lot of details in their sentences. William Strong (1999) asserts that one of the signs of a student's growing maturity as a writer is that he can *say more* in fewer words (79). This

My First Communion with My Sister

The big day has finally come! It was terribly hot on Sunday morning when I woke up. I jumped out of bed and went to get dressed. At nine o'clock my sister and I were dressed in beautiful white dresses. The dress was as white and soft as snowflakes. My dad then, grabbed his camera and we were ready to leave. We walked to the church. Then we got to St. Margaret's church and my parents, grandma, and brothers took a seat up front. While my sister and I sat down with the other kids who were getting their communion.

When church started the children marched in a single line up to the altar. I felt my face turning hot and wondered if my sister would feel nervous too. I could see cameras flashing all over the church. There were also spreading echoes of baby kids playing. Then the kids and I sat up on the front seat and we spoke our prayers. When it was almost time to eat our communion bread, I wondered what it would taste like. It was then time to eat our communion bread. It tasted almost like the smell of chalk. At the end of church my father took pictures of my sister and I in front of a monument of Mary. My father also took a picture of Father Ray, my brother, sister and I.

I was glad I got my first communion with my sister. She gave me more support and confidence to be there in front of the crowds, and not feeling too nervous! This day I'll never forget because I knew that having to do something means having a lot of courage, but if you do what you have to and don't show that you're nervous, it's not half bad after all. Getting my communion with my sister gave me courage to do almost anything.

FIGURE 4.16 *Anya's Piece*

means, in general, that a more experienced writer needs fewer sentences than the inexperienced writer to convey the same number of details. Contrast these two excerpts:

Text 1

I went to the store. It was a grocery store. I bought some bread. It was whole-wheat bread. I also bought some peanut butter.

Text 2

When I went to the convenience store, I bought a jelly doughnut and a cup of coffee.

It took the author of the first text five sentences to communicate the same number of details that the author of the second was able to communicate in just one.

It's not only the author of the second text's ability to pack in more details that demonstrates that he's a more accomplished writer. He's also able to signal readers that there is a relationship between the details in the sentence (the going to the convenience store modifies the buying of the jelly doughnut and cup of coffee).

What enables good writers to pack their sentences with more details—and show relationships between details within sentences—is their ability to compose complex sentences. James Moffat (1992) observed that children move through a rough developmental sequence of being able to write sentences of increasing complexity.

Moffat noticed that young, inexperienced writers typically write texts that are strings of simple sentences:

> I had a sleepover. We had pizza from Dominoes for dinner. We had salad, too. We had ice cream for dessert. We played games in the playroom. We played Twister. I won. We played Hide and Seek. Tanya won. We stayed up until midnight.

As children grow as writers, they are able to write sentences in which they combine some details with conjunctions such as *and, but,* and *or* that let them show that these details are connected:

> One day, my dad took us out on his motorboat. He stopped the engine in the middle of the bay. He told us that dinner was in just a few hours, **and** that we should get in the water to find some clams for dinner. I wanted to go in the water, **but** I didn't like walking around in the cold water. It wasn't so bad once I got in. I quickly found a few clams, **and** my dad told me I could get back in the boat.

As children continue to grow as writers, they begin to signal readers that some details modify other details. They start to use subordinate (or dependent) clauses in their sentences, along with subordinating conjunctions such as *because* and *when*:

> It's never been hard to tell if my little sister is about to get angry. **When** she was a little girl, her face would turn turn redder and redder in the minute before she would fall to the floor and start kicking and screaming. That's how I knew to call my mom, **because** I knew that all heck was about to break loose. **When** she's about to lose it today, she gets ominously quiet. It's a quiet like the one you hear before a thunderstorm hits. That's the signal to get out of her way for a few minutes, or even the rest of the afternoon!

In the previous text, the sentence "When she was a little girl, her face would turn redder and redder . . ." has a subordinate (or dependent) clause ("When she was a little girl") and an independent clause ("her face would turn redder and redder"). The detail in the dependent clause helps us understand when it was that the author's little sister's face got redder and redder. In the sentence "That's how I knew to call my mom, because I knew that all heck was about to break loose," a subordinating conjunction—*because*—signals that the detail that follows ("I knew that all heck was about to break loose") will help us understand the detail that precedes it ("That's how I knew to call my mom").

If we're going to help students learn to write the kinds of complex sentences that will allow them to embed many details and show the relationships between them, we need to assess what kinds of sentences students are now writing. For example, Katie's piece about her aunt's wedding (Figure 4.6) consists of a string of simple sentences; Katie rarely strays from this pattern. She needs to learn how to write more complex sentences that enable her to connect some details and modify some details with others.

William Strong (1999) asserts that syntactic knowledge—that is, a sense of the options for composing sentences—is essential for students to grow as writers. When we assess the complexity of the sentences that students are writing, we're ultimately looking for the ways they are able to weave all the details together into a cohesive, unified text that has something to say.

Using Precise Detail

Good writers write with precision; the details they include are concrete. In *What a Writer Needs* (1993), Ralph Fletcher says, "Writing becomes beautiful when it becomes specific" (47).

What makes some details precise and others general? Specificity has all to do with the words a writer chooses—nouns and verbs that describe exactly what happened or is being talked about, as well as adjectives and adverbs that enhance those nouns and verbs. A writer who includes precise details chooses words that help convey the meaning of the piece.

Consider this passage from Sean's story about seeing Ms. Levinson: "Then I saw her. I saw her smile. I thought, was she looking at me? She waved. I waved back. Now I knew she was looking at me." When I read this scene of reunion between a student and her beloved teacher, I felt joy, not simply because of what happened in the scene, but because of the words Sean chose—*smile* and *wave* describe exactly what happened in this moment. These words also helped Sean communicate the strong bond she felt with Ms. Levinson—that she and her teacher had the kind of relationship in which they would smile and wave at each other if they saw each other at a distance.

Or how about these sentences from Valerie's letter to her mother about not liking chicken soup (Figure 4.8):

- You put too many vegetables. Last time you put tomatoes and cauliflower and I don't like them.
- I do not like the skin of the chicken because it is all slimy. When I see the slimy chicken skin, I want to throw up.

Valerie is using nouns and an adjective that describe exactly what she doesn't like about her mom's soup—*tomatoes, cauliflower,* and *slimy skin.* These words will convince Valerie's mom either to make specific ingredient changes in the future or to serve the soup less frequently. (We can only guess what happened when Valerie shared the letter with her mom!)

Also notice that Sean and Valerie write with precise detail using commonplace words. Many of us are tempted to urge students to use unusual, multisyllabic, "ten-dollar" words in their writing—words students find in a thesaurus and use even when they're not quite sure of their meaning and can't pronounce them. Sean and Valerie were able to write precise details in their pieces not because they wracked their brains or flipped through the pages of a thesaurus, searching for the longest, most complicated words that they could recall, but because they reached for words that helped them convey exactly what they were trying to say. Whatever those words turn out to be—*wave* and *skin,* or *halyard* and *serendipity*—they're well chosen *if* they're specific and concrete and *if* they help convey the writer's meaning.

Of course, many students choose words that are general, not specific, and need to be taught to be more thoughtful about the words they use. Don Graves (1994) writes, "Good nouns are often hard to find in young writers' pieces. They write with a good narrative sense but include very little that sets the tone or conveys the meaning of the action" (218).

However, some students use general words not because they don't have a good vocabulary but because they have other issues as writers. When students aren't trying to communicate meaning in their writing (or aren't sure what they want to communicate), they don't need the precise words that develop meaning. Or perhaps they aren't sure which words to use. In her piece about her aunt's wedding (Figure 4.6), most of Katie's nouns and verbs are very general (*wedding, horseback riding, went, had*). Imagine that Katie wanted us to know how nervous she was to be a junior bridesmaid and had told the story of the wedding ceremony as a way of showing us how nerve-racking the experience was. To do that, she would have needed to use more specific nouns (*sweat, aisle, bride, pew, priest, ring*) and verbs (*shook, kissed, cried*). While it would be easy to conclude that Katie needs to learn to use more specific nouns and verbs after reading this one writing sample, it would be prudent to wait and see what words Katie uses

TEACHER ACTION 4.4

Assess how your students write with detail. Gather some of your students' writing. Try to select several genres. As you read each piece, ask yourself these questions. (You may want to use the checklist "Assessing How Well Students Write" in Appendix 2 to help you record your observations.)

- Do the details that the student includes help develop meaning?
- What kinds of details does the student write in this genre? Which kinds of details does this student need to learn to include when he writes in this genre?
- What kinds of sentences does this student typically write? What does this student need to learn about writing sentences that would allow her to embed more details and show the relationships between details?
- Does the student use precise words that help convey meaning?

in her writing once she starts trying to convey meaning and writes with a stronger sense of genre.

Figure 4.17 lists some of the problems students often have with writing with detail and lessons that address these problems.

Teaching Students About Writing with Detail

If I see this . . .	I might . . .
A student includes detail that is extraneous and doesn't do any work to develop the point he's trying to make.	Tell him that writers cut unnecessary details from their writing.
Students are including some of the kinds of detail that writers typically use in the genre but not others.	Read examples of the genre and analyze the kinds of detail writers typically include and then invite students to try writing details they aren't yet including in their writing.
A student's piece reads like a long string of details that don't seem connected to one another.	Show the student how to combine sentences to show the relationships between the details in her writing.
The words students are using in their writing are general, not specific.	Tell them to make a picture in their head of the topic they're writing about, brainstorm precise words that are connected to the topic, and then try to use them in their writing.

FIGURE 4.17

Voice: The Sound of the Person Behind the Words

It's not hard for us to read a piece of writing and hear the writer's voice in it. However, when we try to define *voice* in our minilessons and describe what good writers do to create it in their writing, many of us find ourselves at a loss for words.

Tom Romano (2004) defines voice as "the sense we have while reading that someone occupies the middle of our mind, filling the space with the sound of a voice, the sense we have while writing that something is whispering in our ear" (6). In "Eminem" (see Figure 4.18), by Sara, a sixth grader, I hear Sara's voice in my head. It's an angry voice, the voice of an adolescent who is troubled by what she sees as the negative effect of certain rappers on members of her peer group. Contrast Sara's piece with Katie's piece about her aunt's wedding (Figure 4.6). I don't hear much of Katie's voice in my head. The tone of the piece seems neutral. I don't feel that Katie *as an individual* is very present in this piece of writing.

If we are going to assess students' writing for voice, we have to know what good writers *do* to convey voice. This will help us see what student writers already are doing to create voice in their writing and what they're trying to do. And we'll be able to identify what we need to teach students to do that they aren't yet doing when they write.

We also need to understand that writers use voice to help them enhance their meaning. Voice, according to Don Murray (1999), is "a clue to meaning the way movie music underlines the action on the screen" (127). In much the same ways as we use our speaking voices to help us get across what we're trying to say (saying some words louder than others to emphasize them, slowing down or speeding up some sentences), writers use voice to help them say what they want to say. Ultimately, it isn't enough for us to assess what children do to write with voice. We also have to ask ourselves how what they are doing helps them communicate meaning.

Creating Voice with Sentence Structure

One way good writers create voice is by writing sentences in ways that cue readers to inflect their actual voice (if they're reading aloud) or their inner voice (if they're reading silently) in certain ways. That is, good writers write sentences in ways that signal us to read them with a certain rhythm, a certain beat, a certain *sound*. Murray (1999) says, "Good writing is not speech written down, but it creates, in the reader's mind, the illusion of speech" (194).

Sara, in her op-ed piece (Figure 4.18), writes many of her sentences in ways that cue me to modulate my reading voice in very particular ways. Her second paragraph is two brief sentences: "I'll tell you straight. Rappers." When I read this, I give *Rappers* greater emphasis than the sentence that precedes it because I know I'm supposed to read

Eminem

I've seen them in my neighborhood, my block, my school . . . everywhere. The boys with the baggy pants hanging down so that their plaid boxers are revealed. The heavy gold chains that weigh a ton. Though, it's not what they're wearing that's pestering me. It's what they're doing. I've heard and watched them. Curse, swear, give the finger, punch and kick. And who do I blame?

I'll tell you straight. Rappers.

I'm talking about Eminem in particular. I'm talking about his need to be vulgar, his need to be violent and his need to be plain cruel.

After all, he's killing his wife and jumping off buildings in the "What I Am" music video and fantasizing about raping his own mother in one of his song lyrics.

Makes you wonder. Makes you think.

Makes you wish that teenagers, mainly of the male gender, would be smart enough to know what's wrong, smart enough to know not to be influenced so easily, smart enough to know that Eminem is WRONG.

Don't gang up on me now! I know what I'm talking about. And I certainly know that I am not talking about *all* teenagers. I definitely know that I am *not* saying that all teenagers would end up in car accidents because of rappers, such as the scene in Eminem's recent music video, "Stan." But, I *am* saying that Eminem is an adult acting like a child. I *am* saying that Eminem is wrong, cruel and mean.

And it's got to stop.

Look, Marshall Mathers is receiving Grammy awards for showing a bad image to little kids. He's getting paid for being cruel and mean. He's being the person parents don't want their children to become.

Mr. Mathers and all you rappers, get this through your head, you need to realize you have young listeners who look up to you, admire you and want to be like you. You have to take the role as a baby-sitter, you have to make sure your album content is appropriate for younger ages, you have to understand that you're supposed to be a role model, you have to act like the adults you are! You have to.

87% of the people I surveyed said they would enjoy Eminem's songs better if they didn't contain the violent and vulgar expressions. So, you see Marshall, lose the "macho man" act and maybe you'll be valued more.

Don't defend him. Don't tell me he's just kidding or joking around. You know I'm right and I know I'm right. And there is nothing left to say.

Wait, yes there is!

You see, I have a brother who is a fan of Eminem and eventually, he's going to become a teenager. And before he does, all this has got to stop.

FIGURE 4.18 Sara's Op-Ed

single-word sentences this way. When I read, "Makes you wish that teenagers, mainly of the male gender, would be smart enough to know what's wrong, smart enough to know not to be influenced so easily, smart enough to know that Eminem is WRONG," I say the repeated word *smart* with increasing emphasis, because I know that when a writer repeats a word like this, I'm supposed to read it this way.

In fact, Sara writes many of her sentences in ways that cue me to modulate my reading voice in very particular ways. One way to test this out for yourself is to read Sara's piece aloud. Listen for the places where you inflect your voice in different ways, and then ask yourself why you did this. Chances are you changed your voice in response to how Sara wrote the sentence you were reading.

Writers who write with voice have a well-developed repertoire of sentence patterns (or syntactic options) that they are able to employ purposefully when they compose a piece. William Strong (1999) writes that "successful writers . . . become increasingly adept at manipulating sentence parts to achieve their rhetorical aims." In contrast, "less successful writers are constrained not so much by deficits of vocabulary or intelligence as by syntactic shackles, a lack of phrase-manipulating skills" (73–74).

Part of assessing a child for what she knows about writing with voice, then, involves assessing her syntactic sophistication. Students like Sara have already learned to write sentences in ways that give their writing voice. A less experienced writer like Katie ("My Aunt's Wedding") uses the same simple sentence pattern over and over, and her piece sounds flat and monotonous when read aloud. Students like Katie have much to learn about the options for writing sentences and how these kinds of sentences give their writing voice.

Whenever I look at writing with teachers, sometime during our conversation we'll discuss what we were taught as children about how sentences are written: *You can't write a sentence that contains just one word. Don't repeat words. Never start a sentence with* but *or* and. And so forth.

Good writers do sometimes write one-word sentences. (Charles Dickens, a rather accomplished writer, begins his novel *Bleak House* with a single-word sentence: "London.") Good writers do sometimes repeat words and phrases, both within a sentence and in the text as a whole. (We remember Martin Luther King's "I have a dream" speech in part because he repeated that phrase many times.) And good writers sometimes begin sentences with *and* or *but*. In *Teaching Grammar in Context* (1996), Connie Weaver points out that nearly one out of nine sentences in informative writing begins with *and* or *but*; in narrative writing the ratio is nearly one out of twenty. Good writers deliberately choose to do these things (and many others we were told never to do) because they want to give their writing voice.

If we're going to assess students' syntactic sophistication, we need to become more knowledgeable about the kinds of sentences writers routinely write. Probably the best way is to look at examples of the genres that our students typically read and write and study the sentences. It's also important to read books about good writing (Katie Wood Ray's *Wondrous Words* [1999] is one of the best) as well as handbooks on usage, such as William Strunk and E. B. White's classic, *The Elements of Style* (2000).

Good writers also use punctuation to help them create voice. Janet Angelillo (2002) says, "Writers use punctuation to shape the way readers read their texts" (8). They deliberately choose certain marks because they know these marks signal us to inflect our voice in a particular way, emphasize a word or phrase, or slow down. We know to pause in our reading when we see a period. We make a shorter pause when we encounter a comma. And so forth.

Alexandra (Figure 4.5) uses the ellipsis several times in her swimming pool story to signal us to slow our reading of certain sentences. On page 5 she writes, "But then . . . I let go of the wall!" And she uses an exclamation point at the end of that sentence to signal us to read the last phrase with added emphasis. Sara uses the ellipsis in her Eminem piece (Figure 4.18) for a different reason. Read this sentence aloud: "I've seen them in my neighborhood, my block, my school . . . everywhere." You probably read the word *everywhere* with added emphasis because it was preceded by an ellipsis.

When we're assessing what a child does to write with voice, we need to look for the ways she uses punctuation to cue us to give her writing the rhythm and sound of spoken language. It's important to assess the kinds of punctuation she regularly uses (and the marks that aren't yet in her repertoire) as well as the effects that she's trying to achieve by using those marks.

Good writers have other ways besides punctuation to cue readers to read their texts in a particular way, and it's important to consider whether or not student writers know about—and do—these things when they write. For example, sometimes writers italicize or boldface a word or put it in all caps (as Sara does in the sentence ending "smart enough to know that Eminem is WRONG") to signal readers to emphasize that word. One reason poets choose to end lines where they do is because they want readers to pause in those places. Writers also use white space to signal readers to pause in their reading.

Creating Voice Through Details

Good writers also convey voice by including details that reveal who they are as individuals: male or female, city or suburban or rural, elderly or adolescent, Asian American or Arab American, rich or poor, and so forth.

When I read the feature article "Deodorant: All You Need to Know" (Figure 4.19), written by fifth grader Matt, I clearly hear the voice of an adolescent. I can identify Matt as an adolescent because of

Deodorant: All You Need to Know

Have you ever imagined what it would be like to be in a crowd and have everyone turn around and say, "Hey, you forgot to put on deodorant!" That is what deodorant prevents. Deodorant is that little container that you keep in your drawer or medicine cabinet, and use daily under your arms to prevent that gruesome smell.

Choosing the Right Deodorant

How do you know which deodorant is right for you? Let's start with the fact that if you're going to buy deodorant, you're going to have to know what type, and what strength you want. If you get the wrong type of deodorant, people just might start saying, "ooh, what's that horrible smell."

How do you know what type you need? It depends on what you do. Do you sweat a lot? Do you play a lot of sports? Do you wear sleeveless shirts? These are some of the questions that you need to ask yourself before going to make your purchase.

The deodorant that you use might depend on what part of the world you're from. For instance, some Asian cultures do not produce body odor, whereas the Irish use the most deodorant per capita because they play the most sports per capita.

Bad Odor, No Odor, or Your Favorite Scent

When you go to a store, you are going to see plenty of deodorants on the shelves. This way you can choose the one that fits your needs best. You could get extra strength, sensitive skin and regular. There are plenty of types of ways for people to put it on like roll on, spray on, stick, and wipe on. Different deodorants also last for different lengths of times. Usually the stronger the deodorant the longer it will last. There are also different scents such as "baby powder," "ocean breeze," and "shower mist."

The best part about deodorant is that there is a better chance that people are not going to say "peeuuu."

Almost Perfect

Deodorant has its problems just like everything else in the world. Let's start with what may be the worst problem and the most dangerous problem. Some studies show that deodorant might increase your chances of getting breast cancer.

Another problem is that if you're wearing a baggy shirt with no sleeves, you are going to look like a jerk with white stuff in your armpits. If you wear clear deodorant nobody will be able to see it.

When Do You Need It

According to Webster, the majority of people begin needing deodorant when they are between the ages of 16–22. If you have ever been in a locker room with a bunch of 11-year-old kids, you know it should be much younger. Other things that help determine when you need to begin using deodorant are how often you play sports, and how much you sweat. If you play a lot of sports (in the summer), you're going to smell a lot more than if you are walking to Key Food (in the winter). If you think about it, it makes sense that athletes use stronger deodorant than the couch potatoes watching them on television.

Isn't deodorant a great invention? Who could live without it? If only they could make this stink buster ever-lasting, like the Ever-Lasting Gobstopper in Willy Wonka and the Chocolate Factory.

FIGURE 4.19   Matt's Feature Article

the numerous details he includes that reveal the anxiety about body odor that is typical of kids this age:

- "Deodorant is that little container that you keep in your drawer or medicine cabinet and use daily under your arms to prevent that gruesome smell."
- "If you get the wrong type of deodorant, people just might start saying, 'Ooh, what's that horrible smell?'"
- "The best part about deodorant is that there is a better chance that people are not going to say 'peeuuu.'"
- "Another problem is that if you're wearing a baggy shirt with no sleeves, you are going to look like a jerk with white stuff in your armpits."

When I read Rusty's memoir about cutting and loading tobacco (Figure 4.3), I hear the voice of a teenage boy raised in Kentucky because, as Matt does, Rusty includes details (in this case, nicknames and idiomatic language common in central Kentucky at the time Rusty wrote the piece) that reveal something about who he is:

- "I heard my grandfather, alias Paw-Paw, talking about his tobacco."
- "'Finally up?' asked Maw-Maw as I walked into the kitchen."
- "They'll bite the heck out of you."
- "Everybody was dog tired."

When we assess what a child knows about writing with voice, we need to ask ourselves whether we can get a sense of who this child is as an individual from reading details that he includes in a piece. Too often, student writing doesn't reveal much, if anything, about the student as a person. The pieces have a generic quality, as if they could have been written by any child, anywhere.

Voice is the quality of writing that gives it authority and power. Ralph Fletcher (1993) writes, "I figure that if [a reader] can get a sense of me as a person he might, in turn, listen to what I have to say" (71). In her piece about swimming across the pool for the first time, Alexandra writes, "I felt as though I was a tiny little fish that had just gotten eaten by a shark." Reading this sentence, I hear the voice of a scared little girl, which helps me understand emotionally what a difficult challenge Alexandra faced on this day and what a triumph it was for her to make it all the way across the pool by herself for the first time.

Creating Voice by Creating Intimacy with Readers

Good writers create the sense that they are having an intimate conversation with their readers. They use techniques that draw their readers in.

One way is sharing the thoughts they were having during the experiences they're writing about. This brings us as close as we can be to them—we're in their minds. When Sean tells her story about Ms. Levinson, she writes, "I thought, would she look different? Was her hair going to be blue? Was she going to have red little streaks? I wonder, I wonder." Sean draws us close to her by allowing us to be privy to her thoughts.

Writers of nonnarrative genres (feature articles, op-ed pieces, etc.) draw their readers in by weaving in their thoughts and reactions to the topic. When Matt wrote his feature article about deodorant, he included some commentary (my italics) along with the facts: "According to Webster, the majority of people begin needing deodorant when they are between the ages of 16–22. *If you have ever been in a locker room with a bunch of 11-year-old kids, you know it should be much younger.*" In her feature article about the uses of grass, Helaina, too, includes some of her own thoughts (my italics) about the information: "Grass . . . keeps soil and sand tied to the ground. *If we didn't have grass then when a wind picked up, woosh, there would go your front yard.*"

Writers also create the feeling of intimate conversation by actively reaching out to their readers. In the middle of his memoir about loading and cutting tobacco, Rusty steps out of his story to address his readers directly:

> I'm going to tell you the pay before the story. You get paid $7.00 an hour. That's 8 $\frac{4}{7}$ min. of work for every dollar. You're probably thinking that's a lot for a little. You just wait and see.

TEACHER ACTION 4.5

Assess how your students write with voice. Gather some of your students' writing. Try to select several genres. As you read each piece, ask yourself these questions. (You may want to use the checklist "Assessing How Well Students Write" in Appendix 2 to help you record your observations.)

- What kinds of sentences does this student write that give his writing voice?

- How does this writer use punctuation to create voice? Which punctuation marks does she use? Which marks can she still add to her repertoire?

- Does this writer include details that reveal who he is as a person?

- How does this writer create a feeling of intimacy between herself and her readers? (This doesn't apply to a genre such as a news story in the school newspaper.)

And in her piece about rappers, there are places where I feel Sara is reaching right out of the page, grabbing my shoulders, and talking to me: "Don't defend him. Don't tell me he's just kidding or joking around. You know I'm right and I know I'm right. And there is nothing left to say."

When I'm assessing children's ability to create voice in their writing, I look for the ways in which they position me to hear their voice. I'm more likely to hear the voice of a writer if I feel that there isn't much distance between us. Conversely, I find it hard to hear a writer's voice if she feels distant. The better I can hear a writer's voice, the better, ultimately, I'm able to understand what she's trying to say to me.

Figure 4.20 lists some common issues students encounter when dealing with voice and some lessons we can teach them to help them deal with these issues.

Conventions: Grammar, Punctuation, and Spelling

As teachers, we want to help students learn to use writing conventions. We want them to divide their texts into paragraphs, use appropriate punctuation marks, make their subjects and verbs agree, spell each word correctly, and so forth. The conventions of written English are tools for writers to help them communicate meaning.

However, it's no secret that students of all ages make errors when they write. Grammatical errors. Punctuation errors. Spelling errors. These errors distract readers from the meaning a writer is trying to communicate. They can also confuse readers, making it difficult for them to understand what a writer is trying to say.

Teaching Students About Writing with Voice	
If I see this . . .	**I might . . .**
The student relies on the same sentence structure in sentence after sentence, and the sound of his writing is flat.	Analyze the kinds of sentences in model texts and nudge the student to try some of these kinds of sentences in his piece.
Students' pieces seem as if they could have been written by anyone, anywhere.	Tell the students that writers include details in their writing that reveal aspects of who they are as people.
The student seems distant from her readers in her writing.	Show the student how to draw readers close to her by including her thoughts in her writing and/or by using pronouns such as *you*.

FIGURE 4.20

The traditional response to student errors has been the red pen. The underlying assumption of this approach is that students *should already know* how to write grammatically correct sentences, use punctuation correctly, and spell the words they use. Teachers who use the behaviorist approach of highlighting the errors that students make and deducting points from their grade accordingly assume that students will be cajoled into not making these errors again. In my high school, for example, my classmates and I automatically received an F on a composition if it contained a single sentence fragment or run-on sentence.

When we go on error hunts in student writing, however, we are missing opportunities to learn about what students *do* understand about writing sentences, using punctuation, and spelling words. Thus, we're missing opportunities to get the information we need to be able to teach students to use the conventions of written English with more and more precision.

The research of educators such as Diane Snowball and Faye Bolton (1999), William Strong (1999), Connie Weaver (1996), and Sandra Wilde (1992) indicates that student errors fall into one of two categories. The first we might call the careless error. As we (all of us, even prize-winning adult writers) compose our drafts, our attention is usually more focused on issues of content and craft. We make some errors in spelling, grammar, and punctuation because our attention is elsewhere. This kind of error usually disappears when we edit our writing.

Students make the second kind of error because, paradoxically, *they are growing as writers*. To understand this kind of error, remember that when people are learning to do new things, they make mistakes. When I was learning to ski, I quickly became proficient at going down the bunny slopes, but when I started down the intermediate slopes, I fell down numerous times (usually rather dramatically). Gradually, with the guidance of a few ski instructors, I was able to navigate even the steeper slopes, and now I rarely fall when I go skiing.

As students grow as writers, they begin to try out more and more complex sentence structures. When they are on what William Strong (1999) calls a "syntactic threshold"—that is, when they are beginning to write new kinds of complex sentences—they make very predictable kinds of errors. Therefore, a seventh grader who is starting to write sentences with subordinate clauses may have more errors in a paper than a third grader who writes only simple sentences. Connie Weaver (1996) points out that while errors disappear after students master writing certain kinds of sentences, new kinds of errors take their place as the students begin to write even more complex sentences. Errors, Weaver asserts, are "evidence of the writer's thinking and, in some cases, clear indicators of the writer's growth in mastering the structures and conventions of written English" (59).

Here's the first page of a story written by fifth grader Khalil about a ride he took on an airplane:

> My family and I were standing in the airport. I couldn't believe the amount of people there. Everyone was rushing around and waiting on long lines. I wondered where everyone was going. I looked over at my mom and dad. They were standing on line to get their tickets. I went over and talked to my brother.
>
> "How does it feel to be on a plane?" I asked.
>
> "It's not a big deal," he said.
>
> When my mom and dad were done getting the tickets. We began walking to the plane. I was getting nervous because I never went on a plane before. We were getting closer to the plane door.

Even though Khalil edited this piece before he published it, there is still an error in the fourth paragraph: "When my mom and dad were done getting the tickets. We began walking to the plane." Khalil should have used a comma to join the subordinate clause ("When my mom and dad . . .") to the independent clause ("we began walking . . ."), not presented the clauses as separate sentences. Let's try to figure out why Khalil made this error when he wrote and why he didn't catch it when he edited his piece.

First, most of the sentences on this page are simple sentences: "My family and I were standing in the airport." "They were standing on line to get their tickets." In two sentences, Khalil joined details together with the conjunction *and*: "Everyone was rushing around and waiting on long lines." "I went over and talked to my brother." These sentences are all correctly punctuated.

The sentence in which Khalil made the mistake is the only sentence on this page that begins with a subordinate clause (indeed, of the thirty-six sentences in Khalil's entire story, only this one and one other begin with a subordinate clause). Khalil probably made this mistake because he is beginning to incorporate a new kind of sentence structure into his repertoire, and he doesn't yet know how to punctuate it. Instead of putting a big red *X* through the sentence, it would be more helpful to point out to Khalil, in an editing conference, that he's writing a new kind of sentence and show him how to punctuate it. William Strong (1999) advises that errors like these "should be welcomed as evidence of [students'] efforts to *develop* their writing skills rather than play it safe" (81).

When I'm assessing students' writing for their knowledge of conventions, I pay particular attention to how they use punctuation. The punctuation marks I see them use—and those I notice they aren't yet using—tell me what students know and haven't yet learned about how to show relationships between the clauses in their sentences. Don

Graves (1994) writes that punctuation marks "keep one meaning unit from interfering with the next"—they "provide separate rooms in the house of meaning" (202).

Figure 4.21 is a piece of writing by Terrence, a fifth grader. What do his punctuation errors tell us about the kinds of sentences he is learning to write? Like Khalil, Terrence knows how to write and punctuate simple sentences:

> My Uncle Jackson drove us there in his car.
> My sisters stayed at a friend's house on the same block as me.

However, when Terrence writes a compound sentence, he doesn't put a comma before the conjunction:

> My mom said she was going to go get the rabbit by herself
> but I wanted to go too.

And in another, more complex compound sentence, Terrence doesn't put a comma after the subordinate clause that begins the sentence and puts a comma after the conjunction:

> When we got to the pet store my mom went to the back
> of the store with the pet store guy but, I stayed in the front
> with my Uncle Jackson.

Clearly, Terrence needs to learn how to use commas to punctuate compound sentences, as well as dependent clauses.

Of particular interest in Terrence's piece is his lead, in which he seems to be trying to write a series of short sentences that will cue us to read dramatically:

> May 16, 2000 the day I got my rabbit, the best day of my life.

The Day I Got My Rabbit

May 16, 2000 the day I got my rabbit, the best day of my life. My mom said she was going to go get the rabbit by herself but I wanted to go too. My sisters stayed at a friend's house on the same block as me. My Uncle Jackson drove us there in his car. I kept on asking my mom if we were almost there, she said "yes." I couldn't wait to get there. When we got to the pet store my mom went to the back of the store with the pet store guy but, I stayed in the front with my Uncle Jackson. My mother walked to the front of the store with a big smile on her face and a big white rabbit in her arms.

That's right May 16, 2000 the best day of my life.

FIGURE 4.21 Terrence's Piece

A more experienced writer might write this part in one of several ways:

- May 16, 2000. The day I got my rabbit. The best day of my life.
- May 16, 2000—the day I got my rabbit. The best day of my life.
- May 16, 2000. The day I got my rabbit—the best day of my life.
- May 16, 2000 . . . the day I got my rabbit. The best day of my life.

When I read this section, I thought Terrence needed to learn something new about using periods—that they can be used to punctuate very short sentences (which Connie Weaver [1996] refers to as "minor sentences"), signaling readers to read them with emphasis. And I thought about how teaching Terrence punctuation marks like the dash or the ellipsis could help him join clauses together in ways that could help him signal readers to read them with more emphasis than others.

It may seem daunting to assess each of your students like this. One thing that helps me make quicker assessments of a student's ability to write conventionally constructed and punctuated sentences is that most of the students in a class are at a similar developmental threshold. They are trying to write the same kinds of sentences, and they make very similar kinds of errors. I expect to see certain patterns of errors when I work in second-grade classrooms and other patterns when I work in eighth-grade classrooms. If you want to learn more about these patterns, Sandra Wilde's *You Kan Red This!* (1992) contains information on children's punctuation development in elementary school;

TEACHER ACTION 4.6

Assess how your students use conventions. Gather some of your students' writing that they have already edited themselves. As you read each piece, ask yourself these questions. (You may want to use the checklist "Assessing How Well Students Write" in Appendix 2 to help you record your observations.)

- What conventions does this student use consistently? What does this reveal about what he knows about writing sentences?
- What kinds of errors do I see in the piece? What do these errors reveal about what this student is trying to learn to do as a writer? What do these errors tell me that I need to teach this student?

Connie Weaver's *Teaching Grammar in Context* (1996) is another excellent resource.

When we abandon the error hunt and see students' errors as signs of their growth as writers, we remove a significant obstacle to their willingness to take syntactic risks in their writing. "One of the problems with overreacting to error," Weaver observes, "is that it stunts our students' growth as writers" (1996, 81). Students who feel the presence of the red pen are often less venturesome as writers and write the kinds of simple sentences that won't get them in trouble with their teachers. On the other hand, when students sense that their teachers are encouraging them to experiment with more complex sentences and will respond to the risks they are taking with *teaching*, instead of with punishment, they will be much more likely to try to write the kinds of sentences they need to learn to become powerful writers.

Teachers of students who are learning English as a second language often ask me how to cope with the number of errors that these students usually make when they are learning to write in English. I approach these children much the same way I do students for whom English is their first language. Stephen Krashen (1985) has noted that one of the conditions for language acquisition is being unafraid to make mistakes. The error hunt has the same detrimental effects on ESL students as it does on students who are native English speakers. It does help to know some of the predictable developmental stages that ESL students move through as they learn to write English, so it's a good idea to read descriptions of these developmental stages, such as the one that Guadalupe Valdes and Patricia Sanders (1999) constructed in response to their research into the writing of Latino students.

Student errors in spelling, too, can be categorized as careless errors and errors that are evidence of their growth as spellers. Teachers of primary-grade children are especially aware that young writers go through a series of developmental stages on the road to spelling words conventionally. The terms *invented spelling* and *constructed spelling* refer to these developmental stages. Sandra Wilde's *You Kan Red This!* (1992) is an extensive discussion of this subject.

Figure 4.22 lists some of the general issues students encounter when dealing with conventions and lessons that address them.

Creating Your Own Definition of What It Means to Write Well

Now that you've spent some time learning how I conceptualize what it means for a writer to write well, it's time for you to step back and think about the words you're going to use to define good writing and what these words mean to you.

Teaching Students About Conventions

If I see this . . .	I might . . .
The student is starting to write a new kind of sentence in her writing but isn't punctuating it conventionally yet.	Show the student examples of the kind of sentence and discuss how they're punctuated.
The student is starting to use a particular kind of punctuation mark (e.g., quotation marks) but isn't yet using it conventionally.	Discuss a model text in which the writer uses this kind of punctuation mark and point out how the writer uses it.
The student misspells frequently used words.	Give the student a list of the frequently used words that he misspells and have him use the list to help him write these words correctly.

FIGURE 4.22

TEACHER ACTION 4.7

Reflect on your own definition of what it means to write well. Construct your own list of traits of good writing.

- Start by brainstorming terms that best describe for you what it means to write well.

- Refer to the official list of qualities of good writing that your school or district may have published for teachers.

- Read the list of traits of good writing that your state has published for teachers. These can usually be found in your state standards or in the scoring guides to your state's standarized writing tests.

- Read some other lists of the qualities of good writing, such as those in this chapter.

- Combine these lists into one that best speaks to you.

- Share your list of traits with colleagues in a study group and ask them to share theirs. Conversations with others can help you refine and extend your thinking.

Learning What Students Know About Writing Well from Conferences

Our writing conferences give us another source of information about what students know about writing well—the students themselves. We expect students to tell us what they're trying to do to write well.

The word *trying* is important. In a writing workshop, students are usually trying out what they're learning about writing well from minilessons and conferences. Because they're trying to do something for the first (or second or third) time, they often aren't able to pull it off successfully. If we have only the students' final drafts, we may not be able to see clearly what new understandings about writing well they are attempting to realize. Therefore, our conversations with students are an important window into how they are constructing new understandings about writing well as they grow as writers. This information, in combination with the information we can gather from reading the actual work in progress, helps us decide what to teach them to help them apply their understanding effectively in their writing.

Consider how much I learned about what Doran, a fifth grader, knew about writing well—or perhaps was just learning about writing well—when I sat down to confer with him. Doran was getting ready to write a feature article on strategies for getting good deals on toys.

ME: How's it going?

DORAN: Well, I'm working on my article.

ME: Working on your article?

DORAN: Well, OK, I'm just getting started.

ME: Does that mean you're ready to start writing your lead?

DORAN: Yeah.

ME: Could you tell me why you think you're ready to start your lead?

DORAN: Well, I made a list of my bullets [subsections].

ME: So you made a plan for your article?

DORAN: Yeah. At first I was just listing the parts, but then I thought a little bit, like, which would go one after the other, to make sense. So I did a part about Toys 'R' Us, then I did one about the difference between stores, and then I have here waiting toys out, and buying toys quick, and then I have coupons over here. I tried to match them near another one so it would kind of make sense.

ME: So you're trying to group the parts together.

DORAN: Right.

ME: Your subject is toys, and your angle is getting the best deal on toys?

DORAN: Right.

ME: And this article will help people get that deal. You know, I can't believe how much toys cost, even for babies, so you're doing people like me—parents—a real service here.

DORAN: Uh-huh.

ME: How are you going to get started with your draft?

DORAN: Well, I guess first I'm just going to think about my lead and write about what my angle is, like at the beginning of the bully article. [*The class' touchstone text was "So a Big Bad Bully Is*

Coming After You," by Candace Purdom.] Once that's done, I'll look back on these entries [in his writer's notebook] and make them bigger and add things on . . . and my mom and I are planning to go to maybe a toy store or something like that and look; I'm just going to do a little research.

ME: So you still have more research to do. . . .

DORAN: Yeah.

ME: Wow, you have a lot of smart plans. You want to write that lead, and then you have some material in your notebook, some entries, that will help you as you draft. You want to stretch those and write them better to create the different sections, the "bullets." These are the kinds of plans that good writers have when they start a draft.

DORAN: Yeah.

ME: How do you think your lead is going to go?

DORAN: Well, I guess I'd start . . . well, I wouldn't say, "My angle is about such and such"; I'd say, "When you're getting toys, either if you're a parent buying gifts or you're a kid trying to get some toys that you're collecting, here are some tips and ways that you can get toys for good deals."

ME: Let me tell you what I'm hearing here. In the lead of a feature article, there's usually that one sentence that's the angle of the whole article, and you really have a feel for how to write that sentence. I want to talk about one other thing you could do. One thing I noticed about the bully article is Candace Purdom does more than what you're planning to do. The sentence you've got is like the one she has right here [*pointing to the last sentence of the lead*], where she says, "Here are tips on making a tough spot easier."

DORAN: I see, but that's at the end [of the lead] for her.

ME: For her it's at the end. What does she do at the beginning here?

DORAN: She kind of describes what some kids think of a big mean bully.

ME: Yeah, and it's fun to read, isn't it? "Bigger than Shaquille. Meaner than the Wicked Witch of the West. Scarier than a Raptor. We're talking about the school bully."

DORAN: Yeah. If I was going to take after that, I could say, "So you want to get a toy that's very expensive. But you don't have so much money. Here are . . ." I could enlarge on that, like she did there.

ME: Good. What you're doing now is not just coming in with the nitty-gritty; you're trying to draw your readers in. So I'd like you to go ahead and write your lead, OK, and as you write, keep the bully lead in your head.

DORAN: OK.

ME: Good talking to you.

DORAN: Good talking with you, too.

> So you want to get that cool new toy, but you only have half the money? It's a major holiday and you have to buy toys for all your nephews, nieces and kids? Anyone who has ever stepped into a toystore has heard kids whining for expensive toys, such as, "I want Pokemon Red, mom. Thats the one for me, or, "I Just have to have Nintendo 64 dad." Here are a few ways to get good deals on toys.

FIGURE 4.23 Doran's Lead

After the conference, Doran wrote a lead that incorporated a more developed hook. (See Figure 4.23.)

In this conference, I was able to learn a great deal about what Doran understood about writing well and what he was actually able to do to write well. The table on the following page describes what I learned.

Most important, Doran understood that his feature article should communicate a meaning about his topic (feature article writers refer to this as their *angle*). He also already knew what his angle was going to be. Therefore, I didn't need to focus this conference on teaching Doran about meaning.

I also learned that Doran knew some things about structuring a piece of nonnarrative writing. He knew that writers order their sections logically in a feature article, and he demonstrated (in his written plan for the piece) that he could do this. Therefore, I didn't need to focus the conference on ordering his piece.

Doran also knew some important things about writing a good lead for a feature article. Even though he understood that writers try to hook their readers into a piece in the lead, I didn't feel that he could do this effectively yet as a writer. Many feature article writers spend one or more paragraphs hooking the reader. Doran, however,

What Doran Said	What I Learned Doran Knows About Writing Well
I made a list of my bullets [subsections].	Doran understands that writers structure their writing.
At first I was just listing the parts, but then I thought a little bit, like, which would go one after the other, to make sense.	Doran understands that in feature articles, writers order their sections logically.
Well, I guess first I'm just going to think about my lead and write about what my angle is, like at the beginning of the bully article.	Doran noticed that feature article writers let readers know their angle in their leads.
I wouldn't say, "My angle is about such and such"; I'd say, "When you're getting toys, either if you're a parent buying gifts or you're a kid trying to get some toys that you're collecting, here are some tips and ways that you can get toys for good deals."	Doran knows that feature article writers try to hook their readers in the beginning of their leads. Doran has an angle on his topic.

was planning a hook that was just the first part of a sentence ("When you're getting toys, either if you're a parent buying gifts or you're a kid trying to get some toys that you're collecting . . ."). Therefore, I decided to teach him how to write a lead with a better developed hook.

The opportunity that a conference provides us to talk with a student about his work in progress, then, gives us information about what a student understands about writing well. That information, in combination with the information we can gather from reading the actual work in progress during the conference about what a child actually does when he tries to write well (or, in conferences like the one I had with Doran, from what students tell us about what they're going to write), helps us decide what to teach him to help him apply his understanding effectively in his writing.

References

Angelillo, Janet. 2002. *A Fresh Approach to Teaching Punctuation.* New York: Scholastic.

Bomer, Randy. 1995. *Time for Meaning: Crafting Literate Lives in Middle and High Schools.* Portsmouth, NH: Heinemann.

Cai, Guanjun. 1999. "Texts in Contexts: Understanding Chinese Students' English Compositions." In *Evaluating Writing: The Role of Teachers' Knowledge About Text, Learning, and Culture*, edited by Charles R. Cooper and Lee Odell, 279–97. Urbana, IL: NCTE.

Cooper, Charles R. 1999. "What We Know About Genres, and How It Can Help Us Assign and Evaluate Writing." In *Evaluating Writing: The Role of Teachers' Knowledge About Text, Learning, and Culture*, edited by Charles R. Cooper and Lee Odell, 23–52. Urbana, IL: NCTE.

Crowhurst, Marion. 1987. "Cohesion in Argument and Narration at Three Grade Levels." *Research in the Teaching of English* 21: 185–201.

Culham, Ruth. 2003. *6 + 1 Traits of Writing: The Complete Guide Grades 3 and Up.* New York: Scholastic.

Diederich, Paul B. 1974. *Measuring Growth in English.* Urbana, IL: NCTE.

Fletcher, Ralph. 1993. *What a Writer Needs.* Portsmouth, NH: Heinemann.

Graves, Donald. 1994. *A Fresh Look at Writing.* Portsmouth, NH: Heinemann.

Krashen, Stephen D. 1985. *The Input Hypothesis: Issues and Implications.* New York: Longman.

Lane, Barry. 1994. *After the End: Teaching and Learning Creative Revision.* Portsmouth, NH: Heinemann.

Moffat, James. 1992. *Detecting Growth in Language.* Portsmouth, NH: Boynton/Cook.

Murray, Donald M. 1982. *Learning by Teaching: Selected Articles in Writing and Teaching.* Portsmouth, NH: Boynton/Cook.

———. 1985. *A Writer Teaches Writing.* Boston: Houghton Mifflin.

———. 1999. *Write to Learn.* New York: Harcourt Brace.

National Center on Education and the Economy and University of Pittsburgh. 1997. *Performance Standards, Volume 1, Elementary School.* San Antonio, TX: Harcourt Brace Educational Measurement.

Portalupi, JoAnn, and Ralph Fletcher. 2004. *Teaching the Qualities of Writing.* Portsmouth, NH: firsthand, Heinemann.

Ray, Katie Wood. 1999. *Wondrous Words: Writers and Writing in the Elementary Classrooms.* Urbana, IL: NCTE.

Romano, Tom. 2004. *Crafting Authentic Voice*. Portsmouth, NH: Heinemann.

Snowball, Diane, and Faye Bolton. 1999. *Spelling K–8: Planning and Teaching*. York, ME: Stenhouse.

Spandel, Vicki. 2001. *Creating Writers: Through 6-Trait Writing Assessment and Instruction*. New York: Addison Wesley Longman.

Strong, William. 1999. "Coaching Writing Development: Syntax Revisited, Options Explored." In *Evaluating Writing: The Role of Teachers' Knowledge About Text, Learning, and Culture*, edited by Charles R. Cooper and Lee Odell, 72–92. Urbana, IL: NCTE.

Strunk, William, and E. B. White. 2000. *The Elements of Style*. Boston: Allyn & Bacon.

Valdes, Guadalupe, and Patricia Sanders. 1999. "Latino ESL Students and the Development of Writing Abilities." In *Evaluating Writing: The Role of Teachers' Knowledge About Text, Learning, and Culture*, edited by Charles R. Cooper and Lee Odell, 249–78. Urbana, IL: NCTE.

Weaver, Constance. 1996. *Teaching Grammar in Context*. Portsmouth, NH: Heinemann.

Wilde, Sandra. 1992. *You Kan Red This! Spelling and Punctuation for Whole Language Classrooms, K–6*. Portsmouth, NH: Heinemann.

Assessing Students' Writing Processes

5

Writing is a craft before it is an art; writing may appear magic, but it is our responsibility to take our students backstage to watch the pigeons being tucked up the magician's sleeve.
—Donald M. Murray, A Writer Teaches Writing

I became a Beatles fan as a teenager and have remained one ever since. Over the years, I've collected every CD I can find with the group's name on it, as well as numerous books that discuss the history of the Fab Four, their music, and their contributions to popular culture.

One of the things that fascinates me about the Beatles is how they wrote their songs. For example, John Lennon was inspired to write "A Day in the Life" (from *Sgt. Pepper's Lonely Hearts Club Band*) after reading two stories in the *Daily Mail*—one about the death of a friend who drove his car into a parked van, the other about potholes in Blackburn, Lancashire (Everett 1999). When George Harrison was writing "Something" (from *Abbey Road*), he was having trouble thinking of just the right word to complete the lines "Something in the way she moves / Attracts me like a _____." John Lennon suggested George use any word for the time being, even *cauliflower,* as a placeholder until he thought of just the right word. Eventually, George completed the line this way: "Attracts me like no other lover" (Hertsgaard 1996). And one week after recording what the band thought was a final version of "Ob-La-Di, Ob-La-Da" (from *Anthology 3*), Paul McCartney decided he was dissatisfied with the song and requested that the band join him in recording a very different version (which you can find on *The Beatles*) (Lewisohn 1988).

In other words, I'm intrigued by John's, Paul's, George's, and Ringo's writing processes. I enjoy learning about how they got their ideas, the strategies they used while drafting, the ways they collaborated with one another, even the kinds of revisions they made to their songs. I am fascinated by the process that each of them went through, because what they did *worked*. The result of all this hard work was one of the greatest musical legacies of the twentieth century.

It should come as no surprise that like other writers, the Beatles, individually and collectively, went through a series of steps in the process of writing their songs. Writing teachers today are well aware that writers typically *rehearse* an idea, write a *draft*, and then *revise* and *edit* the draft before they *publish* it (that is, share it with others). And they teach their students about the writing process—that is, they teach students what to do to compose a piece of writing, from finding an idea to publishing a finished piece.

If we're going to help children develop into lifelong writers who have effective writing processes that work for them throughout a lifetime of writing, we need to start by assessing what they do *now* when they write. With this assessment in mind, we can then figure out what to teach to help them develop more effective writing processes.

What Does It Mean to Have an Effective Writing Process?

Being aware that writers go through various steps doesn't equip us to make in-depth assessments of students' writing processes. True, we can check to see whether students go through all the steps or skip one or more of them. But if we're going to assess whether students have *effective* writing processes, we need to have a clear image of what this means.

Any discussion has to begin by acknowledging that there isn't one writing process that guarantees success for all writers. While it's true that most writers *do* rehearse topics before starting a draft, *do* compose a draft, and *do* revise and edit that draft before they publish it, it's also true that most writers have their own individual ways of working in these different stages of the writing process. As Don Murray (1999) points out, "There is not one writing process but many" (10).

One writer's process may differ from another's in the tools (see Figure 5.1) he uses in some or all stages. Some writers gather ideas for

> **Examples of Writing Tools**
> A writer's notebook
> Pen and paper
> A laptop computer
> Sticky notes (for adding to a draft)
> A dictionary
> Spell-check software
> A thesaurus

FIGURE 5.1

Examples of Writing Strategies

Rereading what you've written

Referring to a model text

Sharing what you've written (or are going to write)
with a friend

Sketching what you're going to write

Boxing out (or circling) the sections of your draft

Making a plan for a piece of writing

Reading your writing aloud

FIGURE 5.2

writing in a writer's notebook while others write their ideas on napkins and scraps of paper that they squirrel away in a drawer. Some writers write best using pencil and paper while others write best using a word processor.

A writer's process may also differ from another's in the strategies (see Figure 5.2) she uses to navigate the steps. Some writers plan their writing in great detail before writing a draft; others plunge into a draft and let its structure emerge as they write. Some writers read their drafts out loud to find errors when they are editing; others rely primarily on others to read their drafts and find their mistakes.

If writers have their own individual writing processes, how can we know whether or not their processes are effective? Easy. A writer has an effective writing process when whatever tools and strategies he uses when he's rehearsing, drafting, revising, and editing help him write well time and time again. That's because an experienced writer's knowledge of good writing shapes the work he does in every step of the process. In other words, he chooses to use particular tools and strategies during the writing process *because* he knows they'll ultimately help him compose a well-written piece.

Take me, for example. Throughout the writing of this book, I used a writer's notebook to help me rehearse the ideas in each chapter. I chose this writing tool in part because I knew that writers communicate meaning in a well-written piece and because I knew that the pages of a writer's notebook would be an excellent place for me to think about the points I wanted to make.

Then, as I wrote each chapter, I used many writing strategies. When I finished a draft of a chapter, I made a list of all the sections on a page in my writer's notebook, because I know that in a well-written piece, each part of the structure helps the writer develop his point. By listing all the parts, I was able to see the whole chapter and judge whether or not each section made a contribution.

And so forth.

What I know about writing well influenced the work I did in every step of the writing process that I went through to write each chapter of this book. I didn't just go through the writing process and—presto!—a well-written text happened to come together magically at the end. I worked on making this book a well-written text from the moment I got the idea until the moment I finished rereading the manuscript for the very last time.

Rehearsal

Writers usually do a lot of work before they start drafting a piece. This work is commonly referred to as *prewriting,* a term I don't like, because so much of prewriting involves writing—writing about a topic in a writer's notebook, taking notes while doing research, making a plan for a piece, and so on. Instead, I refer to this work as *rehearsal,* a term I learned from Tom Romano (1987). I like it because it suggests that writers, like actors preparing for the opening night of a play, have work to do to get ready to draft. Rehearsal involves two different kinds of work: finding topics to write about and developing a topic before starting a draft.

Finding Topics

It's an oft-uttered adage that good writers write about what they know. For many writers, this means that they return again and again to the same topics they've written about before. Don Murray (1999) refers to these topics as a writer's "writing territories." In the journalism world, it's common for reporters to write most of their stories about the same topic—city news, presidential politics, education, sports—which reporters refer to as their *beat.* Many writers of fiction, too, have writing territories; for example, in each of his novels to date, Pulitzer prize–winning novelist Richard Russo has explored small-town life in New England.

Writers acquire their territories in two ways. One is by living their lives. One of my favorite writing topics is my father, whom I began to write about when I was a teenager. I know the topic of my father because he was part of my life for forty years. The other way writers acquire a territory is by learning as much as they can about it. The teaching of writing became one of my writing territories after I spent years learning about the subject by reading professional books, attending workshops, teaching writing for eight years, and being involved in hundreds of hours of conversations with colleagues at the Teachers College Reading and Writing Project.

Good writers return to certain topics again and again because the topics are connected to purposes that are important to them in their lives. They're confident they can return to these topics *and write well about them,* because they understand that it's not just the topic they're writing about that makes a piece of writing good. It's also what they know about writing well and how they use that knowledge that will make their writing good writing. Katie Wood Ray (1999) says, "Good writing will come from finding fresh new things to say about a topic and from knowing how to write about the topic in different ways for different audiences" (93).

The writer's notebook is one of the most important tools that writers use to help them develop their writing territories. Over time in the pages of a notebook, certain topics emerge as particularly important, and writers draw on the thinking they've done about these topics when they write pieces for publication. To help them fill up their notebooks with ideas—and ultimately, to help them discover their writing territories—writers use a variety of strategies (see Figure 5.3).

Not all writers use a notebook, of course, but they often use other tools to help them think about their writing territories. My wife, Robin, for example, used to keep a list of topics that she wanted to write about in a special file on our computer. That file served the same purpose for her as my writer's notebook does for me.

Developing a Topic

Once a writer has decided that he's going to write about a topic, he usually has work to do *before* he starts a draft. Many writing teachers today refer to this work as developing a seed idea. For example, a writer may need to decide the genre in which he's going to write. He also needs to start thinking about what point he wants to make about his topic. He'll then start gathering the details that will help him develop his point. And he'll begin to find the appropriate voice for the piece.

> **Some Strategies for Writing in a Writer's Notebook**
> Freewrite until you find an idea.
> Reread what you've written already to get ideas.
> Write about something you've read.
> Write about something you've seen.
> Write about a meaningful object.

FIGURE 5.3

Many writers use a writer's notebook as a tool for developing their topic. Randy Bomer (1995), whose middle and high school students were using their notebooks in this way, says, "It was perhaps during this phase of sticking to a single topic and writing over and over about it in different ways that the notebook seemed best to be doing its job as a writer's tool. . . The notebook was now, more than ever, a workbench for pieces of writing as yet half-conceived and unassembled" (70).

Of course, not all writers use a notebook to develop an idea. Some collect thoughts and information about their topic in a set of files in their desk drawer or on their computer.

The work that a good writer does to get ready to write a draft is shaped by her knowledge of what it means to write well. This knowledge leads her to ask certain questions as she develops her topic. These questions, in turn, lead her to use writing strategies to help her answer them. (See Figure 5.4 on pages 114–15.)

For example, because she knows that in a well-written piece, an author communicates meaning, she'll ask herself, "What am I going to say about my topic?" In order to figure out what she's going to say about her topic, she might freewrite about it in her notebook, "writing to learn" (Murray 1999) what she will say about the topic to readers.

Or consider the effect genre knowledge has on a writer's rehearsal work. Heather Lattimer (2003) has written that the work a writer does before drafting is dramatically affected by what he knows about the genre in which he'll be writing. Thus, a good writer will ask herself, "What do I need to do to get ready to write in this genre?" Someone who wants to write a memoir about the summers she spent as a child on Cape Cod might answer this question by brainstorming memories about those summers in her writer's notebook or talking to her siblings about what they remember or looking through family photo albums. Someone who wants to write a feature article about cheetahs might answer this question by reading a book on cheetahs and interviewing a wildlife expert at a zoo.

There is no correct order for grappling with these questions while a writer is getting ready to write a draft. Some writers gather a lot of information about a topic and then figure out what they want to say. Others know immediately what they want to say about a topic and gather the details that will help them make their point. Or writers might consider only some of these questions and save the rest for when they are revising their drafts.

Drafting and Revising

It may surprise you that I'm discussing writing a draft and revising it in a single section. In the way we typically think about the writing process, we talk about drafting and revising as being different steps: composing the piece and making changes to improve it. While there does come a point when writers have a draft in front of them on a piece of paper or a computer screen and they revise it, it's also true that even before they reach the end of a draft, they often revise what they've written so far. As Georgia Heard (2002) says, "Students need to understand that revision doesn't necessarily take place after they've finished a piece of writing, but instead revision will most likely occur throughout the writing process". Then, too, while they're revising, writers sometimes need to draft new sections or completely rewrite ones they've already written. The boundary between drafting and revising is a permeable one.

Until the past couple of decades, writers used pen and paper or a typewriter as their tool for drafting and revision. While some writers today still prefer the feel of these tools, many of us now draft on our desktop computers or laptops. And bundled into our word-processing programs are several other tools that make drafting and revision easier—the formatting and cut-and-paste functions, for example.

As writers compose a draft, they use strategies to help them write. A writer might jump-start his writing each day by rereading what he's written so far. Or when making a craft decision about his piece (how to write a lead or an ending, how to write an effective topic sentence), he might refer to a text written by a writer whom he admires (we call these texts *mentor,* or *model,* texts).

When good writers are drafting and revising, they draw on their in-depth knowledge of what it means to write well from the moment they write the first word of a draft to the moment they make their final change to it. As they do during rehearsal, they ask themselves certain questions that grow out of their knowledge of good writing. And to find answers to these questions—that is, to write well—writers then use drafting and revising strategies. (See Figure 5.5 on pages 116–17.)

Naturally, a writer doesn't grapple with all of these questions simultaneously. Certain questions come to mind depending on which part of a draft a writer is currently drafting or revising. For example, when I started writing the lead to this chapter, I asked myself, *How am I going to let my readers know what points I'm going to make in this chapter?* because I knew that I would have to let you know where I was going to take you. I also asked myself, *How do I use what I know about the characteristics of this genre to write well in it?* Because I know that writers who write in this genre (professional books on the teaching of writing) often start chapters with a personal anecdote used as a metaphor, I started by mentioning my interest in the Beatles' writing processes.

Other questions came to mind when I was revising the initial draft of this chapter. When I reread all that I had written, I asked myself, *Is*

What the Writer Knows About Writing Well . . .	Will Lead Her to Ask This Question . . .	Which Will Lead Her to Use Writing Strategies Such as These . . .
A good writer communicates meaning in her writing.	What am I going to say about my topic?	• Write in my writer's notebook in response to the question *What will I say about my topic?* • Reread the writing in my notebook and look for a line that expresses what I want to say about my topic.
A good writer brings her knowledge of genre into her writing.	What kind of work do I need to do to get ready to write in this genre?	• Read examples of this genre and imagine the work I need to do to write a similar piece. • Read what other writers have written about what they did to write in this genre or a guidebook for writing in this genre.
A good writer structures texts in ways that enable readers to grasp her meaning.	What will the components of my piece be? How might I order them?	• Look at examples of this genre and notice the kinds of sections that the authors include in their pieces. • Make a plan for my draft—an outline, a flowchart, a web.

A good writer uses precise detail to develop parts of the structure.	What details do I need to help me say what I want to say?	• Memoir: Brainstorm memories about my topic; look through family photo albums. • Feature article: Interview experts about my topic; read about my topic in books and articles.
A good writer gives her writing an appropriate voice to enhance her meaning.	What voice will I write in?	• Talk about my topic with others. • Write about my topic in my writer's notebook before drafting. • Read the writing of a writer whose voice I admire and try to write like that writer.
A good writer uses conventions to guide the reader through the text and enhance her meaning.	How can I use punctuation to help me craft this text and help me say what I want to say?	• Write about my topic in my writer's notebook, experimenting with punctuation. • Read the writing of a writer who uses punctuation in interesting ways and try to write like that writer.

FIGURE 5.4

What the Writer Knows About Writing Well . . .	Will Lead Her to Ask These Questions as She Drafts and Revises . . .	Which Will Lead Her to Use Writing Strategies Such as These . . .
A good writer communicates meaning in her writing.	How am I going to say what I want to say about my topic? Is what I'm trying to say coming through in this draft? Is what I'm trying to say changing as I write the piece?	• Start with a line from my writer's notebook that sums up what I'm trying to say. • Reread my draft and ask myself if what I'm trying to say is clear throughout the draft. • Have someone else read the piece and tell me what he thinks I am saying.
A good writer brings her knowledge of genre into her writing.	How do I use what I know about the characteristics of this genre to write well in it? How does this draft resemble examples of this genre that I've read? What do I need to do to make this piece more closely resemble the genre I'm writing in?	• Read several examples of the genre and note which characteristics I'll incorporate into my draft. • Compare my draft to an example of the genre. Ask myself what I still need to do to make it resemble the genre more closely.
A good writer structures texts in ways that enable readers to grasp her meaning.	How will I write my lead? Does it work? How do I signal my reader that I'm shifting to a new section? How much attention do I give each part? How will I end this piece? Does it work? Does the way I've organized this draft make sense? Which sections do I need to further develop? Does each section help me make my point?	• Study examples of the genre to see how writers have written leads, endings, and transitions. • Brainstorm several leads or endings. • Box (or circle) each part of the draft. Reread each part and ask myself which parts need more work. • Share the draft with a partner. Ask her which parts need more work.

A good writer uses precise detail to develop each part of the structure.	Which details will help me say what I want to say? Which kinds of details should I use? Do I need to include more detail? Less? Are my details too general? Do the details I've included help me say what I'm trying to say?	• Study examples of the genre to see what kinds of details the authors used. • Reread my writer's notebook for details I could include in my draft. • Reread the draft and highlight details I think help make my point. Delete the rest. • Use a thesaurus to find more specific words.
A good writer gives her writing an appropriate voice to enhance her meaning.	What voice will I write in? Is my voice an appropriate one for the audience for whom I'm writing?	• Try several leads in my writer's notebook and experiment with different voices. • Read my writing aloud. Ask myself where it sounds right and where it doesn't. • Ask a partner if the voice of the piece seems appropriate for my intended audience.
A good writer uses conventions to guide the reader through the text and enhance her meaning.	How can I use punctuation to craft my piece and help me say what I'm trying to say?	• Read my writing aloud. Ask myself how I could use punctuation to signal to readers how I want my piece to sound. • Try to punctuate my piece in the ways that a writer I admire uses punctuation.

FIGURE 5.5

what I'm trying to say coming through? and *Did what I start out trying to say change as I got deeper and deeper into the draft?* Asking these two questions during my initial rereadings helped me identify which sections needed more work.

Editing

Usually, we think of editing as the last step of the writing process. Before they share their writing with its intended audience, writers look over what they've written and decide whether or not to change the way that they're written sentences and used punctuation. However, just as they sometimes revise while they've in the midst of composing drafts, experienced writers often edit while they're drafting and revising.

Sometimes writers make changes to the way they've written sentences and used punctuation in order to craft their writing and enhance their meaning (Angelillo 2002; Ehrenworth and Vinton 2004). A writer might decide to insert an ellipsis into the middle of a sentence to create a sense of drama at that moment. Or he might decide to make the last sentence of a paragraph into a paragraph of its own in order to cue the reader to give that sentence extra emphasis (that is, change his voice at this spot).

When writers edit their writing, they also look for errors in spelling, punctuation, and grammar and correct them. Sometimes the errors are typographical. Often they're careless errors that have crept in because the writer's attention has been focused on other aspects of writing well. And some writers (Charles Dickens, for one) are simply poor spellers.

All these errors would distract or even confuse readers if they were to remain in a published text. This is why newspapers and magazines—which employ some of the best writers in the country—find it necessary to employ copy editors, whose job is to do the final editing of each piece before it goes to press.

When they edit, writers use a variety of tools. Even when they've written and revised a draft on a computer, some writers still edit a printout of their pieces with a pen or a pencil. While the spell-check and grammar-check features of our word-processing programs have made the job of editing easier, many of us also consult dictionaries and stylebooks.

Experienced writers use a variety of editing strategies (see Figure 5.6) and, as they edit, call on their knowledge of spelling, punctuation, and grammar—Sandra Wilde (1992) refers to this as the "language system"—to help them make their final decisions about how to write the sentences in their piece. Usually, after an experienced writer has used several editing tools and strategies—and brought to his editing all that he knows about the written language system—he is satisfied with how he's written each sentence and his piece is finally ready for publication.

Editing Strategies
Read your writing to yourself.
Read your writing aloud, to yourself or to a writing partner.
Give your writing to someone else to edit.
Read your writing backward to help you focus on the spelling
of each word.
Use the spell- and grammar-check features of your word-
processing program.
Find the correct spellings of words by looking them up in a
dictionary or asking a friend who is an excellent speller.

FIGURE 5.6

How Can We Assess Our Students' Writing Processes?

We don't usually know very much about the writing processes of the writers whose work we read in newspapers, magazines, or books, unless we happen to read an interview in which they talk about how they write. Don Murray (1999) says, "Everyone has a writing process, but the process is invisible since writers usually write alone. Because writing is a closed-door activity, we have no way of knowing the difficulty an author has with finding a topic or how many times he revises before publication" (37).

Fortunately, it's possible to gather a great deal of information about our students' writing processes, information that will help us figure out what we need to teach them to encourage more effective processes. That's because in a writing workshop, we spend time with students while they're working on pieces, and we also read their writing before it's in final form. We learn about students' writing processes by observing them as they write, reading their writer's notebooks and drafts, and talking with them in conferences about how they write.

Observing Students at Work

In a writing workshop, we see students' writing processes in action. It's usually obvious in which stage of the writing process a child is. Likewise, we can see which writing tools a child uses. Sometimes, too, we can see which writing strategy he's using.

We know Sammy is getting ready to write a draft because we see him writing an outline. We know Kate is revising her draft because we

Learn about your students' processes through observation. (To help you record what you notice as you observe your students at work, you may want to use the checklist "Assessing Students' Writing Processes" in Appendix 3.)

- Take some time in your classroom to sit and observe students as they write. Where are students in the writing process? What writing tools are they using? What writing strategies are they using?

see that she's writing on sticky notes and sticking them to the page. We see Anayra editing her writing by reading her writing aloud to Bonnie and stopping occasionally to discuss whether or not a word is spelled correctly.

Occasionally it's helpful to sit for a few minutes and observe a child at work. Through this kind of close observation, we can learn about the strategies a child uses that aren't always visible in more casual observations. For example, we can see whether or not a child rereads her writing while she drafts or revises and how frequently she does so.

Observation, however, has its limitations. While it's possible to see where students are in the writing process, as well as the tools and strategies they're using, we can't determine the effectiveness of their processes. To be able to do that, we need to read their work in progress as well as talk with them about their work in conferences.

Reading Student Writing

Student work in process is another window into what children do when they write. When we look at all the work a child has done over time to write a piece, we can get a full picture of which steps a child has gone through. In a child's writer's notebook, we can find evidence that he rehearsed a topic for several days. By reading his draft, we can see evidence that he revised and edited. Some teachers ask their students to make revisions and edits with certain-color pens or markers so that the changes they make stand out from their original drafts.

We can also see evidence of some of the strategies children use when they're working through the various steps of their process. And we can infer from their use of these strategies some of the things they know about writing well. Over time, we hope to see that students have developed a repertoire of strategies to use in each stage. Not all students will use the same strategies, however, since some strategies will work better for them than others. Whatever strategies children make part of their regular writing repertoire, we hope to see that they use them purposefully to help them write well.

Sometimes we look through a child's writer's notebook and notice no evidence that she did any rehearsal work before she drafted. Or we see that a child made no revisions or edits to a draft. When we look at student work, then, we also learn about the gaps in a child's process.

Reading to Learn About Students' Writing Territories

We can learn a great deal about students' writing territories by reading their writing. One way is to look through students' writing portfolios to see which topics they return to again and again. During my daughter Anzia's first-grade year, she wrote several times about her pet hermit crabs. She wrote a story about the death of one of the crabs as well as a nonfiction book about the animal.

We can also read through their writer's notebooks. Many students return to certain topics in their notebooks again and again, and it's these topics that ultimately become their writing territories. As we read, we can keep an eye out for these favorite topics. We might also look for pages where students reflect on topics that matter to them. Nancie Atwell (1998) asks her students to write a list of their territories in their notebook at the beginning of the school year and to revisit that list often.

Let's look at some entries in sixth grader Kanupriya's writing notebook (see Figure 5.7). On September 10, she brainstormed a list of topics she thought she might want to write about during the year. On September 17, she wrote about one of the topics on that list, horses, a topic she returned to again on October 9 and 11.

Then, on October 17, Kanupriya folded over a page in her notebook and wrote on it, "Start of Official Seed Idea/Publishing Piece," and went on to write more entries about horses over the next several school days. Finally, on October 29, she composed a feature article about horses. Thus, during the first two months of sixth grade, Kanupriya used her writer's notebook as a place in which to discover and explore the topic of horses and as a tool to help her get ready to write a piece about this writing territory.

Some students still need to learn to how to identify their own writing territories. I've worked with many students who've said, "I've run out of things to write about. I've already written pieces about my mom and my dog and my best friend. What else is there?" These students often think that a piece of writing will be good only if they pick an "exciting" topic. They need to learn that any topic can be a good one, provided it's important to them in some way and they write about it well. Figure 5.8 details several common difficulties students have with discovering writing territories and lists lessons we can teach to help them.

9/10   Topics
- Best friends
- NSYNC
- Music
- Movies
- TV Shows
- Family

- Horses
- Living Things
- Dreams
- Time
- Sports
- Harry Potter

9/17   The Way a Horse Runs

I think this is an interesting topic. Horses are strong animals, and there are so many of them. They are also graceful and gentle. That's why I love them. I think it's amazing how they run.

For walking, a four-step pace, has a slow rhythm, sounds like a person falling asleep, their heart slowing down.

For trotting, another four-step pace, has a faster rhythm, much like how a person's heart sounds when they're running . . .

10/9   Horses

I really, really love horses. If I could get a horse, I'd want a newborn filly, so I could raise her. She would be completely black, even her hooves. On her forehead, though, she would have a crescent moon star. It would be the only color on her coat besides black. I would name her Mistress. I'd call her Misty for short.

10/11   Horses

I really love palomino and roan horses. I also love feathering. I like quick and graceful horses.

Horses are cute and I love them a lot. I wish I could take horse-back riding lessons. I hope I'm not too tall, if I ever do get to.

I watch horse-racing, but I don't like how people gamble for horses. I'm strongly against that. I wish there was something to change it. Oh, well. Maybe there is.

FIGURE 5.7   Kanupriya's Notebook Entries

Reading to Learn About How Students Develop Topics

Reading student writing can also teach us a great deal about the work students do to develop a topic before they draft. Eighth grader Rusty (his work is shown in Figure 4.3) had been reading memoirs as part of a class genre study. Having learned that memoirs include stories about one's life, during the week and a half before he drafted his memoir about

TEACHER ACTION 5.2

Read students' writing to learn about their writing territories. (You may want to use the checklist "Assessing Students' Writing Processes" in Appendix 3 to help you record what you see and learn.)

- Look through your students' finished folders or portfolios. Which students return to topics again and again—their families, a best friend, a favorite sport? Which students go from topic to topic, rarely if ever returning to one that they've written about before?

- Read through several of your students' writer's notebooks to see who writes about the same topics again and again. Ask your students to read through their writer's notebooks and to write about what they find out about themselves.

- Explain the concept of writing territories to your students and then ask them to make a list of theirs. Which students can do this easily? Which students have trouble imagining topics that they would want to write about many times?

Teaching Students to Develop Writing Territories

If I see this . . .	I might . . .
A student often complains that she has nothing to write about.	Tell her to brainstorm a list of topics that she feels she could write about again and again.
In the pieces in students' writing folders or in entries in their writer's notebooks, they go from topic to topic without returning to any of them.	Ask them to reread the pieces in their writing folders or the entries in their writer's notebooks to find one or two topics they can imagine writing new pieces or entries about.
A student writes about the same topic in the same way again and again.	Have him brainstorm a "Things I Could Write About My Topic" list (e.g., Cape Cod: "The Time I Found a Wounded Seagull," "The Time I Capsized a Sunfish," "Different Kinds of Cape Cod Crabs," etc.).
A student seems surprised to hear that she can write about the same topic again.	Talk about how many writers return to the same topic across their writing lives. Patricia MacLachlan, for example, frequently writes novels set on the prairie.

FIGURE 5.8

tobacco farming, he made several entries in his writer's notebook about his experiences cutting and loading tobacco (see Figure 5.9), such as the time a rafter fell on his cousin Jamie (10/8), checking to see if the tobacco was ready to strip (10/14), and seeing coyotes, falling out of the barn, and driving a tractor for the first time (10/18).

Because Rusty had also learned that memoirists reveal what their memories say about their lives—and because from the beginning of the school year I had been talking with Rusty's class about how good writers have something to say in their writing—Rusty soon started asking himself what his experiences at the tobacco farm meant to him (10/15). In this entry, he came up with two possible meanings—that his experiences had helped him grow into a man and that his experiences had helped him learn about the value of a dollar. Ultimately, Rusty decided that the point of his memoir would be to discuss the latter meaning.

For Rusty, getting ready to write a draft was dramatically shaped by what he knew about good writing. His knowledge of what a memoir is shaped the work he did in his writer's notebook, as did his knowledge that good writers communicate meaning and write with detail.

Consider also the rehearsal work second grader Ben did before he wrote a story about riding on a Coney Island ferris wheel. His teacher had taught him that a well-written story includes a series of scenes and that writers often start a story at an exciting part to create tension in the reader's mind. Before Ben started drafting, he planned out which scenes his story would have and then decided to start his story at the more dramatic point when he was already on the ride (see top of Figure 5.10). His resulting draft is shown at the bottom of Figure 5.10.

For Ben, getting ready to write a draft was shaped by what he was learning about good writing. His knowledge of structure and of the story genre led him to make a plan for his piece and then to revise that plan.

Some children do little or no work before starting a draft. Believing an exciting topic makes a piece of writing good, they find a hot topic and plunge in. To help these students understand the value of rehearsal, we need to nudge them to try rehearsal strategies and talk with them about how and why these strategies can help them write well.

Other students do use rehearsal strategies before they start a draft, but the strategies seem to have little impact on how well they write. Perhaps they have an internal checklist (or an actual checklist their teacher has given them) of strategies they should use before they start a draft. They dutifully use each strategy, one after the other, because they think they're supposed to, not because they understand their purpose. We need to teach these children how they can use strategies in purposeful ways. For example, we could explain to first graders how sketching what they're writing about can help them write with more

10/8 My grandfather and all of his family raise tobacco. This is my way of earning money. I'm a hard worker and get paid seven dollars an hour. Mostly I load and hang tobacco. I'd like to cut, but my grandfather thinks I'm too young. I know I'm not, but that's the way life is. Lots of people work for my grandfather. My cousins Jamie and Stevie to name a few.

This year I worked for 18 hours and made $126. I was happy. This let me buy a lot of things I needed. A fishing pole and so forth.

Last year was different. I only made $84, but had a ton of fun. It just so happens that one of the barn's rafters was loose. As we started to hang, we were startled by a crash. It turns out that one of the rafters had fallen. We got ourselves together and realized that Jamie was in there. Stevie started to the barn when Jamie stumbled out. He was cussing and coughing up a storm. Everybody burst out laughing.

That was my story. You'll only find this story and others like it in the Rusty zone.

10/14 I went to the tobacco barn last night. I went with my uncle and grandfather to see if the tobacco was ready to strip. We drove out at about 9:30. It took us a couple of minutes to get there. Once there we pulled up in front of one of the barns. My uncle left the lights on so we could see the tobacco better. It looked pretty good. We shut a couple of the doors so the air wouldn't mess it up. It wasn't long until we were gone. It was a short trip, but I had fun.

So here I am. Just sitting at home writing in my journal. I've decided to write about my adventures in the tobacco barn. I've got many memories of that place. I think these could make a good memoir. So I'll keep on writing over these memories. Adios Amigos.

10/15 I grew from the years working in the tobacco farm. I went in a boy and came out a man. Not to mention the check I had in my pocket. Those long hours of grueling work in 100 degree weather. Those are what made me grow. Strength and brain wise are two ways I improved. I learned the value of a dollar. You have to work for money.

"Money doesn't grow on trees," says my mom.

I understand that a little better. I still beg for money. After all, you can only work tobacco two weeks out of the year. I mean a boy has got to make a living someway. I'll come out for the better in the long run though. Beg now and work later. That's the way it should be.

10/18 Thinking over the times I spent working in the tobacco fields brought up some memories. I remembered the time when a couple of coyotes were gathering around the barn. There's also the time I fell out of the barn and landed on the wagon. These two memories and many others come to mind when I think of my years in the tobacco fields.

With this memory of past experiences I hope to make a good memoir. If I had any other memories on my mind right now, I'd write them. So far I'm stuck. Let me think on it for awhile . . .

How about the time when I first drove the tractor. I was jerking around all over the patch. Stop, go, stop, go. I went on forever. Now I can drive better.

FIGURE 5.9   Rusty's Notebook Entries

2/2/04

~~Going to Coney Island with camp~~
~~Waiting to get on~~
On the Ferris wheel
On the top swinging back and forth

The Ferris Wheel
①
One day I was on the Ferris Wheel going higher and higher from the ground. I was really happy that I was going on the Ferris Wheel for the first time. I wondered how high it would go? Then I was at the very top I could see the whole place from there. Then it started to shake back and forth. I almost fell down, but I caught a grip of the seat and pushed myself bac onto the seat, close one I said in my mind I hope I won't fall off I thought. Ten seconds later it did it again. I said to myself I could not go on again today. It was a fantastic view. I hoped the ride would end soon.

②
It looked like the ride would not end soon. Then it came to a stop, I wondered why it had stopped before we had got to the end! I really hoped it would start soon. Then it started again. Then I got off.

FIGURE 5.10   Ben's Plan (top) and Story (bottom)

detail or show third graders how writing an outline can help them compose a well-structured piece.

Then there are students whose rehearsal work is shaped by their knowledge of some of the traits of good writing but not all. Reread the feature article that Matt wrote about deodorant (Figure 4.19) and then consider some of the rehearsal work Matt did in his writer's notebook before writing the draft (Figure 5.11). His rehearsal work is clearly influenced by his knowledge of some of the traits of good writing. For example, he finds several sources of information about deodorant and records many of the facts he learns; thus he is able to include a lot of details about his subject in his draft. Matt also writes responses to some of the facts he is learning—"You need it when people around start saying, 'Whew, what's that smell?'"—that are typical of an adolescent boy and give his writing voice. However, he doesn't seem to know that he should have something to say about his topic. While he does a very good job of gathering numerous facts about deodorant, he doesn't decide on a focus for his piece at any time during his research. It doesn't come as a surprise, then, that when he writes his article, he writes all about his topic instead of focusing on one aspect of it. Matt still needs to learn that feature article writers usually write about one aspect of their topic (their angle) and that to do that, he could start thinking about what that aspect will be while doing his research.

Figure 5.12 details several common problems students encounter while developing a topic and lists several lessons that will help them learn to navigate this important part of the writing process.

Reading to Learn About How Students Draft and Revise

Reading student drafts can teach us about what students do when they draft and revise. Remember the piece that fourth grader Sean wrote about her reunion with her third-grade teacher, Ms. Levinson (see Figure 4.9)? Her initial draft, with revisions (see Figure 5.13), shows us that Sean drew on some knowledge of what it means to write well when she composed it. Her very first sentence, in which she immediately creates tension—"'Where is she?!' I asked Lisa"—shows that she knows about some of the characteristics of the story genre. She also includes dialogue and her own thoughts and actions, showing that she knows some things about the kinds of details writers use when they write narratives.

Sean also used several revision strategies. First, she boxed out her draft, breaking it down into its parts, a strategy writers use to help them focus on each part of a piece. And given that she made numerous internal revisions to each part—drawing arrows to the margins and adding her thoughts and actions—it seems likely she used the strategy of rereading her piece to help her identify places where she should add on.

Entry 1

1. Deodorant unlike antiperspirant doesn't clog up your glands.
2. Deodorant just masks the smell, antiperspirant stops your glands from working.
3. Some women get breast cancer from antiperspirant.
4. Deodorant causes no harm to the body because it lets the odors out but making them smell good. Antiperspirant doesn't let the odors out.

Entry 2

1. You can make good deodorant but not as good as store bought deodorant.
2. Deodorant has chemicals so disgusting that if you knew about them you wouldn't use deodorant.
3. If you don't use clear deodorant it makes you look sort of weird.

Entry 3

1. Ireland has the highest deodorant consumption per capita.
2. They have shirts with built in deodorant made by Quizbrain.
3. Hepatitis and AIDS are two of many diseases that can be influenced because of using deodorant.
4. Some hospitals do not allow people to use deodorants and antiperspirants. P.S. That is why hospitals smell bad.
5. In 1995 they started a study on if deodorant influences Alzheimers. Results came out 11-9-01 and deodorant does influence Alzheimers.

Entry 4

1. You need it when people around start saying, "Whew, what's that smell?"
2. Most people start needing deodorant between the ages of 16–22.
3. People that come from hot places usually need more deodorant than people that come from New York.
4. The people that use a lot of deodorant are people that sweat a lot and play sports.

FIGURE 5.11   Matt's Notebook Entries

Teaching Students to Develop a Topic Before Drafting

If I see this . . .	I might . . .
Once a student decides on a topic to write about, she jumps right into a draft.	Show examples of my own or other students' rehearsal work—entries about a topic in a writer's notebook and/or a plan for a piece of writing—and nudge the student to try this work before drafting.
A student isn't sure how to write several entries in his writer's notebook to develop his topic before drafting.	Have him brainstorm an "Entries I Could Write About My Topic" list (e.g., my dad: "When He Taught Me to Ride a Bike," "His Weird Sense of Humor," "When My Dad Brought the Rabbits Home," etc.).
Although a student has written several entries about her topic in her notebook, she isn't sure what she wants to say about her topic.	Ask her to freewrite in response to the question, *What do I want to say about my topic?*
The student knows what he wants to say about his topic but is unsure of how that should impact the work he needs to do to get ready to draft.	Suggest that he brainstorm a list of things he can write about his topic that are connected to what he wants to say about it.
The student knows what genre she wants to write in but isn't sure what work she should do to get ready to draft.	Have her study a text that's an example of the genre and think about what the author may have done to get ready to draft.
The student has written very generally about his topic in his notebook ("My trip was really, really fun," etc.).	Remind him to write about specific events (for a narrative genre) or present facts about the topic (for a nonnarrative piece).
In the entries she's written so far in her notebook, the student hasn't yet found her writing voice.	Suggest that she talk about her topic with several classmates and then try writing about her topic in the way she talked it out.
The student wants to start his draft but isn't sure what the parts are or in which order they should appear.	Teach him to make a flowchart, web, or outline of his draft before he starts writing it.

FIGURE 5.12

It's interesting that she added a detail to her first paragraph—"I have to talk so loud because the kids are screaming"—and then later crossed it out. From this we can infer that Sean knows that writers use detail to help them make their point but decided that this particular detail was trivial.

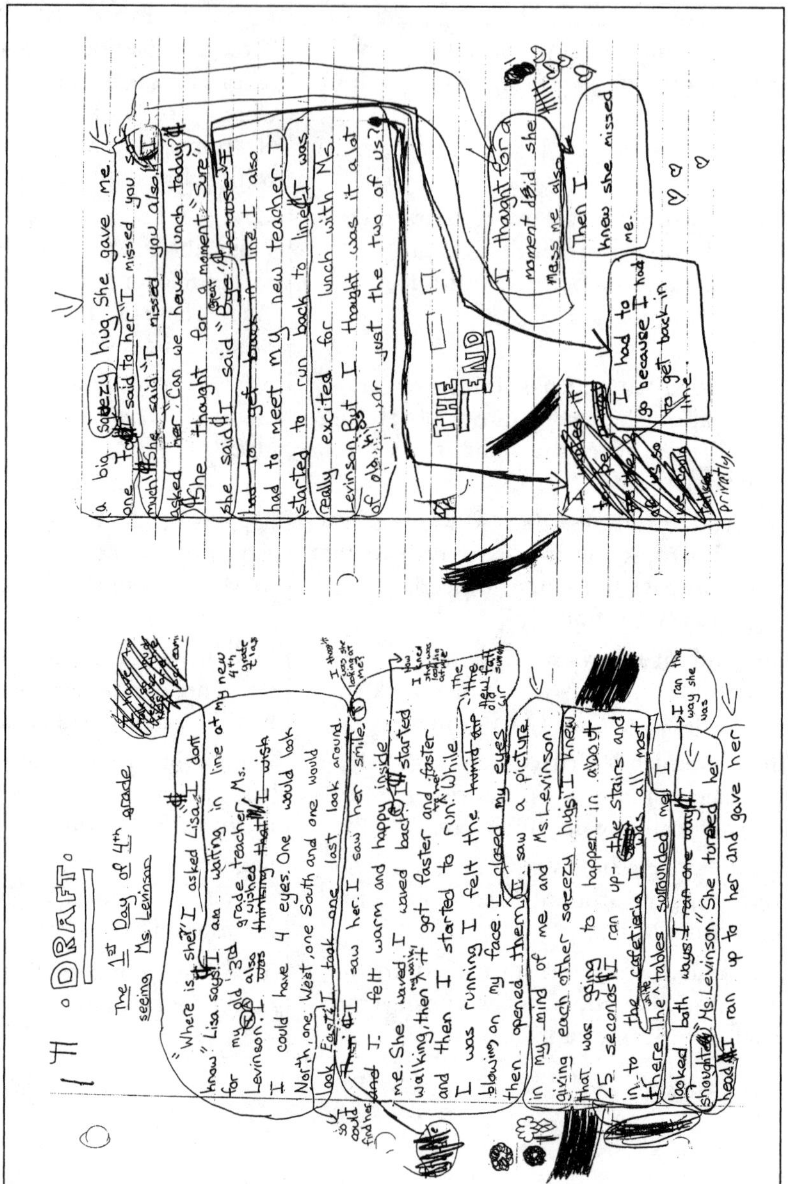

FIGURE 5.13 Sean's Revised Draft

TEACHER ACTION 5.3

Read students' writing to assess how they develop a topic before drafting. (You may want to use the checklist "Assessing Students' Writing Processes" in Appendix 3 to help you record what you see and learn.)

- Gather some of your students' work-in-progress folders and/or writer's notebooks. Look for the work that students did before starting drafts. What strategies do your students use to get ready?

- Now read some of the pieces that resulted from this rehearsal work. In what ways did your students write well in these pieces? What did they do in their rehearsal work that enabled them to write well in the ways they did?

- What do these students' pieces reveal about what they still need to learn about writing well? What do you need to teach them to do when they rehearse to help them compose better-written pieces?

Sean also added several details to two key parts in her draft—when she first saw Ms. Levinson and later when they embraced. From this, we can infer that Sean brings some knowledge of structure—that writers will develop some parts more than others—into her revision work.

Some children, however, see the composing process only as making a draft, often as quickly as possible. They do very little or no revision, either while they're drafting or after they've finished. These children often have yet to experience writing as an activity that can fulfill important purposes in their lives (beyond satisfying their teacher's demands). They do what their teacher says they have to—write a piece—but not much else, because they don't see the need. Teacher pleasers will often make a few halfhearted revisions to a piece, but again, more to satisfy their teachers' requirements than to make their writing good enough so it can *do* something for them.

But I've also worked with plenty of students for whom writing is very purposeful, yet who still have a rudimentary composing process. There are a number of possible reasons to explain this. It may be they believe it's the topic that makes a piece of writing good, and that they simply need to get the story down or write all they know about their topic. They don't yet understand that it's the writer who makes a piece of writing good and that if they're going to compose a quality piece of writing, they have a lot of work to do beyond recording an event that happened to them or some facts about their topic.

Other children just haven't been taught to have a more sophisticated composing process. Students need explicit instruction in the strategies that writers use when they draft and revise. Nancie Atwell (1998) discusses how important it is for teachers to write in front of their students, demonstrating drafting and revision strategies as well as sharing the thinking that they do as they compose (Nancie calls this work "taking the top off of [her] head"!). And if students are going to use what they know about the qualities of good writing when they draft and revise, they also need explicit instruction in those qualities and in how writers use their knowledge of good writing to help them draft and revise. When teachers share many well-written pieces with their students, and discuss what makes them good, students develop an internalized image of what it means to write well that shapes what they do when they write.

In many writing workshops, students are learning to develop a more extensive drafting and revision process. Some students, however, make revisions to their pieces because their teacher has required that they do so. I've visited classrooms in which students are expected to make five add-ons to a draft or write three drafts before they can publish. Students in these classrooms sometimes see revision as some sort of punishment they must endure before they can finally publish their pieces! While it's important to expect students to revise their drafts—it's something most writers do, in fact need to do, if they're going to publish well-written pieces—it's also important to teach them how and why writers revise. Ultimately, students learn to revise not because it's required, but because it's *taught*.

Fortunately, in many classrooms students are developing a repertoire of drafting and revision strategies and are connecting what they

TEACHER ACTION 5.4

Read students' writing to learn about their drafting and revising processes. (You may want to use the checklist "Assessing Students' Writing Processes" in Appendix 3 to help you record what you see and learn.)

- Read several student drafts. What do these drafts tell you about the students' knowledge of writing well and how that knowledge has informed their drafting process?
- Read drafts that your students have revised. What revision strategies did they use? What do their revisions reveal about what they know about writing well and how they use that knowledge as they revise?

> **When We Went to the Beach**
>
> One day, my family and me went to the beach. It was a really fun day there! We went in the car. **It took an hour to get there. My sister got really car sick and almost threw up. I played with my game boy.** I couldn't wait to get to the beach. The first thing we did when we got there was go in the water. It was cold. I played catch the tennis ball with my brother. Then we ate lunch. I had a hot dog and french fries. I put a lot of ketchup on my fries. My mom didn't let us go swimming until a half hour later. I love the beach. I want to go back again.

FIGURE 5.14   Eric's Revised Draft

know about writing well to their drafting and revision work. In many cases, of course, students do not yet have a highly sophisticated sense of what it means to write well. What they do when they draft and revise, then, reveals what they know about the qualities of good writing and what they still need to learn.

Consider the revision work that Eric, a second grader, did when he composed his story about a trip his family took to the beach (see Figure 5.14). When I sat down to confer with him, Eric told me that he added details to the story because "it would paint a picture in a reader's mind." This work (shown in boldface) indicates that Eric knows it's important to include details in his writing. That he adds details to the part when his family is in the car traveling *to* the beach instead of the parts when they are *at* the beach indicates that Eric still needs to learn that to get his point across ("It was a really fun day there!"), he will need to develop the parts that show the fun his family had there.

Figure 5.15 details several common problems students encounter while drafting and revising their pieces and lists several lessons that will help them draft and revise more effectively.

Reading to Learn About How Students Edit

Reading students' edited drafts lets us see the changes they made to their writing before they published it. Alterations to the structure of sentences—perhaps breaking a long sentence into several short ones to create a different voice—reveal students' syntactic repertoire and show they are able to use it to enhance meaning. Changes in punctuation—substituting one mark for another, adding a mark that wasn't there before (perhaps emphasizing a clause by separating it from the rest of the sentence

Teaching Students to Draft and Revise

If I see this . . .	I might . . .
A student is having trouble getting started with a draft or is stuck in the middle of a draft.	Ask him to reread what he wrote about his topic in his writer's notebook or reread what he's written of the draft so far to help him jump-start his writing.
A student is unsure of how to write a part of her draft—the lead, a transition, a dramatic scene, the ending, and so on.	Have her study a model text and see how a more experienced writer wrote the kind of part she's trying to compose.
A student has written a part of his draft but is unsure whether what he's written is good writing.	Suggest that he get feedback from a classmate in a peer conference or from several classmates in a response group.
Students get to the end of a draft, write "The End" at the bottom of the page, and are finished with the piece.	Revise one of my drafts in front of the class and nudge students to make some revisions to their drafts.
A student has trouble identifying which parts of her draft need revision.	Suggest that she reread the draft, putting an asterisk where she thinks she needs to make a change, or box out the draft (circle each part) to break it down and then concentrate on revising one part at a time.
A student wants to add to his draft, but there isn't any room on the page to do so.	Teach students about how arrows, footnotes, Sticky notes, and "spiderlegs" (strips of paper taped to the edges of the draft) can give them more room to add to a draft.
A student has added to her draft, but the add-ons seem superfluous and don't improve the piece.	Teach the student to ask herself, *What can I add to help me make my point more effectively?* when she revises.

FIGURE 5.15

with a dash)—let us know students are able to use punctuation marks to craft their writing. And changes like adding an apostrophe to indicate plural possessive or inserting commas between items in a series indicate that students know the conventions of written language.

We've all experienced the sinking feeling in our stomach when we read students' edited pieces and see the number of errors that remain. *How is it possible they didn't catch these errors?* we ask ourselves incredulously. It's easy to start thinking that our students are lazy.

But perhaps the abundance of errors is a signal that they weren't invested in their pieces. When students are writing to fulfill a requirement and not because they want their writing to have some kind of effect on others, they have little motivation to edit thoroughly. Students who aren't invested in their writing see editing as yet another teacher-imposed requirement instead of a purposeful, important activity. For these students to learn to edit well, they're going to need our help in discovering that writing can be meaningful and that editing is necessary to communicate effectively with an audience.

Sometimes, too, we are partly to blame for the abundance of errors in students' finished writing. Maybe we didn't give them explicit instructions about how to use editing strategies. Maybe we didn't give them the time they needed to use these strategies to find their errors. Maybe we didn't provide the structures that scaffold students' editing—for example, checklists that remind them about the editing strategies we expect them to use and some common errors to look out for.

When children are writing for reasons that are important to them, receive explicit instruction in how to edit, and are given the time it takes to do it, they can and do learn to edit their writing. However, even when children edit well, more than likely they won't locate every error they've made.

Sometimes their editing strategies are ineffective; they need to be taught better ones. For example, some children edit by reading their writing silently once or twice. Suggesting in a writing conference that they read their writing aloud to themselves or to an editing partner—a strategy that helps them draw on their knowledge of how written English looks and sounds—often helps them find more errors.

TEACHER ACTION 5.5

Read students' writing to learn about their editing processes. (You may want to use the checklist "Assessing Students' Writing Processes" in Appendix 3 to help you record what you see and learn.)

- Read through several of your students' drafts after they've finished editing. What kinds of changes did they make? What do these changes tell you about their knowledge of sentence structure, their knowledge of how to use punctuation to craft their writing, and/or their knowledge of conventions?
- Read through the drafts again. What errors remain? Are there a lot of careless errors you feel should have been caught? What editing strategies could you teach students that would help them find these errors the next time they edit?

Then, too, students miss some errors because they don't realize they're errors. Students tend to make new kinds of errors in their writing when they start to write more complex sentences. They make their best guess at how to punctuate them and don't know when they've guessed incorrectly. These kinds of errors don't mean students aren't good editors. It does mean we need to teach them how to punctuate the new, more complex sentences they're beginning to write. As a result of our teaching, students will gradually begin to recognize these errors and later to use these conventions automatically.

Figure 5.16 details several common editing difficulties students encounter and lists lessons that will help them learn to become good editors of their writing.

Teaching Students to Edit

If I see this . . .	I might . . .
Students see editing only as searching for errors in their writing, not as an opportunity to rewrite sentences and use punctuation differently to enhance meaning.	In minilessons, demonstrate how when we edit, we rework sentences and try different ways to use punctuation to help us get our point across.
	In conferences, suggest places in student drafts where they could write sentences and/or use punctuation differently to help them say what they're trying to say.
A student turns in a piece that is filled with careless errors.	Ask her to read the piece aloud to herself and look and listen for errors or read the piece aloud to a classmate to get help in locating errors.
Even after instruction in editing strategies, students don't use the strategies consistently to help them find mistakes.	Have them use an editing checklist to remind them of which strategies to use when they edit.
Students carefully use editing strategies, but some errors still remain in their drafts.	In minilessons and conferences, give explicit instruction on grammar and punctuation rules that will help students identify common errors in their writing.

FIGURE 5.16

Talking to Students About Their Processes

We can also gather information about students' writing processes by asking them to talk about the steps they go through when they compose and the tools and strategies they use during each step. Talking with students is the best way of gathering information about how they connect what they know about writing well to their writing processes. And we need this information to help us decide what to teach them so that they will develop more effective processes.

A writing conference is the best time to talk with students about how they write. When I confer with a student, I ask him early on to talk about his process. Some of the assessment questions I ask include

- What are you doing today?
- Where are you in the writing process?
- What strategies are you using?
- Why are you using these strategies?

Look again at the conference I had with Doran (pages 101–102). Since Doran was just at the point of starting his draft, I was able to

TEACHER ACTION 5.6

Talk to students to learn about their writing processes. (You may want to use the checklist "Assessing Students' Writing Processes" in Appendix 3 to help you record what you see and learn.)

- Ask students about their writing territories. Why did they decide to write about this topic? Is the topic connected to their life? Is it one of their interests? Is their topic one that they've written about before—earlier in the year, at home, or during a previous year?

- Ask students to talk about how they're developing a topic before drafting. What are they doing to get ready to write a draft about their topic? Why are they using the strategies they're using?

- Ask students to describe their drafting and revising processes. What strategies do they use while they're drafting or revising? Why are they using these strategies? How do the strategies help them write well?

- In editing conferences, ask your students to explain how they go about editing their pieces and why they've made the edits they've made.

What the Student Said	What I Learned About the Student's Writing Process	What I Learned About What the Student Knows About Writing Well
"I'll look back on these entries and make them bigger and add things on."	• Doran uses a writer's notebook as a tool to rehearse his writing. • Doran has gathered information about his topic in his notebook. • Doran is planning to refer back to his notebook while he is drafting.	Doran understands that writers write with detail.
"I made a list of my bullets [subsections]."	Doran makes a plan for his writing before he drafts.	Doran understands that writers structure their writing.
"At first I was just listing the parts, but then I thought a little bit, like, which would go one after the other, to make sense."	Doran thinks about the order of his sections before he drafts.	Doran understands that in feature articles, writers order their sections logically.
"Well, I guess first I'm just going to think about my lead and write about what my angle is, like at the beginning of the bully article."	Doran gets ideas for how to write his pieces from studying the writing of other writers.	Doran has noticed that feature article writers let readers know their angle in the lead.
"My mom and I are planning to go to maybe a toy store or something like that and look; I'm just going to do a little research."	Doran continues to gather more information for his draft even after he begins to write it.	Doran understands that writers write with detail.

FIGURE 5.17

learn a great deal about his rehearsal work as well as some of the strategies he was planning to use to write the draft of his article. I was also able to gather some information about how Doran's knowledge of the qualities of good writing was shaping his writing process. (See Figure 5.17.) What I learned about Doran's writing process helped me decide what to teach him in the conference:

- I learned that Doran made a plan for a piece before drafting and that his plan for his feature article was informed by his knowing that nonnarrative writing is ordered by logic. Thus, I didn't need to focus this conference on helping Doran make a better plan for his feature article.

- I learned that Doran was planning to use the information from his writer's notebook to help him write the sections of his article and that he was going to do more research to flesh out these sections. I didn't pursue these aspects of Doran's process because he hadn't yet written these sections.

- I found out that Doran thought about model texts when he drafted—in this case, the class touchstone text. By looking at the model text together—that is, by helping him learn to use this important writing strategy more effectively—I was able to guide him to think about what else he could to do write a lead with a better-developed hook.

Of course, not all children have learned to describe their writing process the way Doran did. When I ask students how they're writing their pieces, they sometimes don't answer, or they shrug, because they haven't yet learned how to talk about how they write. Then I often take a few moments to help them learn how to talk about their process. I might say, "I see you've circled some misspelled words and tried to write them correctly. So you're editing your writing for spelling today." Narrating children's writing processes helps them eventually be able to do this for themselves.

References

Angelillo, Janet. 2002. *A Fresh Approach to Teaching Punctuation*. New York: Scholastic.

Atwell, Nancie. 1998. *In the Middle: New Understandings About Writing, Reading, and Learning*. Portsmouth, NH: Heinemann.

Bomer, Randy. 1995. *Time for Meaning: Crafting Literate Lives in Middle and High School*. Portsmouth, NH: Heinemann.

Ehrenworth, Mary, and Vicki Vinton. 2004. *The Power of Grammar: Unconventional Approaches to the Conventions of Language*. Portsmouth, NH: Heinemann.

Everett, Walter. 1999. *The Beatles as Musicians: Revolver Through The Anthology*. New York: Oxford University Press.

Heard, Georgia. 2002. *The Revision Toolbox: Teaching Techniques That Work*. Portsmouth, NH: Heinemann.

Hertsgaard, Mark. 1996. *A Day in the Life: The Music and Artistry of the Beatles*. New York: Dell.

Lattimer, Heather. 2003. *Thinking Through Genre: Units of Study in Reading and Writing Workshops 4–12*. Portland, ME: Stenhouse.

Lewisohn, Mark. 1988. *The Complete Beatles Recording Sessions*. London: Hamlyn.

Murray, Donald M. 1985. *A Writer Teaches Writing*. Boston: Houghton Mifflin.

———. 1999. *Write to Learn*. New York: Harcourt Brace.

Ray, Katie Wood. 1999. *Wondrous Words: Writers and Writing in the Elementary Classroom*. Urbana, IL: NCTE.

Romano, Tom. 1987. *Clearing the Way: Working with Teenage Writers*. Portsmouth, NH: Heinemann.

Wilde, Sandra. 1992. *You Kan Red This!: Spelling and Punctuation for Whole Language Classrooms, K–6*. Portsmouth, NH: Heinemann.

Linking Assessment and Instruction

Designing Individual Learning Plans for Students

Assessment, like writing, is a process of developing meaning.
—Lucy Calkins, The Art of Teaching Writing

A few months into my first year of teaching I was ready to quit. I became a teacher because I imagined I would get to know the students I was teaching. However, as I stood in front of my classroom in a Bronx elementary school and talked at my students hour after hour that fall, I realized that I knew very little about the children sitting in front of me except their names. The lack of meaningful relationships with any of my students—and my inability to imagine how I could develop such relationships—led me to question my decision to become a teacher.

Luckily, a friend gave me a copy of Lucy Calkins' *The Art of Teaching Writing* in the middle of that school year. As I read the book and, for the first time, learned about writing workshop, Lucy helped me imagine a teaching method in which, to be an effective writing teacher, it would be *essential* to get to know my students. I was captivated by the classrooms Lucy described and began to think that teaching—especially teaching writing—might just be the career for me.

During the past nineteen years, I've been fortunate to get to know several thousand children—my own students in schools in the Bronx, Kentucky, and Illinois and the students of teachers in whose classrooms I've worked as a staff developer all over the United States. And, just as Lucy promised, getting to know these students as writers made it possible for me to help them grow as writers.

What exactly does it mean to get to know students as writers? And why is it essential for teachers to get to know students in order to teach them to become lifelong writers?

A teacher who gets to know students in a writing workshop gathers information about them as writers. She then uses that information to construct multidimensional images in her mind of who the students are as writers at that point in their development. That is, through her everyday assessment, a teacher learns about students as initiators of writing. She learns about what students know about writing well. And she learns about students' writing processes.

When a teacher gets to know a student, she also imagines what kind of a writer she wants that student to become in a few months and by the end of the school year. A teacher constructs an *individual learning plan* for each student in her writing workshop, a set of clearly defined goals—for learning to initiate writing, for learning to write well, and for developing an effective writing process—that she'll work on in writing conferences with that child and in her whole-class curriculum. The payoff for designing individual learning plans for students is that they enable us to be better writing teachers.

Looking for What Students Can Already Do as Writers

To construct images of who students are as writers, we begin by observing them as they write, talking with them about their writing, and reading their writing. We need information about what students are doing as writers *right now*. We can construct pictures of who students are as writers—and then figure out the next steps we hope they'll take—only if we have this kind of information.

Maybe the idea of assessing children by looking for what they are already doing as writers is obvious. However, for many of us, me included, this was a foreign way of thinking when we began our journey as teachers of writing. Instead, we looked for what students were doing "wrong" and judged them as good or bad writers in relation to the number of mistakes we found.

Categorizing students as good or bad writers is a common response, I think, because most of our own teachers played this role with us when we were learning to write. Most of my teachers read my writing searching for mistakes, and whenever they found one, they made a big red mark on the page. When I got my papers back, the message in the numerous red marks—usually the only feedback I received—was that I was a member of the bad-writer club in those particular classes.

Here's the problem with this way of seeing student writers. If our attention is focused on looking for what students are doing wrong, then it's all too easy to overlook all the things that students *do* know about writing. Even our youngest students often know a lot of things about writing. As Brian Cambourne (1991) explains, when children write, they use what they have learned so far about writing to *approximate* what adult writers do. Over time, with a lot of writing experiences and

143
*Linking
Assessment and
Instruction:
Designing
Individual
Learning Plans*

instruction, students' approximations gradually become more and more like the writing of adult writers. Instead of thinking of what students do as wrong, it's more instructive for us to think of the pieces they write as steps along the journey toward becoming accomplished writers.

Since so much of the art of teaching writing is recognizing what children already know and then extending that knowledge over time, we have to be able look at students' approximations and see what they do know about writing. Writes Lucy Calkins (2003), "When we, as teachers, assess a child as a writer, we try to discern what the child can do independently so that we can determine the next step for this child" (85).

If we see students' errors as something bad, we overlook what some of these errors are telling us about the ways that students are growing as writers. For example, when students begin to write longer pieces, they sometimes lose control and include some parts that don't help them make their point. I see this as evidence that students are trying to compose pieces of growing complexity. And so I teach them strategies to gain control of their writing (such as making a plan before they start drafting). Or, again, when students are beginning to incorporate more complex sentences into their writing, they often make certain kinds of punctuation errors, which I see as evidence that students are learning to use new types of sentences in their writing. In response, I teach them how to punctuate these kinds of sentences.

I no longer use the words *good* and *bad* to describe students and their writing. To me, students are simply somewhere on the path (I hope) toward becoming lifelong writers. My job is not to judge them but to figure out where they are on the path and then nudge them forward on the journey.

However, with the pressure that many of us feel to meet district and state standards and to help all our students score well on the high-stakes tests, it's all too easy for us to overlook what students are already doing as writers. How tempting it is to respond to student writing by saying, "But my fourth graders *should* be able to write a focused personal narrative," or "My students *should* be making a plan for their writing before they draft."

I wish that all our students could do what the state and national writing standards say they should be doing at a particular grade level (and I expect that as writing instruction gets stronger and stronger in our country, more and more students will be able to do so). However, most teachers that I work with have at least several students who aren't yet able to compose pieces that meet the standards for their grade.

Standards *are* useful for helping us imagine the kinds of writers we hope students will become by the end of a school year (or by the date of the high-stakes test) and the teaching we need to do to help them get there. However, saying that students should be doing certain things as writers doesn't make it happen. It's our teaching—which begins with assessing who students are right now as writers—that will ultimately help students meet standards.

Let's try looking at a piece of student writing to see what the student who wrote it can do as a writer. Read the picture book Tiffany, a first grader, wrote about a visit to a beauty salon (see Figure 6.1). As you do so, try to name some of the many things she knows about writing well.

When I read Tiffany's book, I see that she seems to know about many of the qualities of good writing and is beginning to incorporate that knowledge into her writing. For example, reading her first and last pages, I learn that Tiffany seems to understand that she should have something to say about her topic of going to the beauty parlor—specifically, that the experience was fun. She also seems to know something about structuring a narrative—there are two scenes, the first outside the beauty parlor, the second inside, in temporal order. She seems to know she should try to signal readers that a new event is about to occur in a story (by using the transition *then*). And she seems to know that she should give readers precise details about her topic; as in many of the picture books she has read, she communicates those details in her drawings of her family's hair before, during, and after the beauty parlor session.

There is, of course, much that Tiffany needs to learn in order to become an accomplished writer, but these things are extensions of what she already knows. Certainly, she needs to learn not only to draw with precise detail but also to write with more precise detail. To do that, she needs to be able to take very general details—"Then they fix[ed] my hair," "Then they fix[ed] my mom['s] hair"—and break them down into specific details, such as what she and her family were saying when they were having their hair fixed, what she was thinking, and what the hairstylist was doing as she cut their hair. In other words, she needs to learn more about a trait of good writing she already knows something about.

Tiffany also needs to incorporate other transitions besides the word *then* into her repertoire. For example, she needs to learn how periods can help her show that she is finished relating one detail to her readers and is ready to move on to the next. Here again, Tiffany needs to learn more about an aspect of writing that she already knows something about.

Without knowing what Tiffany already knows about writing with detail and using transitions, deciding what she needs to learn next to grow as a writer is guesswork. Learning what students already know about writing helps us figure out the next steps that we should help them take.

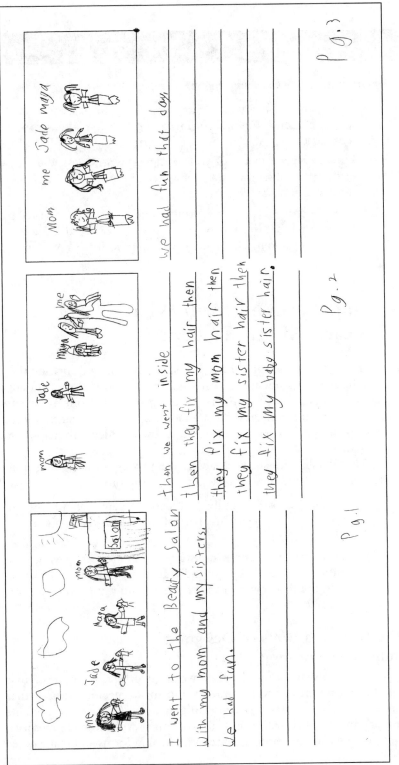

FIGURE 6.1 Tiffany's Story

TEACHER ACTION 6.1

Practice learning what your students can do as writers.

- Take some time in your writing workshop to observe several students at work, jotting down the things that you see that they're able to do as they write.

- Look at several pieces of your students' writing. As you read, make a list of all the things you identify that each student can do as a writer.

- Tape-record one of your writing conferences and listen to it afterward. What did you learn from your conversation with the student about what she or he is able to do as a writer?

Making Meaning from What We Learn About Students

Teachers who are skilled at writing assessment use the information they gather about their students to construct images of who the students are as writers and, as the students grow as writers from month to month, to revise these images. Most important, they use what they learn to make plans for what they want to teach their students to help them grow as writers.

When I talk with teachers about the process of designing individual learning plans, they usually ask two questions:

- How can I construct individual learning plans for students in a *practical* way, so that it's part of my day-to-day work as a writing teacher?

- What information about my students should I be paying attention to when I design individual learning plans for them during the first few months of school and during the rest of the year?

The Nuts and Bolts of Designing Individual Learning Plans

If you were to shadow me during a writing workshop, you'd see that I gather information about students and make meaning out of that information *during the entire time I'm with them*. As I observe students at work and as I talk with them and read their writing in conferences, I jot down what I'm learning on record-keeping forms and make notes about what I think the students need to learn to grow as writers. (I also do this when I read student writing outside writing workshop.) Thus, the process of constructing images of who students are as writers and designing individual learning plans for them unfolds as part of *every* writing workshop period.

My record-keeping forms are my most important assessment tool. Just as a writer jots down ideas in a writer's notebook and, over time, makes meaning from them, I use these forms to record what I learn about students and to reflect on what I learn. James and Kathleen Strickland (2000) write, "When teachers look over their anecdotal notes, they are able to put pieces together and draw conclusions that would have been more difficult to discover had the observations not been recorded . . . [These] records help sort things out; they are a type of writing for discovery" (26).

During the past couple of years, I've been using a form (see Figure 6.2) that supports the kind of thinking about students that I need to be doing if I'm going to teach them effectively. As you can see, this form is for the individual student. I keep a binder that includes one of these forms for every student in a class. When I fill up a form for any student, I put another one right after it and continue writing notes about him.

On the left side of the form, titled *What am I learning about this student as a writer?* I write down what I learn about a student when I observe him at work, when I talk with him in writing conferences, and when I read his writing in conferences and outside writing workshop. In other words, in this column I construct an image of who a student is as a writer and how he changes as a writer over time.

On the right side of the form, titled *What do I need to teach this student?* I record my thoughts about what I want to teach a student during the next few months of writing workshop. When I observe a child at work and realize there's something I want to teach him, I record my idea on this side of the form. Right after a conference, I write down any thoughts I had about what the student needs to learn. And I usually jot down some ideas when I'm reading student writing outside writing workshop. In other words, in this column I imagine my individual learning plan for a student.

Teachers sometimes ask me if it's necessary to use *this* record-keeping form to assess students. Of course not. The professional literature on writing workshop includes descriptions of any number of assessment forms (Kathleen and James Strickland's *Making Assessment Elementary* [2000] has several excellent ones on pages 23–27.) You can also design your own. Whatever the form, it's useful as long as it has space in which to record both what you're learning about students and your ideas for what you want to teach them to help them grow as writers.

Assessment Notes for _____ Dates _____

What am I learning about this student as a writer?	What do I need to teach this student?

Ⓣ is the symbol for Teaching Point.   Ⓖ is the symbol for Instructional Goal.

FIGURE 6.2   Record-Keeping Form

Let's walk through the process of designing an individual learning plan for a third grader named Aurora. I worked in Aurora's class as a staff developer during the first several months of the school year and assessed her as a writer during four of my visits.

September 21

My first encounter with Aurora was in a writing conference on September 21, when she was in the middle of a draft about the time she learned to ride a bicycle without training wheels. As you read the transcript of the conference, think about what you're learning about Aurora as a writer, and also imagine what you would want to teach her if she were your student.

ME: How's it going, Aurora?

AURORA: OK.

ME: What are you doing as a writer?

AURORA: Well . . . I'm writing about the time when my dad took off my training wheels.

ME: And what happened?

AURORA: I rode my bike with no training wheels for the first time. I was really scared, but then I did it!

ME: Why did you decide to write about this? [*Aurora thinks for a moment, then shrugs.*] From the way you just talked about your story, it sounds like it's a really important one. [*Aurora nods.*] How do you feel about what you did that day?

AURORA: I feel . . . good.

ME: Pretty proud of yourself, huh?

AURORA: Yeah.

ME: You know, a lot of kids I work with write stories like this. They tell about a time they were scared to do something, like ride a bike for the first time, swim across a pool for the first time, or go to sleep-away camp for the first time. Sometimes these kids write these stories to tell something important about themselves— that they're the kind of person who has the courage to meet a tough challenge and succeed. I wonder if that might be why you're writing this piece, to tell readers that you're this kind of person? [*Aurora beams.*] So who do you hope will read this when you're finished writing it?

AURORA: [*After thinking for a moment*] The class?

ME: Everyone in the class? Or are there some specific kids in the class that you really hope will read this?

AURORA: Everyone in the class.

ME: How about people not in school? Have you thought of sharing this story with people who aren't in your class?

AURORA: No.

ME: Well, I think it's great that you want the kids in this class to read your story and learn about how you're able to meet tough challenges. [*Aurora nods.*] When I'm writing, I think about the people I'm going to share my writing with. And you know what? Keeping those people in mind as I write helps me write better. That's because I feel that I'm making something that's going to do something to them—make them feel proud of me, make them laugh, help them learn something—and I have to make sure that my piece actually does that. I bet it would help you write really well if you thought about who all the people are that you want to read this story. Who else do you think could read this?

AURORA: [*Looking serious*] My dad? Because he was there?

ME: Excellent idea. I bet he would really enjoy remembering this time with you. And I bet he would feel proud of you all over again.

AURORA: And my mom, too. She likes it when I tell her stories about me.

ME: Yeah, I bet she would love to read your story, too. [*Aurora smiles.*] OK, you're going to share this piece with your class in the writing celebration in a week and a half, and you're also going to give it to your mom and dad to read. You can take your finished piece home in one of those special take-my-writing-home folders that your teacher has for you guys to use.

AURORA: OK.

ME: As you write, try to imagine all the people whom you want to read your story and how you want them to learn that you really can meet tough challenges.

AURORA: OK.

ME: Great talking with you.

AURORA: Thanks.

I learned a lot about Aurora during this conference—specifically about Aurora as an initiator of writing—which I recorded on my record-keeping form for her right after the conference (see the notes for 9/21 on Figure 6.3). On the left side, I wrote that her writing seemed purposeful although she needed me to help her articulate why she was writing the piece. I also wrote that she seemed tentative in naming the class as her audience, as if she hadn't really thought about who was going to read her piece. On the right side, I wrote a note to continue helping Aurora imagine audiences for her writing. Even though this was the teaching point I had focused on in this conference, I felt it was something that I would need to pursue with her in future conferences as well.

September 28

One week later, on September 28, as I was circulating around Aurora's classroom, I noticed that she and her classmate Angelique had ex-

151
*Linking
Assessment and
Instruction:
Designing
Individual
Learning Plans*

Assessment Notes For ___Aurora___ Dates ___9/21 – 11/1___

What am I learning about this student as a writer?	What do I need to teach this student?
9/21 " When I Rode My Bike Without Training Wheels" - Purpose : let people know she's the kind of person who meets challenges - Audience : class (tentative) ⓉReaders for a piece can be outside of class 9/28 " when I Rode..." - editing with Angelique - exchange papers, they read silently 10/3 " When I Rode..." - story : tension, change - detail : dialogue, thinking, body movement - climatic scene undeveloped 11/1 "Butterfly Life Cycle" - audience : "insect club" (!) - lots of voice (asides) - boxed out the article - adds on : idea first, then skims draft to find place to add the idea ⓉWriters look at each part of a piece when they revise	ⒼClearly think out who her readers will be inside and outside of class ⒼRead writing aloud in a peer conference ⒼDevelop important parts (revision) ⒼWork on revising by looking at the parts first
Ⓣis the symbol for teaching point.	Ⓖis the symbol for instructional goal

FIGURE 6.3 Assessment Notes for Aurora

changed drafts and were editing each other's writing by reading the drafts to themselves silently. I wrote this down on the left side of my form for Aurora (and also on my form for Angelique); on the right side I wrote a note to teach Aurora (and Angelique) how to read her writing aloud to a classmate in a peer editing conference, the editing strategy that I find students have the most success with during the last stage of the writing process (see the notes for 9/28 on Figure 6.3).

October 3

On October 3, Aurora's teacher shared with me the pieces her class had just published, and I had a chance to read Aurora's final version of her story (see Figure 6.4). Reading her story, I learned a lot about what Aurora knew about writing well. One of the first things I was struck by was Aurora's genre knowledge. In my notes (see 10/3 on Figure 6.3), I jotted down the word *tension,* because Aurora creates tension in the beginning of her piece, as a good story writer usually does ("One day, I asked my dad to take off my training wheels"). I also jotted down the word *change,* another story element, because in Aurora's piece, her main character (herself) changes from a child who rides with training wheels to one who doesn't need them anymore. Then I wrote down *detail: dialogue, thinking, body movement,* because I noticed that Aurora uses a range of specific details.

On the right side of the form, I jotted down *develop important parts.* As I read Aurora's piece, I learned that she develops some scenes with sufficient detail (the scene with her father loosening her training wheels). However, I also thought she needed to learn to use this knowledge in her climatic scene, when she finally rides her bike without training wheels, and develop it more. I also wrote down the word *revision,* because I thought it would be a good thing for her to learn to think about whether or not she had developed important scenes sufficiently at this stage in the writing process.

November 1

In my next encounter with Aurora, a writing conference on November 1, the work I had done to get to know her as a writer and imagine an individual learning plan for her began to pay off. Aurora was revising the draft of a feature article she had written on the life cycle of a butterfly (see Figure 6.5). Prior to the conference, she had boxed out her draft—circled the parts—a strategy (which she had learned in a recent minilesson) that enables writers to break a piece down and revise it part by part.

As you read the transcript of the first part of this conference, again try to gather information about Aurora and make meaning from it. What is different this time is that you already know some things about Aurora as a writer. What you find out in this conference will deepen your understanding of some of the things you already know about her. You'll also see that what I teach her connects directly to the aspects of the individual learning plan I began imagining several weeks earlier.

ME: How's it going today, Aurora?
AURORA: Good.
ME: What are you doing as a writer today?

153
*Linking
Assessment and
Instruction:
Designing
Individual
Learning Plans*

One day, I asked my dad to take off my training wheels.

"No, Aurora, sweetie," my dad said as he was shaking his head back and forth. "First you have to make your training wheels loose enough," he added.

So, my dad kneeled on one knee, took the screwdriver from the ground and told me to hold the back of the bike. He took the screwdriver and made the training wheels loose by putting the screw in the training wheels and turning it back and forth.

I thought I was going to wobble a lot. When my dad was done making my training wheels loose, I put the screwdriver on the bench. Then I sat on the bike and started pedaling.

I was riding my bike around the whole park but in the gates.

"Whee!" I shouted while I was riding my bike. I thought I was going to fall off but, I didn't.

"Daddy I'm ready to take off my training wheels," I told my dad as I stopped.

"Are you sure? Cause if you are, I'll take them off," my dad said.

"I'm sure," I said. So, my dad took my training wheels loose. I think I can do this, I think I can do this, I think I can do this, I thought to myself. Soon, my dad was done taking off my training wheels. I was sitting on the bench while my dad was checking my bike out, to see if it was safe.

"It's okay. Now you can ride your bike Aurora okay?" my dad told me.

"Alright," I answered him back. So, I sat on the seat, put my hands on the bars. My dad gave me a little push. He was in back of me so I couldn't see him. Soon, my dad was still pushing me in the back of my bike. I saw my dad in another direction.

"Oh my god. I'm really riding a two wheeler," I said to myself every ten seconds.

"Come on Aurora you can do it. You can do it," my dad said to me. I rode my bike one more time and took a break. Then my dad took my bike and put it in the car. Then I went to my dad and gave him a great big hug. And that's the story of how my dad taught me how to ride a two wheeler.

FIGURE 6.4 Aurora's Story

Butterflies

Have you ever seen a butterfly in your whole entire life? Well, I have. Do you know the life cycle of a butterfly? Well, I do. I'll tell you all about it.

First, you many think the butterfly's egg isn't that small. Think again. It is very, very small. When you see the egg hatching, you might want to get a closer look to what's coming out.

If you see something come out the size of a jelly bean, that, would be called a catterpiller. Once the catterpiller hatches from it's egg, it is smaller than one inch. Wow! Talk about small. Also, once the catterpiller hatches, it is very, very, and I mean very, very hungry!

The catterpiller will first eat it's eggshell. Yuck! I bet that eggshell tastes nasty but, I bet it runs in the catterpiller family. Then the catterpiller will search for food. After about 2 weeks, the catterpiller is fully grown. Now, the catterpiller is more than 1 inch. It's 2½ inches. Wow! Catterpillers grow faster than I thought.

Then the catterpiller is ready for it's cocoon. The catterpiller will be in its cocoon for 6 weeks.

After six weeks, the catterpiller will start hatching from its cocoon just like it hatched from its egg.

After the butterfly hatches, it will take off. Good-by, farewell butterfly, and to you, too.

FIGURE 6.5   Aurora's Feature Article

AURORA: I'm working on my butterfly article.

ME: Working on your butterfly article?

AURORA: I'm revising it.

ME: So you're getting your piece ready to publish. Have you thought about who's going to read this piece?

AURORA: [*Thinking for a moment*] Yeah.

ME: You're going to share this article with. . .

AURORA: The other kids in the class who are writing about insects. We're kind of an insect club. [*She smiles.*]

ME: That's great that you have some readers in mind. You said you're revising your article? What kind of revision work are you doing?

AURORA: I was boxing out my . . . paragraphs?

ME: Your sections?

AURORA: Uh-huh. And I was going to read it over to see if I wanted to add something, because usually when I read something over and over, I feel like I need to add something.

ME: What about this piece? Have you found parts you need to add to?

AURORA: I was thinking . . . I wanted to add a fact . . . [*skimming her draft, pointing at each line with her pencil*] I wanted to add something . . . [*Her pencil settles on one part.*] like right before this sentence, I could say . . . [*frowning*] no, I don't think so . . . it doesn't fit there.

ME: You're thinking you need to add on to your draft. Let me take a look at it. [*I skim the draft.*]

AURORA: Well, just now I thought of something . . . I just need to know where to put it. . . .

ME: OK, instead of just randomly thinking of things you can add to your draft and then looking for a place to put them, which is what I think you're doing here, I'd like you to think about a couple of things. First off, one thing I noticed about your piece as I read it is that the parts of your article that you boxed out get shorter on page 2. [*I point to the parts on the first page and then to those on the second.*] Do you see that?

AURORA: Yeah.

ME: One thing good writers do when they revise is they look at each part of their draft and ask themselves, "What does *this* part need?" That's why writers circle or box out the parts of their draft in the first place, to help them do this. I'd like you to try that with this draft instead of just thinking of facts and then reading over the draft to find where to put them.

AURORA: OK.

ME: Why don't you try this first with one of the short parts on the second page? [*I point to one of them.*] What else could you say in this part? [*Aurora thinks for a moment and then shrugs.*] What other facts do you know about this part, the part about what happens in the cocoon?

AURORA: Well, when the butterfly is in its cocoon, it looks kind of weird.

ME: It looks kind of weird. . . .

AURORA: Yeah, it looks like the letter *J* as it hangs from a twig.

ME: That's great, Aurora, you're getting a feel for trying to revise a part of your piece. [*Aurora smiles.*] I'd like you to try to add more facts to this part, and then some of the other short parts in your article. I think that if you use this strategy when you revise, your readers—the kids in your insect club—won't say, "Hey, I want to know more about that part," when they read your article. Are you ready to try this?

AURORA: Yeah.

ME: Good talking with you.

I learned several things about Aurora as a writer in this conference. When I asked her about her audience, she was able to give me a specific answer. This pleased me, since after my first conference with her in September, I had written down in my individual learning plan for her that I wanted her to learn to imagine audiences for her writing. I didn't pursue this, because Aurora was doing exactly what I had hoped she would. And as I skimmed Aurora's draft, I noticed that she got voice into her writing by making little asides on the facts she presented. I jotted this down on the left side of my form for her.

I felt the most important information I learned was about Aurora's revision process. I realized she revised by thinking of a detail she wanted to add and then searching for a place in the draft where she could add it. That's why on the left side of my record-keeping form (see the notes for 11/1 on Figure 6.3), I wrote *adds on: idea first, then skims draft to find place to add the idea* and drew an arrow to what I had written after reading her bicycle piece on October 3; I hypothesized that the way Aurora had been revising her writing might be the reason she didn't develop some of the important parts in her pieces. In Aurora's revision process, a part would be developed by chance, depending on whether she could come up with a detail that fit.

On the right side of the form, I wrote *Work on revising by looking at the parts first,* because this is what I taught her during the remainder of the conference—and because this was something I knew I would want to follow up on in future conferences, especially when she was revising pieces of writing. I thought that once Aurora learned how to look at the parts of her piece when she revised, she would be more likely to write a piece in which she developed each part sufficiently to satisfy a reader.

Even after having just four opportunities to assess her, I was able to figure out some important things about who Aurora was as a writer that fall. And I was able to imagine an individual learning plan for her that informed what I taught her in our final conference. Of course, given that I worked in her classroom for just a few months, there's a lot I didn't get to learn about Aurora. Had I been her classroom teacher, I would have had time to develop a much fuller picture of her as a writer, as well as a more comprehensive individual learning plan. And I would have been able to focus on other aspects of her individual learning plan in other writing conferences.

It can seem overwhelming to think that we need to get to know all of our students as writers in this way. However, as we get to know more and more students at a particular grade level, we start to recognize similarities between the students we're getting to know and the students we've worked with before. Thus, with more and more experience, we are able to construct images of who students are as writers and design individual learning plans for them more and more quickly. To make this same point, Peter Johnston (1997) compares literacy teachers to world chess masters. Like expert chess players, who through experience come to recognize more than fifty thousand board configurations and know instantly what their next move should be, literacy teachers become able quickly to spot the resemblances between students and know intuitively where to take students next as writers.

Where to Begin and Where to Go from There

How do we get started designing individual learning plans for students? Are there some aspects of our students as writers that we should pay special attention to at the beginning of the school year? Are there some aspects that we might assess later?

When I'm working with students during the first month of school, my first assessment priority is to get to know them as initiators of writing. Ultimately, I'm going to be much more successful in helping students grow as writers if they're invested in their writing. It's essential to figure out which students find writing meaningful and which ones still need to learn that writing can serve important purposes in their lives. By gathering information in the ways discussed in Chapter 3, I begin constructing images of each student as an initiator of writing. And when I learn that some students don't seem to be writing for purposes that matter to them or aren't yet choosing genres purposefully to help them realize their purposes for writing or aren't yet writing with audiences clearly in mind (as was true with Aurora), I set goals for them accordingly and then look to help students grow in these ways in future conferences.

My second assessment priority at the beginning of the school year is to get a general picture of students' writing processes. I want to find out which stages they go through in writing their first piece (or first several pieces) and which strategies they use independently to navigate each stage.

One reason I pay particular attention to students' writing processes early on is that for a workshop to run smoothly throughout the year, students need to be able to go through the stages of the writing process independently, without constant hand-holding. Thus, it's important to figure out which students have trouble navigating some stages of the writing process or skip some steps entirely. (It's very common for inexperienced writers to skip revision early in the year.) As I learn about students' writing processes (in the ways described in Chapter 5), I begin to set goals for some of them to learn about particular stages and the strategies they'll need to work through them.

Also, the instructional focus of the first whole-class unit of study is usually on developing a writing process (for inexperienced writers) or developing a more effective writing process (for more experienced writers). To make accurate decisions about what minilessons to teach students about keeping a writer's notebook, planning a piece of writing, or revising or editing a piece of writing, I need information about what they already know how to do when they write in their notebooks, compose their drafts, and revise and edit those drafts. This is another reason I need to learn about students' writing processes immediately.

I don't make a full assessment of what students know about writing well an immediate priority. I usually assess students for one quality of good writing—meaning—during this early time, so that I can learn which students are trying to say something about the topic they're writing about and which ones see writing as retelling an event or writing all about a topic. One of my most important priorities during the next few months will be to teach students who fall into this latter category that writing is about communicating meaning. If I happen to learn something else about what a student does to write well, either in a conference or when I'm reading her writing during that first month—something about her genre knowledge or how she writes with voice—I'll write it down on my record-keeping form and set goals for her accordingly. But during this first month, my attention is mainly on the ways students initiate writing and on their writing processes.

Assessing how well students write and setting goals for helping them learn to write better becomes more of a priority at the end of the first unit of study, when students are publishing their first pieces. As I read their pieces, I pay special attention to what they do to write well and begin to imagine what I need to focus on with them in conferences to help them write better. At this point the notes on my record-keeping forms begin to include detailed assessments of what students do to write well as well as goals for things they need to learn about various aspects of writing well (as you saw in my notes about Aurora).

So a month into the school year I've begun to learn about students as initiators of writing, about what they do to write well, and about their writing processes. And I've decided what steps I want to help my students make as writers during the next few months. What should I pay attention to in my assessments during the next few months? For the remainder of the year?

The aspects of writing I've decided to focus on during my initial assessment become my assessment priorities during these months. For example, if I want to help a student write for new types of audiences, I'll be sure to ask her, in conferences, about with whom she's planning to share her writing (as I did in my second conference with Aurora). Or if I want to help a student learn to use semicolons more effectively, in our next editing conference I'll ask him how he's using this punctuation mark.

159

*Linking
Assessment and
Instruction:
Designing
Individual
Learning Plans*

TEACHER ACTION 6.2

Practice designing individual learning plans for students.

- Take a look at the form you use to record information about what you learn about your student writers. Does this form let you record what you learn about students over time as well as set goals for them?

- Design individual learning plans for a few students in your writing workshop. Watch each of them at work for five minutes and jot down what you learn about them and what you want to teach them in response to what you see. Have a conference with each of them, and do the same. Outside of writing workshop, read a piece of writing that each of them has published, and do the same.

- After several months of taking notes about students, read over some of your record-keeping forms. First, pay attention to what you wrote about them during the first month of school. What do you learn about your assessment priorities during the first month of the school year? Then, focus your attention on what you wrote in subsequent months. How did your initial goals for students influence your assessment and teaching during this time? When did you set new goals for students? What led you to set these new goals?

Over time, in response to my teaching in conferences and minilessons, I'll (I hope) see that students begin to meet the goals I've set for them. At this point I shift my attention to other aspects of students as writers and set new goals for them. (Some students, of course, need the entire year to achieve my initial goals for them, so I assess them in relation to those goals for the whole year.)

Upcoming units of study also nudge me to assess certain aspects of students as writers. If the next unit of study I'm planning is on punctuation or on using a writer's notebook, I pay special attention during the current unit of study to how students are using punctuation in their writing or how they are using their writer's notebooks. This assessment not only spurs me to set new goals for students as writers but also gives me the information I need to decide which minilessons to teach during the next unit of study.

The Qualities of Well-Designed Individual Learning Plans

Over the past decade, I've worked with teachers in yearlong study groups as part of my work with the Teachers College Reading and Writing Project as well as with small groups of teachers in schools across the country. These teachers have shared the individual learning plans they've designed for students and discussed the ways these plans help them improve their teaching.

As part of these discussions, group members give one another feedback on the assessment work they are doing with students. We've come to recognize that a well-developed individual learning plan has certain qualities:

- Over time, while designing the curriculum, the teacher pays attention to all aspects of the child as a writer.
- The teacher constructs the curriculum with information from multiple sources.
- The teacher stays focused on her goals for a student over a period of time that may range from several weeks to the entire year.
- The teacher sets appropriate goals for the student.

Encompassing All Aspects of a Child as a Writer

In a well-designed curriculum, the teacher pays attention to who a student is as an initiator of writing, to what he does to write well, and to his writing process and sets goals for the student to grow in all three of these aspects of being a writer.

It's important that we periodically review our individual learning plans for our students and ask ourselves which aspects of our students as writers we haven't yet paid much attention to. Although we won't be able to focus on every aspect of writing with any one of our students in any one school year, we'll want to be sure that during the year we do help each student with *some* aspects of initiating writing, with *some* aspects of writing well, and with *some* aspects of developing an effective writing process.

Using Information from Multiple Sources

In well-designed individual learning plans, teachers make meaning out of information about students that they've gathered from observing them at work, talking with them in writing conferences, and reading their writing. A complete picture of who a child is as a writer can't be gained from relying on only one of these sources of information.

161
*Linking
Assessment and
Instruction:
Designing
Individual
Learning Plans*

It's valuable to review our individual learning plans and ask ourselves if we're gathering information from all three sources or if we rely on one or two to the exclusion of the others. Should we notice that we're overlooking a source of information, we need to find a way to take advantage of this overlooked source. How can we take time in between our conferences to observe our students at work? How can we make conferring the priority it needs to be each day in our writing workshops? How can we make the time we need outside the writing workshop to read student writing without the distractions of students working around us?

Focusing on a Few Goals at a Time

Given that children need to grow in so many ways to become lifelong writers, it's tempting to list a lot of goals in our individual learning plans. And then it's tempting to try to focus on as many of those goals in as short a time as possible, either by cramming several teaching points into each of our conferences or by focusing each conference with a student on a different issue.

However, teachers who construct well-designed individual learning plans focus on only a few goals for each student over the course of a few months (or, for some students, an entire school year). They gather information about certain aspects of students as writers over and over again and have not just one but several conferences with them on those aspects.

It's crucial to keep in mind that growth in any aspect of writing is gradual. To help a child grow in an appreciable way in writing for a variety of purposes, structuring a piece of writing, or revising effectively, it's usually necessary to revisit that aspect of writing with him several times over a given period.

Including Appropriate Goals

When we set goals for students, we need to be sure they are appropriate—that the goals are reasonable next steps for students to take as writers. To that end we must be knowledgeable about what students who are receiving good writing instruction can reasonably be expected to be able to do at various grade levels. When we know what students can do, our goal setting is less likely to be too ambitious or not ambitious enough. Instead, we'll set goals that are within what Vygotsky (1962) calls students' "zone of proximal development"—goals that students can meet now *with our assistance* and will be able to meet later on their own.

Of course, what students learn in our writing workshops teaches us what children can do as writers. And many educators have written about what students at different ages and in different grades can learn

TEACHER ACTION 6.3

Reflect on the individual learning plans you've designed for students.
Read over several of your individual learning plans for students, and
ask yourself the following questions:

- Have I designed my individual learning plans to help my
  students grow as initiators of writing, learn more about
  writing well, and develop more effective writing processes?
  Have I stressed one of these traits to the exclusion of the
  others? If so, what can I do to pay more attention to the
  neglected traits?

- Have I gathered information about students from several
  sources in my writing workshop? Or have I relied primarily
  on one or two sources? What can I do to begin gathering
  information from the sources of information that I've
  overlooked?

- Have I focused on my goals for students over a period of
  time, or do I jump from one goal to another? How can I
  get better at focusing on just a few goals for students?

- Are my goals appropriate for who my students are as
  writers? Are they too ambitious? Not ambitious enough?
  What sources of information about how students grow as
  writers can I read to help me think about the appropriate-
  ness of my goals?

- What do I need to do to be able to construct even better
  individual learning plans for my students?

to do when writing instruction is part of their day-to-day life in school.
Lucy Calkins (1994), for example, includes a discussion of children's
development as writers from kindergarten through middle school in *The
Art of Teaching Writing*. The performance standards created by the
National Center on Education and the Economy and the University
of Pittsburgh (1997) include descriptions of what children can do as
writers in elementary, middle, and high school. The Education Department of Western Australia has constructed a developmental continuum
for writing (1994). And, as part of state testing programs, many teachers get copies of proficient student writing that give them an image of
what students can do in the grade levels being tested.

Given that the students we teach are in different places as writers,
it's important that we be familiar with what students at various grade

163
*Linking
Assessment and
Instruction:
Designing
Individual
Learning Plans*

levels can be reasonably expected to learn to do as writers. In a third-grade class, it's not uncommon to have a few students who have already surpassed the standards for the grade level and whose writing resembles that of many fifth graders. To set appropriate goals for these students, we need to know what fifth graders can learn to do as writers. Likewise, it would not be surprising to have a few students in that same third-grade class who write like many students do in first grade. To figure out goals appropriate for these students, we need to know something about what first graders can learn to do as writers.

References

Calkins, Lucy. 1994. *The Art of Teaching Writing*. Portsmouth, NH: Heinemann.

———. 2003. *The Nuts and Bolts of Teaching Writing. Units of Study for Primary Writing: A Yearlong Curriculum*. Portsmouth, NH: Heinemann.

Cambourne, Brian. 1991. *Coping with Chaos*. Portsmouth, NH: Heinemann.

Education Department of Western Australia. 1994. *Writing Developmental Continuum*. Portsmouth, NH: Heinemann.

Johnston, Peter H. 1997. *Knowing Literacy: Constructive Literacy Assessment*. Portland, ME: Stenhouse.

National Center on Education and the Economy and University of Pittsburgh. 1997. *Performance Standards, Volume 1, Elementary School*. San Antonio, TX: Harcourt Brace Educational Measurement.

Strickland, Kathleen, and James Strickland. 2000. *Making Assessment Elementary*. Portsmouth, NH: Heinemann.

Vygotsky, L. S. 1962. *Thought and Language*. Edited and translated by Eugenia Hanfmann and Gertrude Vakar. Cambridge, MA: MIT Press.

Linking Assessment and Instruction
Conferring

The word assessment . . . *derives from the Latin word*
assidere, *meaning to sit alongside. This is a useful
metaphor for assessment, particularly in the classroom.*
—PETER H. JOHNSTON, Knowing Literacy

When my wife, Robin, was four months pregnant with our second
child, I accompanied her to her doctor's office for one of her periodic
ultrasounds. Since her pregnancy was far enough along that the ultrasound could reveal the sex of the baby, Robin and I decided beforehand that we would like to know if we were going to have a boy or a
girl.

Throughout the examination, I watched carefully. It wasn't that
hard to figure out what the nurse was doing. With one hand, she was
moving the ultrasound scanner along Robin's belly. With her other
hand, she was using a mouse to position a cursor at different points
on the image of the baby on the monitor. At each point she clicked
on the mouse, and then used it to draw a line to another point on the
image where she clicked again, completing the line. The computer then
calculated the length of whatever part of the baby's body the nurse had
just measured.

For the life of me, however, I couldn't tell what I was looking at
on the monitor. I could make out vague shapes that momentarily re-
sembled a limb or spine or head, but more often I felt as if I were
watching one of those lava lamps from the 1960s. I saw nothing that
would indicate whether the baby was a boy or a girl.

When she finished the exam, the nurse said, "From these mea-
surements, it appears that your baby is fifteen and a half weeks old.
I'm also 99.5 percent sure of your baby's sex. Do you want to
know?" Robin and I nodded. The nurse pointed to a white blob on
the screen. "You see this? This is your baby's behind." As I stared
at the blob, I suddenly could see that I was indeed staring at the
baby's rear end (and I wondered how many times I would be clean-

ing that part of the baby's anatomy during the next several years!). Then the nurse pointed to two other, thinner blobs. "And these are the baby's legs." As I stared at the two thinner blobs, I suddenly saw that I was staring at the baby's legs. "Now look between the legs," the nurse commanded, pointing to a tiny blob in that region. I stared at this blob, not comprehending. The nurse chuckled when she saw the look of puzzlement on my face. Finally she announced, "It's a boy! Congratulations!"

Recently, I've begun to tell this story in workshops based on my first book, *How's It Going? A Practical Guide to Conferring with Student Writers* (2000). In the book (and in the workshops), I focus on what to do in a writing conference with a student. While thousands of teachers have told me they find this how-to information very useful, many of them have also expressed frustration that they still aren't sure what they're supposed to be looking for when they're conferring with a child about her writing. And when they finally do see something, they're not sure how to assess it to help them decide what to teach the child.

Just as I was able to figure out pretty quickly the mechanics of what the nurse was doing during the ultrasound, it's not really that hard to grasp the how-to of a writing conference. But just as I had trouble figuring out what I was seeing on the ultrasound monitor, figuring out what to look for and then making sense of what we're seeing are the hardest challenges in a conference. The most difficult part of conferring is assessing our student writers.

How to Conduct Effective Writing Conferences[5]

Writing conferences—the one-on-one conversations we have with students while their classmates are busy writing—are the most important teaching opportunities we have in the writing workshop. When we confer with children, we're able to differentiate our instruction and fulfill the promise of writing workshop: that we will be able to tailor our teaching to each child's individual needs as a writer.

To have an effective writing conference with a student, we need to be familiar with a few important concepts.

---

5. If you've read one or more professional books on conferring with student writers—which include my own book *How's It Going?* (2000), Douglas Kaufman's *Conferences and Conversations* (2000), and Lucy Calkins, Amanda Hartman, and Zoe White's *Conferring Handbook* (2003) and *One to One: The Art of Conferring with Young Writers* (2005)—you may want to skip this section.

A Writing Conference Is a Conversation About How to Become a Better Writer

Since I launched my first writing workshop nineteen years ago, I have thought of writing conferences as conversations. The word *conversation* suggests the way I believe we should talk with students about their writing—the kind of personal, intimate talk we have with friends and colleagues. Even though we're teachers talking with students, we're also writers talking to writers. In *A Writer Teaches Writing* (1985), Don Murray explains, "[Conferences] are not mini-lectures but the working talk of fellow writers sharing their experience with the writing process" (148).

What are these conversations about? is the crucial question teachers ask me about conferring. Our conferences will go well if we—and our students—know why we're having them.

The point of writing conferences, ultimately, is to help students become lifelong writers. In conferences, we help students write for purposes and audiences important to them, acquire a working knowledge of what it means to write well, and develop more effective writing processes, in the hope they'll make use of what we teach them in the future. In *The Art of Teaching Writing* (1994), Lucy Calkins says that our challenge in conferences is to stay focused on the students and on their growth as writers: "If we can keep only one thing in mind—and I fail at this half the time—it is that we are teaching the writer and not the writing. Our decisions must be guided by 'what might help this *writer*' rather than 'what might help this *writing*'" (228).

When we finish a conference, we should be able to name one thing we taught the student to help her or him become a better writer. We want to be able to say, "I taught Madeline a strategy for figuring out the spelling of an unfamiliar word," or "I helped Terrence learn how to write strong topic sentences," or "I helped Dominique learn about a new purpose for writing."

Consider the following conference, which I had with Smith, a sixth grader. Smith has been writing a personal essay called "Losing Spanish" (his first draft is shown in Figure 7.1). Smith and his classmates have read several personal essays and noticed that in this genre, writers explore an idea by writing about some of their life experiences. As you read this conference, in which Smith and I discuss revisions that he could make to his first draft, try to figure out the one thing I taught Smith to help him become a better writer.

ME: How's it going?
SMITH: Fine.
ME: What are you doing?
SMITH: Writing an essay about forgetting how to speak bilingual.

Losing Spanish

When I came from school I showed my mom my homework. But then I realize that I was talking english only. And was suprize that I wasn't Bi-lingual anymore. Bi-lingual is when you know two language.

The problem is that I might not speak with my family. My mom my cusins and my friends my sister can speak english but I like spanish.

FIGURE 7.1   Smith's First Draft

ME: Uh-huh. Tell me more about that.

SMITH: That if I don't be bilingual anymore, I can't talk to my whole family.

ME: So you're telling a story about a time that you were speaking in English and forgot how to speak in Spanish?

SMITH: Yeah. When I was explaining my homework to my mom.

ME: And how did she react?

SMITH: Kind of weird . . . kind of lonely.

ME: So you're writing about a change in you that makes you worry about your relationships with your family?

SMITH: Yeah.

ME: What are you doing with your essay today?

SMITH: I'm making corrections.

ME: Are you editing—checking spelling and punctuation—or are you revising—adding to your draft, moving parts around?

SMITH: Adding.

ME: So you're revising.

SMITH: Yeah.

ME: Tell me more about what you mean by revising.

SMITH: I'm adding some more new stuff.

ME: What do you mean by "stuff"?

SMITH: Like the important parts that happened.

ME: You're trying to add more to the important parts? [*Smith nods.*] That's very smart that you said that you know there are some important parts that you want to stretch out. Let me take a look at your draft. [*I read it through.*] I have a question for you, Smith. What do you want me to understand after I read your finished essay?

SMITH: That problems can happen if you forget how to speak your other language.

ME: You want us to know that learning a second language can cause problems with your family. And you said you wanted to stretch the important parts. Hmmm . . . I see that your piece has a story—what happened when you showed your mom your homework—and an idea that learning a second language can cause problems with your family. Good personal essays have both of these parts, a story and an idea . . . . One thing I'm noticing about your essay is that you wrote three sentences in the story about you and your mom and the homework.

SMITH: Yeah, that's right.

ME: If people reading this are really going to understand what you're saying about losing Spanish, this story is really important. In a personal essay, the stories help readers understand the ideas. And in writing, you need to stretch the parts that help readers understand what you're trying to say. When I read your essay, I need to be in the room with you and your mom if I'm going to understand the problem, because I'm not bilingual. Let's try this together right now. Tell me more about you and your mom and the homework.

SMITH: [*After thinking for a moment*] My mom was kind of surprised, because I used to talk a lot when I was tiny.

ME: You used to talk a lot in Spanish when you were smaller. How did your mom react now?

SMITH: Her eyes . . . she started glaring at me and I started glaring back.

ME: Did she say anything to you?

SMITH: Yeah. She said something in Spanish, but I don't want to say it.

ME: Can you kind of translate, but in a way that's OK for me to hear?

SMITH: She said, "Oh, my son, what's wrong with you?"

ME: How did you feel when she said that?

SMITH: Kind of embarrassed, because I always like to talk Spanish.

ME: That's really powerful. It must be a hard story to tell, right?

SMITH: Yeah.

ME: I'd like you to do some writing now. Instead of just three sentences, see if you can tell the story of you and your mom and the homework with more sentences, just like you were telling me. The better you tell that story, the better I'm going to understand what you're trying to tell me about losing Spanish. [*Smith nods.*] You're grappling with something that's really powerful. Your idea about losing Spanish will really come across better if you stretch this story in your essay. OK?

SMITH: Yeah.

ME: Go for it.

> **Losing Spanish**
>
> One day when I was doing my homework I was finished, so then I was explaining my homework to my mom I couldn't explain a word. I felt like I wasn't Bi-lingual any more.
>
> Then I realize that I was talking english only but then my mom was suprized. My mom was glaring at me and I glared back. I ran back to my room and slam the door shut. I thought for a while and saw that if I can't talk spanish I wouldn't talk with my family.

FIGURE 7.2   Smith's Revision

The one thing I taught Smith in this conference to help him become a better writer is that it's important to develop the parts of a piece that help him make his point. In a personal essay, this means developing the story (or stories). And that's exactly what Smith did (see Figure 7.2).

There Is a Predictable Structure in a Writing Conference

When I've observed teachers who are good at conferring, I've noticed that there is a structure to their conversations. Because these teachers know in general how they want their conversations with students to go—as do the students, once they've taken part in several of them—the talk flows easily and naturally, with both the teacher and the student holding up their end.

The conference conversation has two parts, both of which grow from the underlying purpose of helping students become better writers. In each part, the teacher and student have certain roles (see Figure 7.3).

The First Part

In the first part of a conference, we talk with students about what they're doing as writers. That is, we talk with them about why they're writing and for whom, about what they're doing to write well, and/or about their writing process. During this talk, which Lucy Calkins (1994; Calkins, Hartman, and White 2003, 2005) describes as the "research" part of a conference, we find our assessment focus. We have four responsibilities:

The Role of the Teacher and the Student in a Writing Conference

The Teacher's Role	The Student's Role
In the first part of the conversation:	
• Invite the child to set an agenda for the conference. • Ask assessment questions. • Read the student's writing. • Make a teaching decision.	• Set the agenda for the conference by describing her writing work. • Respond to her teacher's research questions by describing her writing work more deeply.
In the second part of the conversation:	
• Give the student critical feedback. • Teach the student. • Nudge the student to say how she can use what has been taught. • Link the conference to the student's independent work.	• Listen carefully to her teacher's feedback and teaching. • Ask questions to clarify and deepen her understanding of her teacher's feedback and teaching. • Attempt to apply what her teacher has taught her. • Commit to trying what her teacher has taught her after the conference.

This chart is adapted from my book *How's It Going? A Practical Guide to Conferring with Student Writers* (2000).

FIGURE 7.3

1. We ask an open-ended question that invites the child to set the conference agenda (*How's it going?* or *What are you doing as a writer today?*). The student's response is our first opportunity to find an assessment focus. In my conference with Smith, I asked, "What are you doing with your essay today?" Smith's reply ("making corrections") was too general for me to be able to identify an assessment focus.

2. We ask assessment questions. The student's responses give us information about our assessment focus, or if we don't yet have a focus, help us identify one. In my conference with Smith, I asked what he meant by "making corrections." Smith told me he wanted to revise by adding some "new stuff" to the "important parts." My assessment focus then became what

Smith knew about developing the parts of his essay. To gather more information, I asked, "What do you want me to understand after I read your finished essay?" His response, "That problems can happen if you forget how to speak your other language," showed me he had an idea he was trying to get across.

3. We read the student's writing. If we still haven't decided on an assessment focus, we should be able to after this. When I read Smith's draft, I saw it had the main components of a personal essay. He had an idea (that learning a second language can cause problems in one's family) and a personal story (a time when he was trying to explain his homework to his mother). I also noticed he had written just three sentences in the narrative part of his essay and had not written his idea very clearly.

4. We decide, based on what we've learned, what to teach the child that will help him become a better writer. At this point in my conference with Smith, I knew his plan to work on the parts of his essay was a good one. Having noticed that he had barely developed the story of trying to explain his homework to his mother, I decided to teach him how important it is to develop the parts of an essay that help him make his point.

The Second Part

In the second part of the conference conversation, we talk with students about how to be better writers. Our goal is to teach them something about writing that helps them grow as writers. We have four responsibilities here:

1. We give the students feedback, pointing out what we've noticed about their work and telling them what we're going to teach them. In my conference with Smith, I gave him feedback about his knowledge of the genre. I told him he had a story and an idea in his essay, the components of this kind of writing. And I told him that he had written just three sentences about the time he had tried to explain his homework to his mother.

2. We teach. In my conference with Smith, I taught him something about structure, an aspect of writing well. I explained that in a personal essay, it's important for writers to develop their stories to help readers understand their ideas.

3. We ask the student to have a go—to attempt to apply what he's just learned. That is, we nudge the student to talk

through how he can use what we've taught him. This assisted performance, which Katie Wood Ray (1999) calls "writing in the air," gives students the confidence to continue trying out what we've taught them once the conference is over. In this part of my conference with Smith, I asked him to tell me more about trying to explain his homework to his mother. With my assistance, he was able to stretch out this part of his essay orally.

4. We link the conference to the student's independent writing, letting him know we expect him to try what we've taught. We might say, "I'll check back with you in ten minutes to see how you're doing," or "Would you show me what you've done later in the period?" To end my conference with Smith, I told him that I expected he would now work on stretching out the story part of his essay: "Instead of just three sentences, see if you can tell the story of you and your mom and the homework with more sentences." I also connected what I wanted him to do with my teaching point: "The better you tell that story, the better I'm going to understand what you're trying to tell me about losing Spanish."

In Conferences, We Show That We Care About Students as Writers—and as People

In the end, the success of a conference often rests on the extent to which students sense that we are interested in them as writers—and as people. We enter into most conversations because we care about the person with whom we're talking. Donald Graves (2003) believes the most important thing about a conference is the look of expectation on the teacher's face—the look that communicates that she expects the student to be writing about something interesting, and to be doing interesting work as a writer.

With all the pressure we feel today as teachers to raise test scores and get students to meet standards, it's all too easy to forget to communicate how much we care about them as people and as writers. It's easy to see only the work and not the young writers who are doing it.

In my conference with Smith, I hope he saw a look of expectation on my face as I talked with him. I hope he felt that I was interested in—and concerned about—what he was saying from how I listened when he told me about "losing Spanish" and from how I responded: "So you're writing about a change in you that makes you worry about your relationships with your family?" Likewise, I hope he felt that I was intensely interested in the work he was planning to do as a writer.

In general, we show students we care about them by how we talk with them about their topics and their writing. When we ask *How's it going?* at the beginning of conferences, students can hear in our tone of voice and see by the expression on our face that we really are interested in how their writing is going. As conferences unfold, we listen intently to everything students tell us about what they're doing, because we're genuinely curious to learn more about their work.

By truly listening as we confer with children about their writing, we let them know that the work they're doing matters. It's the way we listen, more than anything else, that will nudge our students to look at us with a smile instead of a frown when we sit down next to them. It's the way we listen that can inspire students to stretch themselves as writers. The way we listen can change students' writing lives.

TEACHER ACTION 7.1

Analyze your conferences with students.

- During writing workshop, take a few minutes after each of your writing conferences to jot down on your record-keeping form the one thing you taught in the conference.

- Prepare a transcript of a conference (either from memory or while listening to a tape recording). Label each of the conversational moves you made (inviting the child to set the conference agenda, asking assessment questions, reading the student's writing, making a teaching decision, giving feedback, teaching, nudging the student to have a go, and linking the conference to the student's independent writing). Which of these moves do you feel you did well? Why? Which ones do you still need to work on? Why? Did you leave out one (or more) of these moves?

- Ask a colleague, your literacy coach, or your principal to observe you as you confer and then give you feedback on what he or she saw you do.

- Look at the work that students did after several conferences. What does this work tell you about the effectiveness of your conferring? What could you do differently to achieve better results with your students?

How Do We Find an Assessment Focus in a Conference?

One of the most difficult challenges in a writing conference is identifying an assessment focus. One reason is that much of the writing on conferring—my own book included—seems to cast teachers in a passive role. We begin conferences by asking *How's it going?* and then wait for students to tell us what they're doing as writers.

But I don't in any way play a passive role. I go into every conference looking for very specific things. Ultimately, I focus on assessing one of the three aspects of a lifelong writer: initiating writing, writing well, or having an effective writing process. And in each conference, I teach something about initiating writing, writing well, or developing an effective writing process. That becomes the line of growth I nudge a child along through my conference teaching. A line of growth is an aspect of writing that I help a child get better at over time. In conferences throughout the school year, I focus on numerous lines of growth with my students, helping each of them as writers in many ways (see Figure 7.4).

Here's what goes on in my mind as I try to identify an assessment focus in a conference. After I ask *How's it going?* I listen very carefully to what a child tells me. I'm hoping to learn something about a child's initiative as a writer, about what he's doing to write well, or about his writing process. In many conferences, children give me information about one (or more) of these aspects of themselves as writers, thereby giving me at least one possible assessment focus.

But what about conferences in which a child doesn't say very much about himself as a writer? Or conferences in which what the child says isn't something I want to help him with?

Those scenarios are not disasters. I just proceed to a repertoire of assessment questions that get students to talk about different aspects of themselves as writers. For example, the question *Why are you writing this?* leads students to talk about their purposes for writing their current pieces. And the question *What does this piece need?* encourages students to talk about what they could do to write as well as possible.

How do I choose which questions to ask? In many conferences, my individual learning plan for the student leads me to ask a particular assessment question. Let's say I've learned that a child doesn't have many reasons to write beyond satisfying his teacher's expectation that he write. In that case, in the next few conferences I make sure to ask him, "Why are you writing this?" I also choose assessment questions connected to the current unit of study. For example, if I've spent the last few weeks teaching students to give their writing voice by using

Student ____Alex____

Conferences Across the Year

Trait	Line of Growth	1	2	3	4	5	6	7	8	9	10	11	12...
Initiative	Purpose	9/7									1/4		
	Audience												
Writing Well	Meaning								12/8				2/2
	Genre knowledge			10/7									
	Structure						11/15						
	Detail											1/18	
	Voice												
	Conventions				10/21			11/22					
Process	Rehearsal					10/28							
	Drafting/revising		9/23							12/20			
	Editing												

Figure 7.4

certain sentence structures, I ask, "What are you doing to try to get your voice into your writing?"

A possible teaching point becomes my definite teaching point when what the child tells me about what he's doing as a writer matches a goal in that child's individual learning plan or is connected to the current (or a recent) unit of study.

Bearing in mind that we're looking for one of three specific assessment focuses when we confer, let's take a look at conferences on initiating writing, writing well, and the writing process.

Conferences on Initiating Writing

In these conferences, we teach students to see writing as a meaningful action that will *do* something for them in the world. We help students grapple with purposes for writing, genres in which they could write, or audiences for whom they might write.

Many teachers tell me that students talk much more about their writing process and what they're doing to write well than about why they're writing and for whom. I point out that students may indeed have purposes for writing and audiences in mind but don't know we want them to tell us these things. It's important that we let students know we want them to share this kind of information. One way is by presenting minilessons about the reasons writers write and the audiences for whom they write. Students are much more likely to imagine purposes and audiences for their writing—and talk about them—when we address these issues explicitly in our teaching.

Some of the questions I ask to prompt students to talk about their initiative as writers include

- Why are you writing this?
- Which genre are you planning to write in? Why?
- Which genre are you writing in? Why?
- Who do you hope will read this?

I had the following conference on initiating writing with Teddy, a sixth grader. Teddy's class was studying feature articles. One of the reasons Teddy's teacher decided to study this genre was so students could explore a new purpose for writing: teaching others about a topic.

ME: How's it going?
TEDDY: Good.
ME: What are you doing today as a writer?
TEDDY: I'm going to write about vegetables.
ME: So you're an expert on vegetables. . . .
TEDDY: Yeah. They're good for you.
ME: And you want to teach people about them in your article. . . .

[*Teddy shrugs.*] I'm curious. Why do you want to write about vegetables? [*Teddy shrugs again.*] Are you really excited to write about them?

TEDDY: [*With surprise*] No.

ME: Teddy, I'm getting the feeling that you aren't really that interested in writing about vegetables. Am I right?

TEDDY: [*Sheepishly*] Yeah.

ME: Your class has read quite a few feature articles. Why do you think the authors wrote them?

TEDDY: [*After thinking for a moment*] I don't understand the question.

ME: Why do you think people write feature articles?

TEDDY: [*Shrugs*] Because they know a lot about the topic?

ME: The thing to know about feature articles is that people write them about topics they're really interested in, so they can teach others what they know. One of the reasons your class is studying feature articles is so you can experience what it's like to teach others with your writing. [*Teddy nods.*] So I'd like you to think about what you really know something about and might enjoy telling others.

TEDDY: [*After a moment*] Well . . . football.

ME: Football. Do you play football? Or like to watch football?

TEDDY: Both.

ME: Do you think you might want to write a feature article about something you know about football, something about football that you're really interested in?

TEDDY: Yeah, like the different positions. Or maybe . . . some of the really good teams. What makes them good.

ME: I think you're on to something. You seem much more interested in writing about football than about vegetables. You might want to list some other things you know a lot about in your notebook and then make a decision about the topic for your article. Maybe it will be something about football; maybe it will be something else you really know and care about. Remember, though, that you'll want to write a feature article about something you're really interested in and really know a lot about, so that you can really teach your readers about your topic.

TEDDY: OK.

ME: Good talking to you.

TEDDY: Thanks.

In this conference, I found out that Teddy didn't seem to have any purpose for writing about his topic except to meet the requirement that he write a feature article, nor did he seem to understand why writers write feature articles. In response, I taught him about an important reason

TEACHER ACTION 7.2

Try conferences on initiating writing.

- Make it a point to ask students assessment questions that will give you information about them as initiators of writing. When you identify one of the scenarios listed in Figure 7.5, teach the corresponding lesson to the student.

- If your students don't talk as much about themselves as initiators of writing as you would like, teach a minilesson on how they might do this. Give examples of how they can talk about their purposes for writing, why they decided to write in the genre they've chosen, and the audiences for whom they're writing.

writers write in the genre, helped him find a topic in which he was genuinely interested, and helped him try out this purpose for writing.

There are several different kinds of conferences focusing on initiating writing (see Figure 7.5). While I could have any one of them at any time during the school year, there are some times in which I expect to make students' initiative the assessment focus of many conferences. One is when I launch writing workshop. It's imperative to assess students' initiative as writers *right away,* identifying those students who find writing to be a meaningful activity and those who do not. Those who don't find writing meaningful will need help discovering what writing can do for them. These students are much more likely to be receptive to our teaching throughout the year if they are invested in their writing.

I also expect to have conferences on initiating writing when a class is studying a genre students haven't written in before. Requiring all the students in a class to write in one genre limits the kinds of purposes they can have. Students who have no previous experience writing in the genre may have no sense of what the genre can do for them. While the genre study gives them the opportunity to discover a new purpose for writing or a new means for realizing a purpose for which they've already written, it's nonetheless important to ask students why they're writing. If they shrug or say, "Because you're telling me I have to," we need to help them find purposes that matter.

Conferences on Writing Well

In these conferences, we teach children about one of the traits of good writing. Given that there are numerous traits, one of the challenges is

Purposes for Writing

If I learn this . . .	I might . . .
The student isn't able to articulate why he's writing the piece he's working on.	Talk with the student about some of the reasons he could have for writing the piece.
The student doesn't seem to be invested in writing about his topic.	Help the student discover a worthwhile purpose for writing about the topic or help the student think of a new topic that would give him a good reason to write.
The student writes for the same purpose again and again.	Talk with the student about other purposes for writing and nudge the student to try writing for one of these purposes.

Genre

If I learn this . . .	I might . . .
The student has a purpose for writing but isn't sure of which genre to use.	Suggest genres that would be good vehicles for the student's purpose for writing.
The student is writing in a genre that doesn't seem like a good fit for his purpose.	Help the student imagine a different genre that would better match his purpose.
The student writes in the same genre over and over again.	Suggest other genres the student can write in to help him experience some new purposes for writing.

Audience

If I learn this . . .	I might . . .
The student isn't able to name an audience for whom he is writing.	Help the student imagine an audience—a person, group, or readers of a particular publication—to share his writing with when he is finished.
The student is writing for the same audience again and again.	Suggest other audiences with whom the student could share his writing.
The student has an audience in mind for his piece but doesn't realize that it could be shared with other kinds of audiences.	Talk about how a piece of writing might be shared with several different audiences and help the student imagine who those audiences could be.

FIGURE 7.5   Examples of Conferences Focused on Initating Writing

picking one on which to focus, especially when most children need help with every one of them. There are a couple of ways to decide.

Sometimes the student tells us he's working on one of the traits of good writing and this trait becomes the focus of the conference. But if a student says things are going fine or that he's done, we can nudge him to tell us about what he's doing to write well by asking assessment questions like these:

- What are you doing to write well as you draft?
- How are you crafting this piece?
- What does your draft still need to be a good piece of writing?
- What did you do to write really well in your draft?
- What revisions did you make? Could you explain why you made these revisions?

When a student is editing—the final stage of the writing process, in which it makes sense to teach the child something about using conventions—we can ask one of these assessment questions:

- What kinds of edits are you making? Why?
- What kinds of errors are you discovering as you edit?

In some conferences we ask more specific questions that nudge students to talk about a particular trait of good writing (see Figure 7.6). Our individual learning plans for students will lead us to ask these specific kinds of assessment questions. If I know that a student tends to write about every single part of an experience (a bed-to-bed story) instead of just the parts that help get her point across, I'll be sure to ask, "What are you trying to say in this piece?" and "How are the parts you're writing about helping you say this?" Or if I know a student isn't consistently capitalizing the first word of each sentence in his writing, I'll ask, "How are you doing with capitalizing in your draft?" in an editing conference.

We also ask these specific questions when we're focusing on a particular trait in a unit of study and expect the students in the class to be paying attention to that trait in their writing. For example, if I've spent the last week teaching minilessons about how to write with different kinds of detail—dialogue, a character's thoughts, characters' actions—I'll be sure to ask, "How are you writing with detail in your draft?" If I've given several minilessons on using semicolons, I'll ask students, "How are you using semicolons in your writing?"

When I visited Marge Coughlin's fifth-grade classroom, Marge was concerned because many of her students weren't paragraphing their writing. Therefore, I taught a minilesson on paragraphing in which I showed the class an excerpt from Jean Little's *Little by Little* (1987; see Figure 7.7) and discussed why Little paragraphed where she did.

When the Conference Is Focused on This Quality of Good Writing	These Are Specific Research Questions You Can Ask
Meaning	• What are you trying to say in this piece? • What do want readers to know about your topic when they read your piece?
Genre	• What genre are you writing in? • In what ways is your piece like the ones we've read in this genre?
Structure	• Why have you included this section? • What kinds of parts have you included in this piece? • What are you trying to do in your lead? • What are you trying to do in your ending? • How is your piece organized? • Which parts are the really important ones that help you make your point?
Detail	• Why have you included this detail? • Are there any details you don't think are necessary? • What kinds of details have you included in your piece? • Which words have you selected to help you give readers a picture of what you're talking about?
Voice	• How have you tried to get your voice into your writing? • How have you written your sentences to give your writing voice? • How have you been using punctuation to give your writing voice?
Conventions	• What are you looking for as you edit? • What kinds of edits have you made? Why? • How have you been using semicolons [or any other punctuation mark that you've given minilessons about] in your writing?

FIGURE 7.6   Specific Research Questions We Can Ask in Conferences on Writing Well

"This is Jean Little," my new teacher told the class. She led me to a desk.

"This is Pamela, Jean," she said, smiling at the girl in the desk next to mine. I smiled at her, too.

Pamela's cheeks got pink. She looked away. I thought I knew what was wrong. She was shy. I sat down and waited for lessons to start. I was glad that reading was first.

When it was my turn to read out loud, I held the book up to my nose as usual. The other children giggled. The teacher hushed them. Then she turned to me.

"Are those your reading glasses?" she asked.

I was not sure. I snatched the glasses off and switched. But I still had to hold my book so close that my nose brushed against the page. Everybody stared. Nobody noticed my good reading.

That afternoon when the teacher left the room, Monica pointed at me.

"Look!" she crowed. "She's got black all over her nose!"

I clapped my hand to my face. The class burst into peals of laughter. They only broke off when the child nearest the door hissed, "Shh! She's coming."

When the teacher walked into the room, I longed to tell, but I didn't. I knew tattletales were despised by everyone. I spat on the corner of my handkerchief and scrubbed my short nose until it felt raw. But a red nose was better than a nose smudged with printer's ink.

The next morning nobody sat with me at break. That afternoon, Jane waved her hand before my face.

FIGURE 7.7   Excerpt from Jean Little's *Little by Little*

After the minilesson, I had a conference with Mohammed, who was writing a story about his family's vacation to Orlando, Florida (see Figure 7.8). Marge told me he needed help with paragraphing.

ME: What are you doing as a writer today?
MOHAMMED: Editing.
ME: How's that going?
MOHAMMED: Good.
ME: What kinds of things are you looking for as you edit?
MOHAMMED: I'm checking my paragraphing.
ME: Tell me about it.

On My Vacation

On my vacation we drove all the way to Orlando Florida. It took us 16 hours to get to our hotel. We stayed at a five star hotel. The name of the hotel was Rosen Central Hotel.

The first day we went to Seaworld. We saw two shows. The first show was with killer whales. The people were standing on the whales while the whale jumped up in the air. When the show was over my whole family except for me got wet. The next show was a sea lion show. This show was really funny because they messed up so much. After that it started raining really hard but we didn't go home because it ended really quick. After the rain we went to a ride called Journey to Atlantis. We would go up and then go really fast down. My nephew started to cry.

On the second day I went to Universal Studios. We went on a lot of rides. My favorite ride was Jurassic Park. It is basically like Journey to Atlantis except that T-Rex pops out as soon as you fall. We also saw two shows in Universal Studios. One of the shows was something about Neptune and an evil guy fighting in a battle 100 centuries ago. The coolest part of the show was when the water circled around us. The second show was Matt Hoffman. . . .

FIGURE 7.8   Mohammed's First Draft

MOHAMMED: Well . . . I've paragraphed here [*pointing to his first sentence*] and here [*pointing to the sentence beginning "The first day . . ."*] and here [*pointing to the sentence beginning "On the second day . . ."*].

ME: [*After skimming Mohammed's draft*] Why did you paragraph in these places?

MOHAMMED: Because . . . those were the places where new days started.

ME: Well, that's smart that you did that. Writers do start new paragraphs to help let readers know that some time has gone by, like one day turning into the next. Where do you think you need to do more paragraphing?

MOHAMMED: [*Skimming his draft*] I'm not sure.

ME: That's OK. But you're right to think you should break up your story into some more paragraphs. [*I take out the excerpt from* Little by Little.] Here, take a look at the first part of the Jean Little piece, in which one whole day goes by. Do you see that there are a whole lot of paragraphs in this section, though? [*Counting them*] Eleven paragraphs, actually.

MOHAMMED: Yeah.

ME: [*Pointing*] In the first paragraph, the teacher is leading Jean Little to her desk. In the second, the teacher is smiling at Pamela. In the third, Jean and Pamela are sitting next to each other at their desks. In the fourth, some time seems to have gone by, and it's Jean's turn to read aloud. Are you following me?

MOHAMMED: Yes.

ME: I think Jean Little made a new paragraph every time something new happens in the story—a new action or when some time has gone by. Making a new paragraph is a way to let readers know that something new is happening in a story. [*Mohammed nods.*] Here's what I'd like you to do now. Read the part of your story that starts right here [*pointing to the section beginning "The first day . . ."*]. As you read, look for places where something new is happening. Stop and tell me when you find them. Those will be the places where you need to make some new paragraphs.

MOHAMMED: OK. [*He reads the section.*] Well . . . here. [*Reading aloud*] "The next show was a sea lion show." That's something new. And this part about when it rained, that could be a paragraph.

ME: Do you see any other places where something new happens? [*Mohammed shakes his head.*] What about this part here? [*I point to the sentence beginning "After the rain . . ."*] Isn't something new happening in your story here, too?

MOHAMMED: [*Smiling*] I think so.

ME: Good. There are a couple of things I want you to do when we're finished talking. Read through the rest of your piece, and keep doing what you're doing, thinking about where you need to paragraph. Remember to look for places where something new happens in the story. Something else I'm noticing is that some of your paragraphs will be just a sentence long. You might need to stretch out those paragraphs and add more detail, OK?

MOHAMMED: OK.

ME: It was good talking with you.

MOHAMMED: Thanks.

In this conference, I found out that while Mohammed did indeed know some reasons for paragraphing, there were others he needed to learn. In response, I used Jean Little's writing to help him learn about one of these reasons. After the conference, Mohammed reread his draft and decided to start a new paragraph in several places in his story (see Figure 7.9).

There are many kinds of conferences on writing well, each connected to one of the traits of good writing (see Figures 7.10a and 7.10b), and they make up the majority of my conferences during the school year. However, during the first few weeks of school, I have very

On My Vacation

On my vacation we drove all the way to Orlando Florida. It took us 16 hours to get to our hotel. We stayed at a five star hotel. The name of the hotel was Rosen Central Hotel.

The first day we went to Seaworld. We saw two shows. The first show was with killer whales. The people were standing on the whales while the whale jumped up in the air.

When the show was over my whole family except for me got wet.

The next show was a sea lion show. This show was really funny because they messed up so much.

After that it started raining really hard but we didn't go home because it ended really quick.

After the rain we went to a ride called Journey to Atlantis. It was a water ride. We would go up and then go really fast down. My nephew started to cry.

On the second day . . .

FIGURE 7.9   The First Part of Mohammed's Final Draft

few conferences that fall into this category; my early conferences are often geared to helping students become more invested in writing or to teaching them to use the tools and strategies they'll need to write independently (process conferences).

TEACHER ACTION 7.3

Try conferences on writing well.

- Make it a point to ask students assessment questions that will give you information about what they do to write well. When you identify one of the scenarios listed in Figures 7.10a and 7.10b, teach the corresponding lesson to that student.

- If your students don't talk as much about what they are doing to write well as you would like, present a minilesson about how to do this. Give examples of how they can talk about what they're doing or are planning to do to write their pieces as best they can.

Meaning

If I learn this . . .	I might . . .
The student knows what she wants to say about her topic, but she hasn't communicated her point anywhere in her draft (this applies to genres in which the writer typically makes her point explicit).	Show her several model texts in the genre she's writing in and point out where in these texts the writer lets readers know her meaning.
The student has tried to communicate what she wants to say about her topic in her draft, but her meaning isn't clear.	Nudge her to clarify her meaning in her draft.
The student isn't sure of what she wants to say in her draft.	Ask her what she wants to say about her topic and teach her to write this in an appropriate place in her draft.

Genre

If I learn this . . .	I might . . .
The student knows about some of the features of the genre she's writing in but not others.	Point out another feature in a model text and suggest that she incorporate this feature in her writing.
The student knows some things about a feature of the genre she's writing in, but there's more to learn about this feature.	Look at a model text with her and discuss other aspects of the feature in question.

Structure

If I learn this . . .	I might . . .
The student has included sections that don't seem to help develop her meaning.	Teach her to delete unnecessary sections or to rewrite these sections so that they do help develop her meaning.
The student gives equal weight to all sections of her piece.	Teach her to stretch the parts of the piece that best develop her meaning.
The order of the sections in a student's piece seems random.	Teach the student to order her piece by time (in a narrative) or by logic (in nonnarrative genres).
The student knows to grab the reader's attention in her lead, but she doesn't let readers know where she's going in the rest of the piece.	Teach the student how to write a lead that states her meaning or puts the reader on a path toward meaning.
In nonnarrative genres, the student abruptly shifts from one section to another.	Teach the student to use subheadings or to write topic sentences that signal the shift from one section to the next.

FIGURE 7.10A   Examples of Conferences on Writing Well

Details

If I learn this . . .	I might . . .
The student includes details that don't develop her meaning.	Teach her to delete extraneous details.
There is little detail in the student's piece that helps develop her meaning.	Show her how to add detail that develops her meaning.
The student relies on just one or two kinds of details in her piece.	Teach her about other kinds of details that writers use in this genre.
The student's sentences are very simple in structure.	Teach the student to combine simple sentences into more complex sentences.
The student uses very general nouns and/or verbs.	Teach her to use more specific nouns and/or verbs.

Voice

If I learn this . . .	I might . . .
The student's writing lacks voice because she relies on the same sentence structures throughout the piece.	Teach her new sentence structures (by looking at sentences in a model text) that will increase her repertoire of sentence types and help give her writing voice.
The student relies on just a few kinds of punctuation marks.	Show the student how some new punctuation marks (elipses, commas, dashes, etc.) can signal to a reader how she wants the piece to be read.
The student's writing sounds like anyone could have written it.	Teach the student to include details in her writing that define who she is as an individual.

Conventions

If I learn this . . .	I might . . .
The student is not punctuating a certain kind of sentence correctly (e.g., a compound sentence).	Teach the student how this sentence is conventionally punctuated.
The student is not yet using a particular kind of punctuation mark correctly (e.g., quotation marks).	Point out in a model text how a writer uses the punctuation mark.
The student doesn't understand a grammatical convention (e.g., she uses *me* as the subject instead of *I*).	Teach the student how to use the grammatical convention correctly.
The student misspells frequently used words.	Give the student a list of the frequently used words that she misspells and have her use the list to help her write these words correctly.

FIGURE 7.10B   Examples of Conferences on Writing Well

Process Conferences

In a process conference, we help a child develop a more effective writing process, perhaps teaching him how to use a writing tool (such as a writer's notebook or the cut-and-paste function of a word-processing program) or a writing strategy (such as making a plan for a piece or rereading a draft).

There are several reasons we can decide to have a process conference with a student. Sometimes, when I ask a student *How's it going?* she tells me what stage of the writing process she's in ("I'm prewriting") and what tool or strategy she's using ("I'm making a plan for my piece"). Teaching her something about how to use the tool or strategy then often becomes the focus of the conference.

In other conferences, a student tells me what he's doing to write well ("I'm adding detail"). As I talk to him and look at his writing, I may realize that he needs to learn how to use a particular strategy ("Reread your piece, and stop at the end of each sentence to think about whether it makes sense to add a line of dialogue") to help him write well in the way he is attempting.

Sometimes we need to ask students assessment questions to nudge them to talk about their writing process:

- Where are you in the writing process—rehearsing? Drafting? Revising? Editing?
- What are you doing as you're rehearsing? Drafting? Revising? Editing?
- How are you doing the work you're doing?
- What tools are you using as you write? How is each tool helping you write well?
- What strategies are you using as you write? How are these strategies helping you write well?

Sometimes we need to ask specific questions to gather information about how students are using particular tools and strategies. Often these questions are based on the goals we've written down for these students on their individual learning plans. If I've written down, "Help Amanda with planning," then I'll be sure to ask her, "Have you made a plan?" the next time she's getting ready to draft or has just started a draft. Or if I've devoted a series of recent minilessons to teaching a tool or strategy, I'll ask students if they're using it in their writing and how it's going. If I've taught the class how to box out their drafts during revision—circle the sections of a draft to help them focus on each part—I'll ask, "Did you try boxing out your draft?" and/or "How has boxing out your draft helped you revise it?"

One afternoon I visited Dawn Walsh's third-grade class when they were in the middle of a poetry unit. In recent minilessons, Dawn had

> **Fox**
> Creeping in the brushes
> Fur as red as a rose,
> his eyes transfixed on a
> chipmunk,
> Then,
> at the last second
> pounces,
> and swallows in one
>
> Gulp!

FIGURE 7.11   First Draft of Caleb's Poem

been teaching that one reason poets end lines—that is, make line breaks—is to cue their readers to pause slightly in their reading. In my minilesson that day, I showed how poets put spaces between lines— that is, add white space—for the same reason. After the minilesson I had a process conference with Caleb, who was working on a poem about a fox hunting prey (see Figure 7.11).

ME: Hi, Caleb, how's it going? What are you doing with your poem?

CALEB: I don't know. I think I could use a lot more line breaks and white space.

ME: Sounds as if you're thinking you might want to craft your poem by working on your line breaks and white space.

CALEB: Yeah.

ME: How are you going to do this?

CALEB: [*After reading the poem to himself*] I think I'm going to put a line break . . . one's going to go there [*pointing to the space after the word* eyes *on the third line*].

ME: OK . . . why do you want to do that?

CALEB: Well . . . to make the reader read it like it's really happening . . . like they're watching it.

ME: You want to sound like it's happening, so you're going to make some shorter lines to put in pauses and slow the poem down.

CALEB: Yeah.

ME: And what else . . . you said you want to use some more white space, too?

CALEB: Yeah. [*Reading*] "At the last second / pounces" . . . white space right there.

ME: After the word *pounces*?

CALEB: Yeah.

ME: Caleb, could you read your poem to me?

CALEB: Sure. [*He reads the poem aloud dramatically.*]

ME: Well, I think you've got some good plans for this poem. What I like about this poem about the fox is that it gives a really dramatic image of a fox creeping up on this chipmunk and all of a sudden it pounces on it and—gulp!—the chipmunk is history. [*Caleb smiles.*] So you want the poem to sound like it's happening when people read it. You know, when you read the poem, it sounded just like that—you read it slowly, with a lot of pauses, just the way a fox would creep up gradually on a chipmunk. But I noticed that when you read it aloud, you paused in places where you're not planning on putting line breaks and white space. When I've got a draft of a poem, I read the poem out loud and listen for the places where my voice pauses. If it's a short pause, I'll try a line break at that point. If it's a longer, more dramatic pause, I might add some white space right there.

CALEB: OK.

ME: Try reading it again, and this time listen for where your voice pauses. [*Caleb reads the poem aloud a second time.*] What did you hear?

CALEB: I'm going to read it again. [*He does.*]

ME: What did you hear?

CALEB: Maybe . . . [*reading*] "At the last second" . . . white space . . . "pounces" . . . then white space again . . . "and swallows" . . . then a line break right there, after "swallows."

ME: Wow. This is a really dramatic part of your poem, where the fox is pouncing on the chipmunk. Putting white space before and after the word *pounces* and the line break after *swallows* really slows the poem up there, and helps create a feeling of tension and drama. I think you've got some good ideas.

CALEB: Yeah.

ME: Why don't you read the poem out loud a couple of more times and listen for pauses that tell you where you might break more lines and add more white space.

CALEB: OK.

ME: I can't wait to see what you come up with.

In this conference, I found out Caleb knew that line breaks and white space help guide the way a reader reads a poem. But he didn't seem to have a strategy that would enable him to hear where he wanted to break his lines and use white space. In response, I taught him the strategy of reading his poem aloud and listening for where he paused. After the conference was over, Caleb reread his poem and, using this

Fox
Creeping in the brushes
fur red as a rose,
his blood-curdling eyes
transfixed on a chipmunk

then,
at the last second

springs,

into the crisp air and
swiftly hits the ground
with a loud thump
    and
swallows in one

Gulp.

FIGURE 7.12   Second Draft of Caleb's Poem

strategy, found a way to use line breaks and white space to signal to readers how to read his poem (see Figure 7.12).

There are numerous kinds of process conferences (see Figure 7.13). Although I have process conferences throughout the school year, most of my conferences during the first month of school are about the writing process. One of the goals of launching a writing workshop is to help students write independently, so that we don't need to take time each day to explain to students what they should be doing. Therefore, they need to develop a repertoire of writing tools and strategies. In my early conferences I teach students what they need to do to navigate the various stages of the writing process.

Once my students are able to move through the writing process with a degree of independence, the focus of my conferences shifts to helping them write well. As students begin to try out what I've taught them about writing well in minilessons and conferences, I often need to teach them a strategy to help them use these lessons in their writing. Caleb is a good example. He understood the *why* of line breaks and white space but needed help with the *how*. Conferences with students who understand an aspect of writing well but not how to apply that concept as they write become process conferences.

Rehearsal

If I learn this . . .	I might . . .
The student has a topic but isn't sure about what he wants to say about his topic.	Ask him to freewrite in his writer's notebook in response to the question, *What do I want to say about my topic?*
The student knows his topic and has a sense of what he wants to say but, when asked, seems short on specifics of his topic.	Have the student write several entries in his writer's notebook in order to gather some of the details he will need to write well about his topic.
The student is ready to plunge into a draft, but he hasn't done much thinking about how the draft will go.	Teach the student to make a plan for his writing—a flowchart, a web, or an outline.

Drafting and Revising

If I learn this . . .	I might . . .
The student is having trouble getting back into his draft when he returns to it each day.	Teach the student to reread his draft before he tries to write each day.
The student is trying to craft a part of his draft (the lead, a scene, a topic sentence, an ending, etc.) but isn't sure of how to do it well.	Have the student look at a model text to get an image of how to craft his writing in the way he wishes.
The student wants to add to his draft but doesn't have room on his paper to do this work.	Teach him a revision strategy that will allow him to add on to his draft—carets, arrows, footnotes, Sticky notes, spiderlegs (taping strips of paper to the side of the draft).
The student isn't sure that he's done a good job with an aspect of his draft—his lead, the amount of detail in a section, his tone, the specificity of his words, and so on.	Have the student read his writing to a writing partner or response group to get feedback.

Editing

If I learn this . . .	I might . . .
The student edits by reading his writing to himself.	Teach the student how reading his writing aloud can help him hear missing words or errors in punctuation.
After self-editing, careless errors remain in the student's draft.	Teach the student how to have an effective peer conference to get help in identifying careless errors.
There are certain words the student has trouble spelling.	Help the student create a list of these troublesome words to refer to when he edits.

FIGURE 7.13   Examples of Conferences on the Writing Process

TEACHER ACTION 7.4

Try a process conference.

- Make a point to ask students assessment questions that will give you information about their writing process. When you identify one of the scenarios listed in Figure 7.13, teach the corresponding lesson to that student.

- If your students don't talk as much about their writing processes as you would like, present a minilesson about how to do this. Give examples of what they can say about the stage of the writing process they're in and the tools and strategies they're using in that stage.

How Do We Decide What to Teach a Student in a Conference?

Once we've identified our assessment focus, we're on the path to making a decision about what to teach the student with whom we're conferring. In the instant that we figure out the focus, we ask ourselves two questions:

- What have I learned so far in this conference about what the student knows about this aspect of writing?

- What do I still need to learn about what the student knows about this aspect of writing to help me make my teaching decision?

The first question pushes us to make sense of what we have learned so far about the student as a writer from his responses to both the open-ended *How's it going?* and our more specific assessment questions. If we needed to look at the child's writing to help us find a focus for the conference, then we have learned some things about the child from that source of information, too.

The second question pushes us to gather more information about the child. We might want to ask more assessment questions about the aspect of writing on which we're focusing. Or if we haven't yet looked at the child's writing, we'll want to do that to gather more information about what the student knows.

Ultimately, our goal in asking these two questions is to help figure out where a child is as a writer on the line of growth the conference is focusing on and what the appropriate next step for him as a writer should be to move him forward on this line.

Let's take another look at the first few minutes of the conference I had with Teddy. This time, I'll include the thinking I was doing as the conference unfolded.

ME: How's it going?
TEDDY: Good.
ME: What are you doing today as a writer?
TEDDY: I'm going to write about vegetables.
ME: So you're an expert on vegetables. . . .
TEDDY: Yeah. They're good for you.
ME: And you want to teach people about them in your article. . . .
    [*Teddy shrugs.*]

Teddy's shrug is the first clue that he doesn't have a purpose for writing about his topic that really matters to him. I decide to ask Teddy some assessment questions about his reasons for choosing his topic.

ME: I'm curious. Why do you want to write about vegetables? [*Teddy shrugs again.*] Are you really excited to write about them?
TEDDY: [*With surprise*] No.
ME: Teddy, I'm getting the feeling that you aren't really that interested in writing about vegetables. Am I right?
TEDDY: [*Sheepishly*] Yeah.

At this point I decide to make Teddy's initiative as a writer the focus of the conference. So far, I've learned that Teddy isn't invested in writing about the topic he's chosen. To help me decide what to teach Teddy about the purposes he could have, I need to know what he knows about the purposes for writing a feature article. So I ask him.

ME: Your class has read quite a few feature articles. Why do you think the authors wrote them?
TEDDY: [*After thinking for a moment*] I don't understand the question.
ME: Why do you think people write feature articles?
TEDDY: [*Shrugs*] Because they know a lot about the topic?

While Teddy is right that feature article writers know a lot about their topic, he doesn't seem to understand that these writers write to share what they know with others. Thus, I decide I want Teddy to learn about this purpose for writing. To do this, I need to help Teddy find a topic on which he really is an expert and about which he is genuinely enthusiastic. By writing about such a topic and sharing his finished article with readers—his classmates—Teddy has the best chance of learning that he can teach others through writing. That becomes the focus of teaching in the rest of the conference.

Let's also take another look at the first few minutes of the conference with Mohammed. Even though this conference had a different focus—writing well—I still went through the same assessment process in my mind.

ME: What are you doing as a writer today?
MOHAMMED: Editing.
ME: How's that going?
MOHAMMED: Good.
ME: What kinds of things are you looking for as you edit?
MOHAMMED: I'm checking my paragraphing.

> At this point I decide to focus the conference on paragraphing. I'm able to make such a quick decision in part because I had given a minilesson on paragraphing at the beginning of the writing workshop and also because Mohammed's teacher told me that he needs some help with paragraphing. Since all I've learned so far is that Mohammed is going to think about paragraphing when he edits, I need to get him to explain what he knows about the reasons for paragraphing; I also need to look at his writing to see where he's paragraphed.

ME: Tell me about it.
MOHAMMED: Well . . . I've paragraphed here [*pointing to his first sentence*] and here [*pointing to the sentence beginning "The first day . . ."*] and here [*pointing to the sentence beginning "On the second day . . ."*].
ME: [*After skimming Mohammed's draft*] Why did you paragraph in these places?
MOHAMMED: Because . . . those were the places where new days started.
ME: Well, that's smart that you did that. Writers do start new paragraphs to help let readers know that some time has gone by, like one day turning into the next.

> I've now learned that Mohammed has written several paragraphs in his first draft, each of which signals a major time shift—a new day. Looking at his writing, I also see places where he should start new paragraphs to signal other, smaller time shifts. I'm curious whether Mohammed knows that he can use paragraphs to signal minor time shifts, so I ask him where else he's planning to paragraph.

Where do you think you need to do more paragraphing?

MOHAMMED: [*After skimming his draft*] I'm not sure.

> Now I have enough information. I decide to teach Mohammed that paragraphs can signal minor time shifts to readers.

TEACHER ACTION 7.5

Analyze the assessment work you do in conferences.

- Have a fellow teacher or your literacy coach join you during writing workshop. When you think you've identified a focus for a conference, stop and say something to your colleague about what you've learned so far and what you feel you still need to learn about the student to make a teaching decision. Once you feel that you've gathered enough information, stop once again and tell your colleague what you've decided to teach the student.

- Prepare a transcript of a conference (either from memory or while listening to a tape recording). Underline the place at which you identified a focus for the conference and also the places at which you obtained the information you needed to make your teaching decision.

As you see, there's a lot to think about during the first few moments of a writing conference! This thinking isn't haphazard or random. Once I find a focus for the conference, I think carefully about what I've learned so far about the child and then gather more information. My teaching decisions flow logically out of this information-gathering process.

If you're new to teaching writing—or even if you've been teaching writing for several years—it may be intimidating to peek inside a more experienced writing teacher's mind like this. As you have more and more conferences, however, you'll find that your current students resemble the students you've taught in previous years. Conference assessment becomes a matter of recognizing patterns—the typical ways students write at the grade level you teach. Over time, the process will feel more and more intuitive and automatic. In almost all your conferences, you'll be able to figure out where you're going to take a student quickly and feel confident that you've made an accurate assessment and a good teaching decision.

Reflecting on the Child's Individual Learning Plan After the Conference

Years ago, I heard Lucy Calkins say that our role as teachers in a writing conference is to change a child's life as a writer forever. She meant

TEACHER ACTION 7.6

Reflect on how your conferences change how you see your students as writers.

Review several of your record-keeping forms for students in your writing workshop, paying particular attention to the notes you took about your writing conferences with them. Which conferences led you to understand aspects of your students as writers in deeper ways? Which conferences led you to think about aspects of your students as writers that you hadn't assessed before the conferences?

the same thing as when she says that we teach the writer, not the writing. That is, we teach a child about an aspect of writing—a purpose for writing, a craft technique, a writing strategy, a language convention—that she can use in the piece she's currently working on and, more important, whenever she writes in the future, for the rest of her life.

I've come to believe that our lives as teachers should also be changed forever by what happens in a writing conference. What we learn about a child should change how we see her as a writer. We should end most conferences knowing something we didn't know before about a child's initiative as a writer, about what she does to write well, and/or about her writing process. And what we learn should lead us to reflect on the individual learning plan we've constructed for her based on previous conferences and her earlier writing.

When a conference is over, a few questions nudge me to think about this child's individual learning plan:

- What did I learn that confirms one or more of the learning goals I have for this child? And how does what I learned help me understand more about what this child needs to learn?

- What did I learn that leads me to set some new learning goals for this child?

Once I've come up with answers to these questions, I jot them down on my record-keeping form.

Figure 7.14 contains the notes I wrote down after my conference with Smith. Besides the things I learned about Smith's knowledge of structure, I also learned about his willingness to revise (an aspect of process) and intuited the purpose he had for writing (an aspect of initiative). As a goal for future conferences, I made a note to help him learn to stretch the parts of a piece that develop meaning. I also jotted down that to be able to develop a story, he would need to learn about narrative details—dialogue, thoughts, actions.

Assessment Notes For _Smith_   **Dates** _1|5_

What am I learning about this student as a writer?	What do I need to teach this student?
1/5 "Losing Spanish" - personal essay - meaning : " problems happen when you forget your other language - idea & story sections - wants to add to "important parts" - story : 3 sentences (T) "show" your point by developing narrative part	(G) "stretch" parts that develop meaning (G) communicate meaning clearly (G) range of narrative detail

(T) is the symbol for teaching point.   (G) is the symbol for instructional goal

FIGURE 7.14   Assessment Notes for Smith

My conference with Smith affected how I saw him as a writer. The goals I created for him would affect future conferences with him. And in those future conferences, there would be more to learn about him as a writer and more goals to set for him. Over the course of the school year, the individual learning plan for Smith would become more and more detailed and be more and more a help in guiding the assessment and decision-making process in future conferences.

References

Anderson, Carl. 2000. *How's It Going? A Practical Guide to Conferring with Student Writers.* Portsmouth, NH: Heinemann.

Calkins, Lucy. 1994. *The Art of Teaching Writing.* Portsmouth, NH: Heinemann.

Calkins, Lucy, Amanda Hartman, and Zoe White. 2003. *The Conferring Handbook. Units of Study for Primary Writing: A Yearlong Curriculum.* Portsmouth, NH: *first*hand, Heinemann.

———. 2005. *One to One: The Art of Conferring with Young Writers.* Portsmouth, NH: Heinemann.

Graves, Donald. 2003. Keynote address, the Writing Conference at University of Connecticut, "Celebrating the Work of Donald Graves," Hartford, CT.

Johnston, Peter H. 1997. *Knowing Literacy: Constructive Literacy Assessment.* Portland, ME: Stenhouse.

Kaufman, Douglas. 2000. *Conferences and Conversations: Listening to the Literate Classroom.* Portsmouth, NH: *first*hand, Heinemann.

Little, Jean. 1987. *Little by Little: A Writer's Education.* Ontario, Canada: Penguin.

Murray, Donald M. 1985. *A Writer Teaches Writing.* Boston: Houghton Mifflin.

Ray, Katie Wood. 1999. *Wondrous Words: Writers and Writing in the Elementary Classroom.* Urbana, IL: NCTE.

8

Linking Assessment and Instruction
Designing Units of Study

Of course we can plan and live toward units of study in our writing workshops and still be student-centered.
—LUCY CALKINS, The Art of Teaching Writing

I'm jealous of writing teachers today. Jealous because there are so many books available in which the authors share the yearlong curricula they've designed for their writing workshops. Jealous because there are so many books available in which the authors describe units of study they've designed to help their students engage in in-depth studies of various aspects of writing. Jealous because there are so many books available in which the authors describe minilesson after minilesson that they've taught to classrooms full of young writers.

Mainly I'm jealous because writing teachers no longer have to worry about what units of study they *could* teach as part of their writing curriculum or what minilessons they *could* teach in each unit of study. They can devote their energy to deciding which units of study and which minilessons they *should* teach.

To answer the question of what we *should* focus on in our whole-class teaching, we need to consider all that we learn from assessing our students. It's what we've learned about our students' needs as writers that helps us decide the focus of our whole-class teaching.

Designing a Curriculum for the Writing Workshop[6]

Back in 1987, when I was a novice writing teacher, conversations about whole-class instruction in the writing workshop were about minilessons. There was little talk about constructing a yearlong curriculum for our young writers. (In fact, many of the first writing workshop teachers considered themselves "anticurriculum"—against the scripted curricula provided by basals.) There was very little talk about units of study, either. For most of us, the minilesson was the largest curriculum unit.

In my classroom—and in those of many other writing teachers— the topic for a minilesson changed from day to day (or sometimes every couple of days). Over the course of a week, I might give a minilesson on leads on Monday, on using dialogue on Tuesday and Wednesday, on rules for using the comma on Thursday, and on a revision strategy on Friday.

It probably doesn't surprise you that this kind of whole-class instruction didn't have the effect on my students' growth as writers that I had hoped. Just as one or two lessons on fractions aren't enough teaching to help students learn much about this challenging mathematical concept, one or two minilessons on writing leads or using revision strategies aren't enough teaching to enable students to learn about these aspects of writing. Katie Wood Ray (2001) describes this kind of whole-class instruction as "a hit-and-miss series of bits of teaching, isolated sound bites that don't come together into larger, more lasting understandings" (130).

Today, we think of whole-class instruction in the writing workshop in much more ambitious ways. Instead of envisioning the year as a series of minilessons, we see it as a series of *units of study*. Lasting two to eight weeks, a unit of study is a series of minilessons on one topic.[7] A unit of study can focus on a genre or how to use a writer's notebook or how to write with a particular audience in mind. Isoke Nia (1999) writes, "A unit of study in writing is not unlike a unit of study in science or social studies. It is a line of inquiry—a road of curriculum, a trail of teaching, an excursion of knowing something about writing. It is some big thing that you and your class are digging into over time" (3).

Devoting this amount of time to a focused study of one aspect of writing gives students the chance to respond to our minilessons and learn about the topic in deeper, more meaningful ways. It also gives us the time *we* need to assess our students as they try to understand what we're teaching and then present additional minilessons to help them learn even more.

During the past decade and a half, writing teachers and staff developers have created numerous units of study in their classrooms and

6. If you're familiar with this topic because you've read one or more professional books that address this issue—which include Lucy Calkins and colleagues' units of study for the primary (2003) and upper grades (2005), JoAnn Portalupi and Ralph Fletcher's *Teaching the Qualities of Writing* (2004), Katie Wood Ray's *The Writing Workshop* (2001), Heather Lattimer's *Thinking Through Genre* (2003), and Judy Davis and Sharon Hill's *The No-Nonsense Guide to Teaching Writing* (2003)—you may want to skip this section.
7. Some educators use the term *writing cycle* instead of *unit of study*. The meaning is the same.

written about them in professional books. The first units of study to be developed and discussed were genre studies: memoir, poetry, feature articles, op-ed pieces (persuasive writing), the literary essay, and more, for elementary, middle, and high school classrooms. More recently, units of study have focused on keeping a writer's notebook, the craft of writing, collaborating with other writers, and punctuation. In fact, a unit of study can focus on any aspect of taking initiative as a writer, writing well, or the writing process—any of the lines of growth students need to move along in order to become lifelong writers (see Figure 8.1). (Appendix 5 contains a list of units of study and professional books that discuss them.)

It's very common today for teachers of writing to compose a *curriculum calendar*—a plan for all the units of study they will present during the year. (Figure 8.2 is one example.) Some teachers write their curriculum calendars by themselves; others do so in collaboration with the teachers at their grade level. Sometimes everyone follows these collaborative efforts to the letter; sometimes the teachers decide they will do some units together but also diverge and do different studies at other times.

Many teachers look at the sample curricula provided by authors of professional books to help them envision how their writing workshop

Trait	Some Possible Units of Study
Initiative	• Creating an Independent Writing Life • Exploring Different Purposes for Writing • Writing for Social Action • Writing for an Audience
Writing well	• Genre Studies • Structure • Writing with Detail • Writing with Voice • Using Precise Words • Punctuation
Process	• The Writing Process • Keeping a Writer's Notebook • Using a Writer's Notebook to Write to Learn • Collaborating with Other Writers • Revision • Reading Like Writers • Using Mentor Texts • Strategies for Taking the High-Stakes Literacy Test

FIGURE 8.1

Curriculum Calendar		
Unit	**Start Date**	**Publication(s)**
1. The Writing Process	September 13	Varied genres
2. Personal Narrative	October 11	Personal narratives
3. Reading Like Writers	November 8	Varied genres
4. Collaboration	December 6	Varied genres
5. Feature Articles	January 3	Feature articles
6. Writing with Voice	February 9	Varied genres
7. Op-Ed Pieces	March 14	Op-ed pieces
8. Punctuation	April 11	Varied genres
9. Short (Fictional) Stories	May 2	Short (fictional) stories
10. Using Mentor Texts	May 31	Varied genres

FIGURE 8.2 Sample Curriculum Calendar for an Upper-Elementary-Grade Writing Workshop

curriculum could go. In some school districts, the central office (often in consultation with lead teachers from the district) designs districtwide curriculum calendars that all teachers in that district are expected to follow.

There isn't one right curriculum calendar that will guarantee success in any grade in any school in any state. Ultimately, it's up to teachers to design calendars that will be just right for them and for their students. Ralph Fletcher and JoAnn Portalupi (2001) write, "Of course, there isn't a single right way to plan a yearlong writers' workshop. You will find your own pace, and your own areas to focus on, connected to your particular curricular and setting demands" (125).

When teachers construct curriculum calendars, they need to decide which units of study to include as well as in what order to teach them. Some teachers write a complete curriculum calendar before the school year begins. Others decide what the first few units will be but put off figuring out which ones they will include in the later part of the year until they've gotten to know their students as writers.

Which Units Should We Teach?

To help make decisions about which units to teach, teachers ask these questions:

What Are Our Students' Needs?

Once the school year is under way and we've had a chance to get to know our students as writers, we will probably see that many of the children in our class have similar needs. It makes sense to include some units of study that directly address those needs. For example, we might notice that students tend to write mostly personal narratives. In response, we might decide to study some nonnarrative genres. Or we might notice that students mainly use commas and periods in their writing. In response, we might decide to do a unit of study focused on developing a more extensive repertoire of punctuation marks and understanding why writers use them.

What Are Our Sudents' Interests?

Many teachers include units of study that match their young writers' interests. For example, they may not be wild about teaching short fiction but know their students will jump up and down with excitement when they learn that they'll be studying the genre. Or sometimes, as the year unfolds, a teacher will notice that her students have fallen in love with a certain author. In response, she might revise her curriculum calendar to include a unit in which the students will study the craft of that author's writing.

What Have the Students Studied in Previous Grades?

When planning a yearlong curriculum for the writing workshop, it's important to be aware of what the teachers who have come before us have taught the students we're about to teach. We'll revisit some of those studies, taking students deeper into the subject, but we'll also include different studies that will give them opportunities to grow in new ways as writers. Katie Wood Ray (2001) writes, "We will want to plan for studies that both *extend* what our students have been learning and studies that *introduce* them to important new ideas" (134).

In many schools, students are fortunate to participate in a writing workshop year after year. Teachers in each grade level meet with the teachers from the previous grade level at the end of the school year to learn about what the students in the lower grade studied that year. These cross-grade discussions ensure that students don't feel that they've heard it all before in next year's writing workshop.

What Units of Study Do We Know Well Enough to Teach?

It doesn't make sense to include a unit of study we know little or nothing about unless we know we'll have an opportunity to learn about it soon. Perhaps a colleague, literacy coach, or staff developer knows something about the unit and will help us learn how to teach it, or a study group will read a professional book on the topic, or we'll attend a workshop on it during the year.

Many teachers include units for which they have a special passion. They feel their year would be incomplete if they didn't include a unit on writing poetry or about writing for social justice. When a teacher combines knowledge of and passion for a unit, students will engage most deeply with the study—and learn the most.

What Curriculum Mandates Are We Required to Meet?

State education departments determine literacy standards that students at the different grade levels are expected to meet. One of the most common writing standards is that students become proficient in various narrative and nonnarrative genres. To satisfy these requirements, writing teachers make sure that their curriculum calendars include several genre studies. In all grades, teachers usually teach personal narrative; in grade 2 and above, they often include other narrative studies, such as short fiction. In primary grades, students study all-about nonfiction books; in grades 3 and above, they study other nonfiction genres, such as feature articles, op-eds, and essays.

In What Order Should the Units Be Taught?

When teachers construct curriculum calendars, they also need to decide what the order of their units will be. To help themselves think about how to sequence the units, teachers ask these questions:

Which Units Are Appropriate for Certain Times of the Year?

The school calendar will have some influence on when teachers do certain units of study. For example, many upper-grade teachers launch their writing workshops with a unit on how to use a writer's notebook because they want their students to use notebooks as a tool for rehearsing their writing throughout the year. Primary teachers launch their writing workshop with a unit on the writing process—the various steps and grade-appropriate strategies for navigating these steps.

The dates of high-stakes literacy tests can influence teachers' curriculum planning. Often, teachers study test-taking strategies during the month before the test; in earlier months they'll study the genres children will be asked to write in on the test.

The curriculum in other subject areas also impacts the writing curriculum. For example, if a big study of insects is planned for April, it might make sense to schedule a nonfiction study at the same time, focusing on how to take the results of students' science research and put them together in a well-written text.

What Are Our Students' Previous Experiences as Writers?

Students' previous experiences in writing workshop influence the order of the units in a curriculum calendar. When students are new to writing workshop, it's helpful to spend the first several months writing personal narratives, the genre in which inexperienced writers typically have the most strength. Writing personal narratives, students are often more able successfully to apply what they learn about structuring their writing or writing with detail than if they were writing in brand-new genres, like literary essays or feature articles. Units of study that provide dramatically new challenges might best be planned for mid-year or even later. For example, in the sample curriculum calendar Ralph Fletcher and JoAnn Portalupi provide in their book *Writing Workshop: The Essential Guide* (2001), studies of nonfiction genres are scheduled during the middle of the school year.

In some schools, students have been participating in writing workshops for several years. When students have already studied a wide variety of genres—some of them for several years—it is not as important to begin with narrative genres. Starting the year with new challenges can be a way of reenergizing the writing workshop for students who may feel that they have been there, done that.

Are We Providing Time for Students to Pursue Their Own Writing Purposes?

It's vital to balance genre studies with other kinds of studies. One of the reasons for including genre studies in our curriculum is to help students learn through experience why writers write in specific genres. However, by requiring students to write in a genre for several weeks, we limit the range of writing purposes each student can have during that time. A student who wants to write about the day his pet hamster died in order to express his feelings about that sad event can't do so during a genre study of feature articles. We need to make sure our curriculum calendars include other units besides genre studies so that students have time to write in genres of their choice, for any reason that matters to them. These studies give students the time they need to grow as initiators of writing throughout the school year.

Many teachers have told me that given the number of curriculum mandates in their district, they have no choice but to string several genre studies together in their curriculum. In her book *Independent Writing* (2004), Colleen Cruz discusses how she taught her students to construct writing lives in which they wrote "independent" pieces in addition to the pieces they were writing as part of the current unit of study. Using Colleen's approach, a teacher would encourage her student to write about the death of his hamster at the same time he was writing a feature article about paper airplanes.

When Will We Have the Opportunity for Staff Development This Year?

The staff development schedule for the year will impact our curriculum calendar. If we find out at the beginning of school that the school's

207
*Linking
Assessment and
Instruction:
Designing Units
of Study*

TEACHER ACTION 8.1

Plan a whole-class curriculum for your writing workshop.

- Design a whole-class curriculum for your writing workshop. (A blank curriculum calendar is provided in Appendix 6.)

- Reflect on the curriculum you've already designed for your writing workshop this year. In which ways could you improve it? (If you designed your curriculum with your colleagues at your grade level, do this as a group.)

literacy coach or a writing consultant will be working with us in November on the craft of writing, we'll plan that unit of study for that month. Or if we know we're going to attend a workshop on writing poetry, we'll schedule the poetry unit after the workshop.

How Assessment Can—and Should— Inform Units of Study

Although I'm jealous that teachers today have such easy access to numerous descriptions of units of study, I'm nervous, too. The teachers and staff developers who have written these books have done so magnificently—in many cases, describing each minilesson, relating the order in which they presented them, and explaining their rationale for choosing each lesson. It can be hard to imagine teaching these units any differently.

For teachers who are new to writing workshop or new to certain units of study, the descriptions of these units of study are an excellent *starting place*. I remember how reassured I felt as a young teacher when I attended the Teachers College Reading and Writing Project's summer institutes and listened to Katherine Bomer, Randy Bomer, and Katie Wood Ray describe genre and craft studies they had taught in classrooms. Walking away with images in my head of how these units could go, I had the knowledge and confidence to attempt the studies with my own students.

However, once in the middle of teaching a unit of study for the first time, I had to grapple with a critical issue: *my students were not Katherine's or Randy's or Katie's students*. While some of the minilessons I had learned were just right for my class, others were not, either because my students already knew how to do what I was teaching them or (more common) because they weren't ready to learn what I was teaching them to do.

I had to face a difficult truth: ultimately, *I* had to become a designer of each unit, too. If the units of study I was planning to teach were going to be effective—if they were going to help the students in my class take the next logical steps for themselves as writers—I had to decide which minilessons to include based on all I had learned about my students as writers from my ongoing assessment.

What we read about a unit of study is one way the unit *could* go in a classroom. How a unit *should* go with *our* students can only be determined by *us,* by linking assessment to curriculum design. As Lucy Calkins says in *The Nuts and Bolts of Teaching Writing* (2003), "The end goal, of course, is not the teaching we describe but the teaching that you, your colleagues, and your children invent together" (3).

Focusing Units of Study on Just a Few Lines of Growth

One of the problems we have when we design a unit of study is abundance. Educators have written about so many minilessons that way too many could be taught during any given unit. Let's say I was planning a genre study of personal narrative. Off the top of my head, I can imagine more than thirty lessons I could teach, and if I were to browse Ralph Fletcher's *What a Writer Needs* (1993) or Lucy Calkins and Abby Oxenhorn's *Small Moments: Personal Narrative Writing* (2003) or Barry Lane's *After the End* (1993) or Don Murray's *Write to Learn* (1999), I could come up with at least another fifty.

We can't teach all these minilessons in one unit of study! Most units go on for about four weeks. At the most, then, we can devote just twenty minilessons to each one. How do we decide which minilessons to present during any given study?

The answer is we focus a study on just one or a few lines of growth in writing—aspects of taking initiative as writers, writing well, or the writing process—and teach minilessons that connect to these lines of growth. For example, most of the minilessons in a study of personal narrative might focus on teaching students to include a range of narrative details in their pieces—dialogue, a character's thoughts, and characters' actions. A study of feature articles might focus on teaching students how to structure nonnarrative writing or how to write with voice. And a study of how to use a writer's notebook might focus on how students can use the notebook as a tool for figuring out what meaning they want to communicate about the topic they've chosen.

Although in any one unit a teacher will focus on just one or a few lines of growth, across the many units that make up the year's curriculum, she'll focus on most if not all of the lines (see Figure 8.3). Depending on the students and their needs, a teacher will probably focus on some lines in several units—areas in which her students need

209
*Linking
Assessment and
Instruction:
Designing Units
of Study*

Trait	Line of Growth	Unit of Study									
		1 Launch	2 Pers. Narr	3 Craft	4 Collab-oration	5 Feature Article	6 Voice	7 Op-Ed	8 Punctu-ation	9 Short Fiction	10 Mentor Texts
Initiative	Purpose	X	X			X		X		X	
	Audience	X						X			
Writing Well	Meaning		X			X		X		X	
	Genre knowledge		X			X		X		X	
	Structure		X	X		X		X			
	Detail		X	X		X		X		X	
	Voice			X			X		X		
	Conventions		X	X	X	X	X	X	X	X	X
Process	Rehearsal	X	X	X	X	X		X	X	X	X
	Drafting/revising	X	X	X	X		X	X	X		X
	Editing	X			X				X		

FIGURE 8.3 A Record of the Lines of Growth That a Teacher Focused On in Her Units of Study Across the School Year

the most support—and on other lines just once or perhaps not at all. Given that every unit of study ends with several periods in which students edit their pieces for publication and that on these days teachers give minilessons on grammar and mechanics, teaching students about conventions occurs in almost every unit. (The exception is the first unit, in which teachers usually give minilessons on editing strategies while students are editing their first piece.)

The benefit of focusing a unit of study on just a few lines of growth is that students will have the time they need to understand what we're teaching them and we'll be able to teach in response to their emerging understanding. However, it's easy to lose one's focus in a study. As we confer with students and read their writing, we can't help but notice other issues students have as writers. It helps to remember that we'll be able to address these other needs in subsequent units— or that the students will have another writing teacher next year! And even though many of the conferences we have with students during a unit will be connected to the focus of that study, we can use some of our conferences to address those issues we're not talking about in minilessons.

Deciding on Which Lines of Growth to Focus

To help us decide on which lines of growth to focus in a unit of study, we need to consider everything we've already learned from assessing the students in our class *as individuals*. We've been creating individual learning plans for them since the very first day of school. Now we need to review these individual learning plans and look for needs that many of the students have in common.

At the end of the first unit of study, and again after several more units of study have been completed, and then again several units later, I read through my record-keeping forms and note which goals I've set relative to initiating writing, writing well, and developing a more effective writing process (see the checklists in Appendixes 1, 2, and 3). Once I've finished, I look for needs that are common to many members of the class. Some of these common needs become the focus of the next unit of study, the others, subsequent units.

On the checklist in Figure 8.4, which I filled out for a fourth-grade class after the first month of school, I checked off similar goals for many of the students: to learn to communicate meaning in their writing, to focus on a part of the topic that will enable them to communicate their meaning, to develop a wider repertoire of details, and to break their writing into paragraphs. Therefore, during the next unit of study I would consider giving some minilessons on communicating meaning in a piece of writing, some on how writers focus on the aspects (or parts) of their topics that help them say what they want to say, and/or some on the

Assessing How Well Students Write

Trait	Goal	Jimmy	Allison	Jade	Michael	Jane	Jacob	Jack	Anna	Matt	Molly	Ruby	Robin	Terri	Harry	Isabel	Robert	Annabel	Sophia	Max	Alex
Meaning	The student communicates meaning in her writing.	+	+	+	+	+	⊕	⊕	+	⊕	⊕	+	+	⊕	+	⊕	+	+	+	+	+
	The student's meaning influences (or controls) other decisions she made in composing her pieces.	+	+	+	+	+	+	+	+	⊕	+	+	+	+	+	⊕	+	+	+	+	+
Genre	The student's writing has the typical features of the genres in which she writes.	+		+	+	+	⊕	⊕	+	⊕	+	+	+	+	+	⊕	+	+	+	+	+
	The parts of the student's writing each help develop meaning.	+	+	+	+	+	+	⊕	+	⊕	+	+	+	+	+	⊕	+	+	+	+	+
	The student's pieces contain the kinds of parts specific to the genres in which she writes.	⊕	⊕		⊕		⊕	⊕				⊕	⊕			⊕		⊕	⊕		⊕
	The student orders her writing in genre-specific ways.						⊕														
Structure	The student writes leads and endings that guide readers toward meaning.		⊕				⊕	⊕				⊕			⊕	⊕			⊕		⊕
	The student uses transitions effectively.																				
	The student weights parts that are most important in developing her meaning.	+	+	+	+	+	+	+		+	+										
Detail	The student includes details in her piece that help develop meaning.	+	+	+	+	+	⊕	+	+	⊕	⊕	+	+	+	+	⊕	+	+	+	+	+
	The student writes with a range of genre-specific details.	+	+	+	+	+	⊕	+	+	+	⊕	+	+	+	+	⊕	+	+	+	+	+
	The student embeds and connects details in her sentences effectively.							⊕			⊕			⊕							
	The student uses specific words in her details.	⊕			⊕					+	⊕		⊕	⊕							
Voice	The student uses a variety of sentence structures to give voice to her writing.				⊕		⊕	⊕		+				⊕		+					⊕
	The student uses a variety of punctuation marks to give voice to her writing.			+			+	⊕						⊕		+					
	The student includes details that reveal who she is as an individual.	⊕	⊕	⊕		⊕	⊕	⊕													
	The student uses techniques to create intimacy between herself and readers.																				
Conventions	The student uses punctuation marks correctly in the kinds of sentences that she is writing.	⅃	⅃	⅃	⅃	⅃	⅃	⊕		⅃	⅃	⅃	⅃	⅃	⊕	⊕	⅃	⅃	⊕	⅃	⊕
	The student uses grammatical conventions correctly in the kinds of sentences she's writing.					⊕	⅃	⊕			⅃	⅃s		⅃		⊕	⅃s	⅃	⊕	⅃s	

+ Goal for student   ⊕ Goal achieved   ⅃'s, ", etc. Convention student needs to work on   ① Goal achieved

FIGURE 8.4

kinds of details writers use to develop these parts. At the end of the unit, when the students were editing their pieces for publication, I would also consider giving a few minilessons on paragraphing.

For many teachers, the challenge isn't figuring out what needs their students have in common but deciding on which of their many common needs to focus. There isn't a right or wrong way to do this. Ultimately, we each have to decide which lines of growth to make a priority in our teaching *right now* based on a combination of factors: what we most want children to learn to do as writers, what we know how to teach, and what resources are available. When we focus on several lines of growth in a study, we aren't able to give as many minilessons about each one as we can when we focus on just one or two lines. And focusing on just a few lines of growth during a study doesn't mean we're ignoring students' other needs; it means we'll focus on those needs in later studies.

Planning a Unit of Study That Will Focus on Just a Few Lines of Growth

Planning a unit of study involves moving from thinking in general about our goals for what we'd like students to learn about writing to determining the specific minilessons we'll teach to help them meet those goals. There are two parts to the planning process: deciding which lessons to teach in the unit and figuring out in what order these lessons might logically be sequenced.

Deciding Which Lessons to Teach

To come up with a list of minilessons I'm going to teach in a unit of study, I draw from two sources. First are the lessons I've developed during the years I've been teaching. Second are professional books that discuss the unit of study and/or include descriptions of related minilessons.

I begin by asking myself, *Which lessons in my teaching repertoire fit the focus(es) of this study?* Then I do some brainstorming. If I've taught the study before, I also look at those lesson plans and any notes I wrote down. As I come up with ideas for minilessons, I jot them down on a planning sheet (see Figure 8.5).

I also ask myself, *How could I teach these lessons?* These ideas, too, I'll jot down on my planning sheet. There are several options. I could teach by showing students a text that illustrates the point I want to make, either a published text by a well-known author or one written by me or by a student. I could teach by writing in front of the students to make my teaching point. Or I could teach by giving students an explanation of the aspect of writing on which I'm focusing.

| Unit _____ | Dates _____ |
| | |

Lines of Growth _____

Possible Minilessons	How Could I Teach This Lesson? (show a text, demonstration, etc.)
1.	
2.	
3.	
4.	
5.	
6.	
7.	
8.	
9.	
10.	

FIGURE 8.5   Unit of Study Planning Sheet

Once I've drawn ideas for minilessons from my teaching repertoire, I also like to read what other educators have written about the unit of study. Seeing what lessons other writing teachers have taught often inspires me to teach some new ones myself.

To show you how this works, I'll walk you through how I envision which minilessons I could teach in a unit on personal narrative that's focused on communicating meaning, developing the parts of an event that help communicate meaning, and using a variety of details.

First, which lessons in my teaching repertoire connect to these lines of growth? To teach students that personal narratives have a point, I could read them some stories and talk about the point each author is making. To help them figure out what they want to say in their own stories, I could talk about how writers ask themselves *What do I want to tell readers about this event?* as they are writing a piece. I might teach students to use this strategy when they're starting their draft or when they're revising. As these lessons come to mind, I jot them down on my planning sheet for the unit (see Figure 8.6).

Unit Personal Narrative   **Dates** Oct. 11–Nov. 5

Lines of Growth Meaning, Structure, and Detail / Conventions = Paragraphing

Possible Minilessons	How Could I Teach This Lesson? (show a text, demonstration, etc.)
1. Writers tell stories to get a point across.	Show students texts and discuss the points the authors seem to be making ("Shortcut," by Crews; "Eleven," by Cisneros)
2. To discover meaning, writers ask themselves, "What do I want to tell readers about this event?" before and after they draft.	Demonstrate this with a story from my writer's notebook. Demonstrate this with one of my own rough drafts.
3. Narrative structures: write about one moment of an event or write about several parts of an event.	Show students texts. ("Maybe a Fight," by Little, for focusing on a moment; "Eleven," for focusing on several parts of an event)
4. Writers make a plan for their story before they draft.	Show students some of the plans for stories I've written or demonstrate the planning process during the lesson.
5. Make a time line of an event as a strategy for deciding on which parts of that event to focus. (Fletcher)	Demonstrate this with an event from my life during the lesson.
6. Write important scenes as dramatic scenes with dialogue, characters' thoughts, and characters' gestures and actions. (Fletcher)	Analyze a dramatic scene from "Eleven."
7. Write less important scenes as summary scenes. (Fletcher)	Analyze a summary scene from "Eleven."
8. Paragraphing. (when students are editing)	Show students "Maybe a Fight" and discuss the reasons Jean Little paragraphed where she did.
9.	
10.	

FIGURE 8.6   Unit of Study Planning Sheet

215

*Linking
Assessment and
Instruction:
Designing Units
of Study*

Then I think about which lessons I could teach to show students how having something to say about an event forces a writer to decide on which part (or parts) to focus. I imagine teaching students a lesson on ways of structuring a personal narrative—focusing on one moment or focusing on several parts of the event. Also, I realize that it will be important to teach students some strategies for laying out the structure of their stories, so I envision teaching a lesson on making a plan or an outline of a piece before drafting. I add these lessons to my planning sheet.

As these lessons—and others—come to mind, I am also thinking about which model texts would be good examples of the points I am planning to make. An all-time favorite comes to mind immediately—"Eleven," in which Sandra Cisneros (1991) focuses on several parts of an event (the day the narrator's teacher makes her wear a sweater that isn't hers). I also think of a story that Jean Little (1989) wrote—"Maybe a Fight," from *Hey World, Here I Am*—because it's focused on just one moment.

Once I've combed through my mental repertoire of lessons, I browse my professional books, looking for other lessons that would fit the focus of this study. I pick up my all-time favorite source of lessons for teaching children about writing personal narratives—Ralph Fletcher's *What a Writer Needs* (1993)—and open it to Chapter 11, "A Playfulness with Time," where I know Ralph discusses structuring narratives. Ralph, as usual, doesn't disappoint.

I jot down Ralph's idea that we could teach students to write a time line of an event and then circle the parts of the experience they think they should focus on in their stories (the parts that help them say what they want to say). I also jot down Ralph's suggestion that we teach students to strike a balance between writing parts of their stories as "dramatic scenes", in which we "show" readers the action by writing dialogue, describing characters' gestures, and sharing characters' thoughts, and others as "narrative summaries," in which we "tell" the readers what happened.

And so forth.

For some studies, I'm able to think of many lessons and model texts off the top of my head, and I read the professional literature to extend my repertoire. When I'm doing a study for the first time, however, reading the professional literature is especially important, because my repertoire of lessons and model texts is limited.

Planning a Logical Sequence

Once I have a sense of which lessons I'll be teaching and the texts I'll be using as models, it's time to sit down with a calendar and plan out the study day by day. There are several decisions I need to make:

1. The starting and ending dates for the study
2. How many days to devote to immersion
3. How many days to devote to revision and editing
4. A sequence for the lessons

Deciding the Starting and Ending Dates for the Study

I think hard about how many weeks to devote to the unit. While many of the units I've designed over the past decade have had an average length of four weeks, a few have been as short as two weeks, and others have gone on as long as eight weeks. Ultimately, there is no right number. Sometimes I give a study five or even six weeks because I know from past experience that it's particularly challenging. Genre studies of short fiction or feature articles can easily go this long. Other times, my decision is based on the idiosyncrasies of the school calendar. There are three weeks between the November unit and the winter holidays, so the December unit gets three weeks.

The personal narrative study I'm envisioning in this chapter will take four weeks. Once I've decided how many weeks to give a study, I mark the starting and ending dates on my calendar (see Figure 8.7). Knowing the ending date helps me stay focused on the lines of growth I've identified. Time feels limited and precious, and I'm less likely to teach lessons on other aspects of writing.

Deciding How Many Days to Devote to Immersion

I usually begin a unit of study by immersing students in the texts I'll be using as models in my minilessons—I read these texts with the class. In a genre study, I read examples of the genre to give the students a sense of it. In other kinds of studies, I read texts in which the authors did what I'm going to teach students to do. For example, I could begin a unit on writing with voice by reading texts in which the authors' sentences give their writing a beat. In a unit on what kinds of things writers write about in a writer's notebook, I could read aloud entries from my own notebook and from notebooks kept by former students.

For the personal narrative study, I've decided to spend the first two days of the study immersing students in good examples of this genre (see Figure 8.7). By reading the texts, I mean just that. I read the texts aloud. Students have copies of the texts so they can follow along, or they can just listen. After I finish, I give students time to respond *as readers* by jotting down their thoughts in their writer's notebooks, talking with a classmate, sharing their thoughts in a whole-class discussion, or a combination of these activities.

After reading several texts—usually over the course of several days—I lead a class discussion in which students respond to them *as writers,*

Unit of Study Personal Narrative

Dates 10/11–11/15

Monday	Tuesday	Wednesday	Thursday	Friday
10/11 Immersion	10/12 Immersion	10/13 Writers have something to say in their stories (4 days) Today: Show texts	10/14	10/15
10/18	10/19 Narrative Structures (3 days) Today: Show texts	10/20	10/21	10/22 Writing Dramatic Scenes (8 days) Today: Show a text
10/25	10/26	10/27	10/28	10/29
11/1 (Revising by further developing dramatic scenes)	11/2 ELECTION DAY—NO SCHOOL	11/3 (Revising by further developing dramatic scenes)	11/4 Editing Paragraphing	11/5 Editing Paragraphing
11/8 Publishing Celebration				

Figure 8.7 Plan for Personal Narrative Study

sharing what they've noticed about how the texts are written. As students talk, I record the things they've noticed on a piece of chart paper.

I may spend all of an immersion period reading texts with students or still give them half the period in which to write. During the first few days of a genre study, it's unreasonable to expect students to start writing in the genre, especially if it's a new one for them. In that case, students use their writing time to work on independent projects, as Colleen Cruz details in her book *Independent Writing* (2004).

Deciding How Many Days to Devote to Revision and Editing

The last day of a study is usually a writing celebration in which students share a piece (or several pieces) with classmates, parents, school administrators, or another class. Therefore, during the last several days of the study, students will be getting their writing ready for an audience by revising, editing, and making a final copy (either by rewriting their draft neatly or by typing it on a computer).

I plan this time before the study begins. If I don't, I run out of time to teach students about revision and editing and they don't have time to do it. Editing, especially, is shortchanged in many writing workshops; students don't get the editing practice they need and, no surprise, publish pieces that contain too many careless errors. And students need lessons on grammar and mechanics in order to learn the conventions of written English and use that knowledge as they edit.

I also decide which points of grammar or mechanics I want to focus on in minilessons during those days. Usually, I decide what to teach based on the kinds of errors I've been noticing many of the children making in their writing so far during the year. For example, I might decide to spend two days on how to punctuate compound sentences or on when to use *I* and *me* in a sentence.

For the personal narrative study, I've decided to devote the entire last week to revision and editing. I've also decided to give minilessons on paragraphing on the two days I expect most students will be editing. I've marked these days accordingly on my planning calendar, and I've designated the last day as a writing celebration (see Figure 8.7).

Deciding on a Sequence for the Lessons

Last, and most important, I think about how to sequence the lessons I'm going to teach during the study. I devote several days to each of the teaching points I want to make. One minilesson isn't enough teaching for most students to understand a writing concept and be able to do something new as writers. Several days of minilessons give students more time to grasp a concept and put it to use in their writing.

Teaching several minilessons about the same aspect of writing lets me react to students' initial attempts to understand a writing concept.

In my conferences after the first day's minilesson, I assess what students do in response to that lesson. On the second day, I teach a minilesson that takes into account what I learned. I continue to assess what students are doing on the second day and teach a minilesson on day three that takes into account that assessment. And so on.

Let's say I've decided to do a series of minilessons on how to write a dramatic scene. On the first day I show students an example of a dramatic scene in a text we've read and point out how the writer included dialogue, the thoughts of the main character, and descriptions of the main and secondary characters' actions. Then, as the students work on their stories, I confer with several students and find that they are writing a lot of dialogue but aren't yet including the other kinds of details. Thus, on day two, I make the point that writers balance dialogue, characters' thoughts, and characters' actions in a dramatic scene. As I confer with students after this minilesson, several tell me they want to include their main character's thoughts but aren't sure how to write them. On day three, I teach a minilesson on ways that writers write characters' thoughts.

Sequencing the teaching points I want to make can be tricky. In some units—genre studies, especially—many students are in the same stage of the writing process as the study progresses. Most students spend a week or two rehearsing their topic in their writer's notebook and then spend several days writing a draft, several days revising it, and several days editing it. In these studies, I consider which teaching points it makes sense to teach while students are in a particular stage of the writing process. For example, if I wanted to teach students about the structure of the genre they're writing in, I would give several minilessons on this topic as most of the students were getting ready to draft.

In other units, students will be writing in different genres and will be in different stages of the writing process. In these cases, I look at my list of possible lessons and ask myself whether some of the points are more important to make than others. I also ask myself whether there are logical reasons to make some teaching points before others. I then order the lessons accordingly.

Let's look at my planning calendar for the personal narrative study (Figure 8.7). The first teaching point I want to make is "writers have something to say in their stories," and I'm planning to devote four days to this concept. I've decided to start with this teaching point because I think it's the most important one I'll make. I've also decided to start with this concept because I imagine that most of the students in the class will be rehearsing the stories they'll be writing, either by rereading their writer's notebooks and looking for entries that can become well-developed drafts or by writing new entries in their notebooks that can then be developed into well-written stories. Since part of rehearsal for most experienced writers involves thinking about what they're going

219

*Linking
Assessment and
Instruction:
Designing Units
of Study*

to say in their pieces, it makes sense to introduce this concept while most students are at this stage in the writing process.

I call my next teaching point "narrative structures," and I plan to devote three minilessons to it. I hope to teach students that they have several structural options when they write a story—focus on one moment, write about a series of moments, and so on. I've decided to focus on this concept second because at this point many students will be starting to write drafts. Since many writers decide on a structure for their pieces just before they draft, it makes sense to focus on structure when many students are moving from rehearsal into drafting.

I call my third and final teaching point in this study "writing dramatic scenes"; I'll spend eight days on this. In these minilessons, I hope to teach students that writers weight some parts of their pieces more than others by writing them as dramatic scenes. I'll also show them the techniques they'll need to do this. At this point, most students will be writing drafts of stories and revising these drafts (some students may write one lengthy story during this time; others may write several shorter pieces). I think this teaching point will make the most sense to students when they are in the midst of drafting and revising.

I make an educated guess about how many days to allot to each series of minilessons. Once I've begun a unit, I may find that I want to spend another day or two on a teaching point, or I may find that I don't need to spend as many days on a point as I thought I would. Although I try to finish a study by the date I originally intended, sometimes I need to extend a unit a few days in order to be satisfied that I've done the teaching my students need from me.

I've written a specific minilesson down on my calendar only on the first day of each series. On the first day, I try to give students the big picture of the particular concept. Most often, I show them a text—one of the ones I read aloud during the first few days of the study, some entries from a writer's notebook, a revised draft—that is a good example of the concept I'm going to teach.

I leave the subsequent days of each series of minilessons blank because I can't be sure what I'll be teaching on these days until I assess, in conferences, what students are doing in their writing. After you've taught a number of units of study and see how students react to your teaching, you'll be increasingly better able to predict how a series of minilessons will play out. Even so, I still leave these days on my calendar blank so that I'm open to the possibility that the students I'm teaching today might respond in unexpected ways or that a series of minilessons won't go exactly as I've imagined it will.

Figures 8.8 and 8.9 will help you imagine how two of the series of minilessons in this personal narrative study could develop over several days.

Day	Minilesson	Conferring Observations
1	Teach students that writers write stories to communicate meaning by showing and discussing several model texts ("Eleven," "Maybe a Fight").	When I ask them, "What are you trying to tell readers in your story?" most students have trouble coming up with a response.
2	Teach students how to discover meaning by writing in response to this question in their writers notebooks: *What do I want to say to readers in my story?* Demonstrate this strategy myself.	Some students are able to come up with a response to the question, but others are still struggling to figure out what they want to say about their topics.
3	Teach students another strategy to discover meaning: reread what they've written about their story so far in their writer's notebook, looking for "focusing lines"—that is, sentences that already express a meaning for the story. Demonstrate the strategy with my own notebook entries.	More students are able to figure out what they want to say about their stories. Some of their points, however, are simplistic ("I had fun!").
4	Teach students to reach for more complex meanings by writing an entry exploring what they're trying to say. Show them examples of students' notebook entries in which they've already tried this.	Some of the students in question are able to compose more complex meanings.

FIGURE 8.8   A Series of Minilessons for Teaching Students to Discover Meaning

Day	Minilesson	Conferring Observations
1	Teach students several narrative structures by showing them the structures of several model texts ("Maybe a Fight" focuses on one scene; "Eleven" focuses on several scenes).	Many students are jumping into drafts without taking the time to think about the structure for their stories.
2	Teach students to make a plan for their stories by demonstrating how I make a flowchart for a story I'm planning on writing.	Most students have made a plan for their stories, but they're including parts that don't connect to what they're trying to say in their stories.
3	Teach students to decide which parts of their stories will help them get their point across by demonstrating how to make a time line of the event you're writing about and circling the parts that you need to say what you want to say before you make a plan for your piece or before you make revisions to the piece.	Many students are using the time line strategy to help them think about which parts to include in their stories or which parts they should keep in their drafts.

FIGURE 8.9 A Series of Minilessons for Teaching Students to Structure Narratives

TEACHER ACTION 8.2

Plan a unit of study for your writing workshop.

- Read through your record-keeping forms and look for needs that many of the students in your class have in common. (Use the unit planning checklists in Appendixes 1, 2, and 3 to help you record what you notice.) Which lines of growth will you need to focus on in upcoming units of study?

- Design a unit of study for your writing workshop using the process I've discussed in this chapter. (There is a blank planning sheet in Appendix 7 and planning calendar in Appendix 8.)

223

*Linking
Assessment and
Instruction:
Designing Units
of Study*

TEACHER ACTION 8.3

Reflect on the effectiveness of a unit of study.

- Every couple of days during a unit of study, gather some of your students' writing and look for evidence that they are responding to your minilessons. What are students learning? What do you learn from this assessment that helps you decide which minilessons you should teach during the remainder of the study? Record your minilesson ideas on your planning calendar for this unit of study.

- In your conferences during a unit of study, look for evidence in your students' talk of new understanding they've gained about the aspects of writing you've been focusing on in your minilessons. What do you learn from this assessment that helps you decide which minilessons you should teach during the remainder of the study? Record your minilesson ideas on your planning calendar for this unit of study.

- Gather some of your students' writing and look for evidence that students are still incorporating what they learned a month or several months ago. Do you think that your students need more work on lines of growth you focused on in previous units of study? In which upcoming units of study could you focus on these lines of growth again?

Did We Achieve Our Goals for the Unit?

The traditional way teachers measure whether or not students have met their instructional goals for a unit of study in most subjects is to give them a test on the last day of the unit. In a unit of study on writing, the pieces of writing that students publish give us some information about how far students have moved along the lines of growth on which we've focused our teaching.

However, we don't need to wait until a writing unit of study is over to assess what students have learned. As soon as we start observing and conferring with students during the beginning days of a unit of study, as soon as we start collecting writer's notebooks and drafts in process to read during our prep periods, we're gathering information about what students are learning to do in response to our whole-class teaching. Because of the assessments we make of our students each day, we probably won't be surprised by what we see when we read their published drafts at the end of the unit. We'll already know what most of our students have learned to do.

The *real* measure of success is whether students continue to do what they learned *after* the unit is over. Thus, each unit of study should change the way we assess students for the rest of the school year. One way our assessment will change is that in our conferences, we'll ask students questions connected to our teaching points in previous units. In the units that follow the study of personal narrative I've detailed in this chapter, I'll be sure to ask, "So what are you going to say to readers in this piece?" "Why have you decided to write about these parts of your story?" and "How are you writing with detail in your piece?" And as I read the pieces that students publish during the remainder of the school year, I'll be looking for evidence that students are continuing to do what I taught them earlier.

Of course, we hope students not only continue to do what we teach in a unit but also learn more about the things we've taught them. Sometimes, we decide to focus on a line of growth again in a later unit (or units); this gives us a chance to help all the students in our classes move further along this line. And even though we may not focus on a line of growth again, we still have the opportunity, in writing conferences, to help individual students improve in this area.

References

Calkins, Lucy. 1994. *The Art of Teaching Writing*. Portsmouth, NH: Heinemann.

———. 2003. *The Nuts and Bolts of Teaching Writing. Units of Study for Primary Writing: A Yearlong Curriculum*. Portsmouth, NH: *first*hand, Heinemann.

Calkins, Lucy, and Abby Oxenhorn. 2003. *Small Moments: Personal Narrative Writing. Units of Study for Primary Writers: A Yearlong Curriculum*. Portsmouth, NH: *first*hand, Heinemann.

Calkins, Lucy, and Colleagues. 2003. *Units of Study for Primary Writing: A Yearlong Curriculum*. Portsmouth, NH: *first*hand, Heinemann. Nine unnumbered volumes.

———. 2005. *Units of Study for Upper Grade Writing: A Yearlong Curriculum*. Portsmouth, NH: *first*hand, Heinemann.

Ciseros, Sandra. 1991. "Eleven." In *Woman Hollering Creek and Other Stories*. New York: Random House.

Cruz, M. Colleen. 2004. *Independent Writing: One Teacher—Thirty-Two Needs, Topics, and Plans*. Portsmouth, NH: Heinemann.

225

*Linking
Assessment and
Instruction:
Designing Units
of Study*

Davis, Judy, and Sharon Hill. 2003. *The No-Nonsense Guide to Teaching Writing: Strategies, Structures, and Solutions.* Portsmouth, NH: Heinemann.

Fletcher, Ralph. 1993. *What a Writer Needs.* Portsmouth, NH: Heinemann.

Fletcher, Ralph, and JoAnn Portalupi. 2001. *Writing Workshop: The Essential Guide.* Portsmouth, NH: Heinemann.

Lane, Barry. 1993. *After the End.* Portsmouth, NH: Heinemann.

Lattimer, Heather. 2003. *Thinking Through Genre: Units of Study in Reading and Writing Workshops 4–12.* Portland, ME: Stenhouse.

Little, Jean. 1989. "Maybe a Fight." In *Hey World, Here I Am.* New York: Harper and Row.

Murray, Donald. 1999. *Write to Learn.* New York: Harcourt Brace.

Nia, Isoke T. 1999. "Units of Study in the Writing Workshop." *Primary Voices K–6* 8, no. 1 (August): 3–11.

Portalupi, JoAnn, and Ralph Fletcher. 2004. *Teaching the Qualities of Writing.* Portsmouth, NH: *first*hand, Heinemann.

Ray, Katie Wood with Lester Laminack. 2001. *The Writing Workshop: Working Through the Hard Parts (And They're All Hard Parts).* Urbana, IL: NCTE.

Afterword

Assessment is what we do when we
teach to meet our students' needs.
—KATHLEEN AND JAMES STRICKLAND,
Making Assessment Elementary

Imagine this. It's the first day of school, and your principal hands you a class roster that includes these names: William Shakespeare, Langston Hughes, Abraham Lincoln, Toni Morrison, Thomas Jefferson, Rachel Carson, Gabriel Garcia Marquez, Robert Frost, Jane Austen, Stephen Hawking, Charles Dickens, Martin Luther King Jr., John Lennon, Spike Lee, Maurice Sendak, Tony Kushner, and J. K. Rowling. It's your responsibility to make sure these students grow up to become the writers they're supposed to be.

How would you teach if you knew ahead of time who your students would become as adults, what pieces of writing they would compose, and what powerful effects their writing would have in their communities and the world?

I'd feel an incredible sense of urgency as these students' teacher, knowing their development as writers was in my hands. How momentous would be my decisions about which units of study to teach—and how to design them—knowing that the choices I made would help young Shakespeare grow into the writer who would compose *Hamlet* and Abraham Lincoln, the Gettysburg Address. How important the decisions about what to include in my individual learning plans, knowing that the goals I set would help young Rachel Carson someday write *Silent Spring* and Toni Morrison, *Beloved*.

I'd feel compelled to get to know these students as well as I could so I could make just the right decisions about what to teach them. I would pay such attention to everything they did in my writing workshop. I would listen carefully to every single word they spoke in writing conferences. And I would oh so carefully read every word they wrote. All the while, I'd look for signs—in what they did and said and wrote—that they were becoming the kinds of writers who would rise to meet my (and the world's) expectations of them. I would think hard about what they needed to learn in order to develop into those writers. I would do the best assessment work of my career to ensure that what I taught them was exactly what they needed as I guided them on their paths to greatness.

Of course, when we get our next class roster and read the names—Sarah, Anthony, Cheyenne, Netrice, Quincy, Rebecca, Max, Connor, Alex, Khalil, Kayla, Jose, Tyreese, Edmund, Jasmine, Michael, Tiffany, Emily, Yulisa, Kenyon, Libby, Austin, Tara, Damian, Keagan, and Xavier—we don't know their futures. Still, it's our job as teachers to imagine their futures for them, futures in which each of them is a lifelong writer. Like Stephen Hawking did in his book *A Brief History of Time*, Quincy *might* grow up to write a book that makes the most complex scientific concepts understandable to us all. Like Charles Dickens did in *Oliver Twist*, Tara *might* grow up to write novels that help us understand the injustices in our society.

Even though I don't know my students' futures, I feel an awesome responsibility to them. Their development as writers is in my hands. My decisions about their writing curricula and individual learning plans are momentous ones. I want to do my best possible assessment work every day I'm with them.

We are instrumental in creating our students' futures as writers. We help create those futures by observing them at work, listening to all they have to say in writing conferences, and poring over their words. We do this assessment work every single day of writing workshop and use what we learn to teach them exactly what they need to know to become lifelong writers.

Now it's your challenge to do the best assessment you possibly can, every day. Dream of your students' futures as writers. And then get to know your young writers so well that you can help them take the next steps toward the glorious futures you've imagined for them.

Reference

Strickland, Kathleen, and James Strickland. 1999. *Making Assessment Elementary*. Portsmouth, NH: Heinemann.

Assessing Students' Initiative as Writers

Trait	Goal	Names															
	Student writes about topics that are connected to who she is as a person.																
Purpose	In conferences, student articulates her purpose(s) for writing.																
	Student uses workshop time productively.																
	Student is self-directed and works through the writing process independently.																
	Student makes plans for how she's going to complete her pieces.																
	Student writes outside of school.																
Genre	Student writes in clearly recognizable genres.																
	In conferences, student explains how her choice of genre is connected to her purposes for writing.																
	In her writing, student uses naming moves to signal her intended audience (in genres where this is typically done).																
Audience	In conferences, student names the audience(s) for whom she is writing.																
	Student shares her writing with members of the class.																
	Student shares her writing with people outside of the class.																

+ Goal for student   ⊕ Goal achieved

Appendix 2

Assessing How Well Students Write		Names				
Trait	**Goal**					
Meaning	The student communicates meaning in her writing.					
	The student's meaning influences (or controls) other decisions she made in composing her pieces.					
Genre	The student's writing has the typical features of the genres in which she writes.					
Structure	The parts of the student's writing each help develop meaning.					
	The student's pieces contain the kinds of parts specific to the genres in which she writes.					
	The student orders her writing in genre-specific ways.					
	The student writes leads and endings that guide readers toward meaning.					
	The student uses transitions effectively.					
	The student weights parts that are most important in developing her meaning.					
Detail	The student includes details in her piece that help develop meaning.					
	The student writes with a range of genre-specific details.					
	The student embeds and connects details in her sentences effectively.					
	The student uses specific words in her details.					
Voice	The student uses a variety of sentence structures to give voice to her writing.					
	The student uses a variety of punctuation marks to give voice to her writing.					
	The student includes details that reveal who she is as an individual.					
	The student uses techniques to create intimacy between herself and readers.					
Conventions	The student uses punctuation marks correctly in the kinds of sentences that she is writing.					
	The student uses grammatical conventions correctly in the kinds of sentences she's writing.					

+ Goal for student ⊕ Goal achieved   ¶, 's, ", etc. Convention student needs to work on ⑨ Goal achieved

Appendix 3

Assessing Students' Writing Processes

Trait	Goal	Names									
Rehearsal	The student uses writing tools to rehearse his writing (for example, a writer's notebook).										
	The student uses strategies successfully to help him find topics and develop writing territories.										
	The student uses strategies effectively to help him develop topics and plan pieces before drafting.										
	The student can talk about his rehearsal work and explain why he's using the strategies he's using.										
Drafting and revision	The student uses writing tools to help him draft and revise.										
	The student effectively uses drafting and revision strategies.										
	The student can talk about his drafting and revising work and explain why he's using the strategies he's using.										
Editing	The student uses writing tools to help him edit (the spell checker, a dictionary).										
	The student effectively uses editing strategies.										
	The student can talk about his editing work and explain how and why he's using the strategies he's using.										

+ Goal for student   ⊕ Goal achieved

Assessment Notes for _____ Dates _____

What am I learning about this student as a writer?	What do I need to teach this student?

Ⓣ is the Symbol for Teaching Point.   Ⓖ is the Symbol for Instructional Goal.

May be copied for classroom use. © 2005 by Carl Anderson from *Assessing Writers*. Heinemann: Portsmouth, NH.

Appendix 5

UNIT OF STUDY	SOURCES OF INFORMATION ABOUT THE UNIT
THE WRITING LIFE (also called Launching Writing Workshop or A Study of the Writing Process)	*Launching the Writing Workshop* by Lucy Calkins and Marjorie Martinelli (*Units of Study for Upper Grade Writing*) (Portsmouth, NH: *firsthand*, Heinemann, upcoming) *Launching Writing Workshop* by Lucy Calkins and Leah Mermelstein (*Units of Study for Primary Writing*) (Portsmouth, NH: *firsthand*, Heinemann, 2003) *Writing Workshop: The Essential Guide* by Ralph Fletcher and JoAnn Portalupi (Portsmouth, NH: Heinemann, 2001) *. . . And with a Light Touch* by Carol Avery (Portsmouth, NH: Heinemann, 2002) (primary) *The No-Nonsense Guide to Teaching Writing* by Judy Davis and Sharon Hill (Portsmouth, NH: Heinemann, 2003) (grades 3–8) *Time for Meaning* by Randy Bomer (Portsmouth, NH: Heinemann, 1995) (secondary) *In the Middle* by Nancie Atwell (Portsmouth, NH: Heinemann, 1998) (secondary)
PERSONAL NARRATIVE	*Personal Narrative* by Lucy Calkins and Ted Kesler (*Units of Study for Upper Grade Writing*) (Portsmouth, NH: *firsthand*, Heinemann, upcoming) *Small Moments: Personal Narrative Writing* by Lucy Calkins and Abby Oxenhorn (*Units of Study for Primary Writing*) (Portsmouth, NH: *firsthand*, Heinemann, 2003) *Teaching the Qualities of Writing* by JoAnn Portalupi and Ralph Fletcher (Portsmouth, NH: *firsthand*, Heinemann, 2004) *Significant Studies for Second Grade* by Karen Ruzzo and Mary Anne Sacco (Portsmouth, NH: Heinemann, 2004) *What a Writer Needs* by Ralph Fletcher (Portsmouth, NH: Heinemann, 1993) *Craft Lessons* by Ralph Fletcher and Joanne Portalupi (Portland, ME: Stenhouse, 1998) *After the End* by Barry Lane (Portsmouth, NH: Heinemann, 1993)
MEMOIR	*Writing a Life: Teaching Memoir to Sharpen Insight, Shape Meaning—and Triumph Over Tests* by Katherine Bomer (Portsmouth, NH: Heinemann, 2005) *The Art of Teaching Writing* by Lucy Calkins (Portsmouth, NH: Heinemann, 1994) *Thinking Through Genre* by Heather Lattimer (Portland, ME: Stenhouse, 2003) (grades 4–12) *In the Middle* by Nancie Atwell (Portsmouth, NH: Heinemann, 1998) (secondary) *Time for Meaning* by Randy Bomer (Portsmouth, NH: Heinemann, 1995) (secondary) *Lessons That Change Writers* by Nancie Atwell (Portsmouth, NH: *firsthand*, Heinemann, 2002) *Living Between the Lines* by Lucy Calkins and Shelley Harwayne (Portsmouth, NH: Heinemann, 1990)

ESSAY	*Nonfiction Writing: Idea-Based Essays* by Lucy Calkins and Cory Gillette (*Units of Study for Upper Grade Writing*) (Portsmouth, NH: *firsthand*, Heinemann, upcoming) *Write to Learn* by Donald M. Murray (Harcourt Brace, 2001) (secondary) *Lessons That Change Writers* by Nancie Atwell (Portsmouth, NH: *firsthand*, Heinemann, 2002)
SHORT FICTION	*Realistic Fiction* by Lucy Calkins and Colleen Cruz (*Units of Study for Upper Grade Writing*) (Portsmouth, NH: *firsthand*, Heinemann, upcoming) *Time for Meaning* by Randy Bomer (Portsmouth, NH: Heinemann, 1995) (secondary) *In the Middle* by Nancie Atwell (Portsmouth, NH: Heinemann, 1998) (secondary) *Thinking Through Genre* by Heather Lattimer (Portland, ME: Stenhouse, 2003) (grades 4–12) *Lessons That Change Writers* by Nancie Atwell (Portsmouth, NH: *firsthand*, Heinemann, 2002) *A Fresh Look at Writing* by Donald H. Graves (Portsmouth, NH: Heinemann, 1994)
HOW-TO BOOKS	*Nonfiction Writing: Procedures and Reports* by Lucy Calkins and Laurie Pessah (*Units of Study for Primary Writing*) (Portsmouth, NH: *firsthand*, Heinemann, 2003)
ALL-ABOUT NONFICTION BOOKS	*Nonfiction Writing: Procedures and Reports* by Lucy Calkins and Laurie Pessah (*Units of Study for Primary Writing*) (Portsmouth, NH: *firsthand*, Heinemann, 2003) *About the Authors* by Katie Ray (Portsmouth, NH: Heinemann, 2004) (primary) *Is That a Fact? Teaching Nonfiction Writing K–3* by Tony Stead (Portland, ME: Stenhouse, 2002)
FEATURE ARTICLE	*The No-Nonsense Guide to Teaching Writing* by Judy Davis and Sharon Hill (Portsmouth, NH: Heinemann, 2003) (grades 3–8) *Thinking Through Genre* by Heather Lattimer (Portland, ME: Stenhouse, 2003) (grades 4–12) *Time for Meaning* by Randy Bomer (Portsmouth, NH: Heinemann, 1995) (secondary) *Nonfiction Matters* by Stephanie Harvey (Portland, ME: Stenhouse, 1998) *Nonfiction Craft Lessons* by JoAnn Portalupi and Ralph Fletcher (Portland, ME: Stenhouse, 2001) *Lessons That Change Writers* by Nancie Atwell (Portsmouth, NH: *firsthand*, Heinemann, 2002)
OP-ED (Persuasive Writing)	*Thinking Through Genre* by Heather Lattimer (Portland, ME: Stenhouse, 2003) (grades 4–12) *Time for Meaning* by Randy Bomer (Portsmouth, NH: Heinemann, 1995) (secondary) *Is That a Fact? Teaching Nonfiction Writing K–3* by Tony Stead (Portland, ME: Stenhouse, 2002)
LITERARY ESSAY	*Writing About Reading* by Janet Angelillo (Portsmouth, NH: Heinemann, 2003) (grades 3–12) *Thinking Through Genre* by Heather Lattimer (Portland, ME: Stenhouse, 2003) (grades 4–12)

(*continued*)

UNIT OF STUDY	SOURCES OF INFORMATION ABOUT THE UNIT
POETRY	*For the Good of the Earth and Sun* by Georgia Heard (Portsmouth, NH: Heinemann, 1989) *Awakening the Heart* by Georgia Heard (Portsmouth, NH: Heinemann, 1998) *Poetry: Powerful Thoughts in Tiny Packages* by Lucy Calkins and Stephanie Parsons (*Units of Study for Primary Writing*) (Portsmouth, NH: *firsthand*, Heinemann, 2003) *A Note Slipped Under the Door* by Nick Flynn and Shirley McPhillips (Portland, ME: Stenhouse, 2000) *The No-Nonsense Guide to Teaching Writing* by Judy Davis and Sharon Hill (Portsmouth, NH: Heinemann, 2003) (grades 3–8) *About the Authors* by Katie Ray (Portsmouth, NH: Heinemann, 2004) (primary) *Lessons That Change Writers* by Nancie Atwell (Portsmouth, NH: *firsthand*, Heinemann, 2002)
PICTURE BOOKS	*In the Company of Children* by Joanne Hindley (Portland, ME: Stenhouse, 1996) *The No-Nonsense Guide to Teaching Writing* by Judy Davis and Sharon Hill (Portsmouth, NH: Heinemann, 2003) (grades 3–8) *Living Between the Lines* by Lucy Calkins and Shelley Harwayne (Portsmouth, NH: Heinemann, 1990)
READING LIKE A WRITER (also called Authors as Mentors)	*Wondrous Words* by Katie Wood Ray (Urbana, IL: NCTE, 1999) *A Writer's Tool Kit: Using Tools and Strategies* by Lucy Calkins and Mary Chiarella (*Units of Study for Upper Grade Writing*) (Portsmouth, NH: *firsthand*, Heinemann, upcoming) *Authors as Mentors* by Lucy Calkins and Amanda Hartman (*Unit of Study for Primary Writing*) (Portsmouth, NH: *firsthand*, Heinemann, 2003) *Independent Writing: One Teacher—Thirty-Two Needs, Topics, and Plans* by M. Colleen Cruz (Portsmouth, NH: Heinemann, 2004) *About the Authors* by Katie Ray (Portsmouth, NH: Heinemann, 2004) (primary)

PUNCTUATION	*A Fresh Approach to Teaching Punctuation* by Janet Angelillo (New York: Scholastic, 2003) *Writing for Readers: Teaching Skills and Strategies* by Lucy Calkins and Natalie Louis (*Units of Study for Primary Writing*) (Portsmouth, NH: firsthand, Heinemann, 2003) *The Power of Grammar: Unconventional Approaches to the Conventions of Language* by Mary Ehrenworth and Vicki Vinton (Portsmouth, NH: Heinemann, 2005) *About the Authors* by Katie Ray (Portsmouth, NH: Heinemann, 2004) (primary) *You Kan Red This!* by Sandra Wilde (Portsmouth, NH: Heinemann, 1991) (K–6)
LIFTING THE QUALITY OF THE WRITER'S NOTEBOOK	*Write to Learn* by Donald M. Murray (Harcourt Brace, 1999) (secondary) *Time for Meaning* by Randy Bomer (Portsmouth, NH: Heinemann, 1995) (secondary) *The No-Nonsense Guide to Teaching Writing* by Judy Davis and Sharon Hill (Portsmouth, NH: Heinemann, 2003) (grades 3–8)
REVISION	*Making Revision Matter* by Janet Angelillo (New York: Scholastic, 2005) *Looking at Revision with New Eyes* by Lucy Calkins and Natalie Louis (*Units of Study for Upper Grade Writing*) (Portsmouth, NH: firsthand, Heinemann, upcoming) *The Craft of Revision* by Lucy Calkins and Pat Bleichman (*Units of Study for Primary Writing*) (Portsmouth, NH: firsthand, Heinemann, 2003) *The Revision Toolbox* by Georgia Heard (Portsmouth, NH: Heinemann, 2002) *The Reviser's Toolbox* by Barry Lane (Discover Writing Press, 1999) *The No-Nonsense Guide to Teaching Writing* by Judy Davis and Sharon Hill (Portsmouth, NH: Heinemann, 2003) (grades 3–8) *About the Authors* by Katie Ray (Portsmouth, NH: Heinemann, 2004) (primary)
CREATING AN INDEPENDENT WRITING LIFE	*Independent Writing: One Teacher—Thirty-Two Needs, Topics, and Plans* by M. Colleen Cruz (Portsmouth, NH: Heinemann, 2004)
COLLABORATING WITH OTHERS	*Independent Writing: One Teacher—Thirty-Two Needs, Topics, and Plans* by M. Colleen Cruz (Portsmouth, NH: Heinemann, 2004) *In the Middle* by Nancie Atwell (Portsmouth, NH: Heinemann, 1998) (secondary) *About the Authors* by Katie Ray (Portsmouth, NH: Heinemann, 2004) (primary)
WRITING FOR SOCIAL ACTION	*For a Better World: Reading and Writing for Social Action* by Randy Bomer and Katherine Bomer (Portsmouth, NH: Heinemann, 2001)

Appendix 6

Curriculum Calendar		
Unit	Start Date	Publication(s)
1.		
2.		
3.		
4.		
5.		
6.		
7.		
8.		
9.		
10.		

Unit of Study Planning Sheet

Unit _____

Dates _____

Lines of Growth _____

Possible Minilessons	How Could I Teach This Lesson? (show a text, demonstration, etc.)
1.	
2.	
3.	
4.	
5.	
6.	
7.	
8.	
9.	
10.	

May be copied for classroom use. © 2005 by Carl Anderson from *Assessing Writers*. Heinemann: Portsmouth, NH.

Appendix 8

Unit of Study _____

Dates _____

Monday	Tuesday	Wednesday	Thursday	Friday

Index